The Luxury Empire

Yves Hanania
Isabelle Musnik – Philippe Gaillochet

The Luxury Empire

Accelerations and Disruptions

DUNOD

© Dunod, 2022

11, rue Paul Bert, 92240 Malakoff

www.dunod.com

ISBN : 978-2-10-084164-6

Contents

Part 2

The Luxury Sector: An Empire Under Pressure

Forewords

"Preserve, enrich and transmit"

At the dawn of our civilizations, luxury was first and foremost an aspiration towards the divine, a quest for the sublime, the magnificence of a unique object charged with symbols and powers. Luxury is today an expression of status and success. It is a quest for recognition, something superfluous, a "*very necessary thing*" as Voltaire called it. Luxury is also something intimate, a sublimation of the senses, of the emotions linked to beauty and good. In the end, luxury is about culture, about the hand of the craftsman who shaped the item, aided by their creativity and the power of their imagination. It is a heritage handed down over the centuries, as demonstrated by the 18,000 years of accumulated know-how of the *maisons* of the Comité Colbert. It consists of many timeless characteristics and aspirations which join together with the major evolutions in our modern society.

The first major change is the growing role of digital technology in distribution structures and the world of communication. The field of possibilities is constantly expanding and becoming increasingly sophisticated. A double phenomenon is taking place – ever greater proximity and immediacy, hand in hand with the creation of areas of communication nourished by updated stories aimed at carefully keeping desire flowing. It is worth noting that the luxury industry is often one of the first sectors to adopt new technologies. Let's take the example of blockchain, which provides a concrete response to the problem of counterfeiting, the real scourge of luxury brands. Or the meta-verse, a new universe in which luxury players naturally feel very comfortable. What could be more logical as luxury feeds on the imagination and seeks to break down the limits of what is possible.

The second major change is the explosion of the second-hand market, especially among young people. Is this due to a sudden awareness of our frenetic way of consuming fashion that quickly goes out of date? Or is it a return to roots? There was a time when the rarity or even uniqueness of a product was what made it a luxury product. Timelessness and durability have always been the main pillars of luxury.

The third major change is sustainability. Luxury is beco-ming increasingly responsible. By their nature, luxury brands have time at the heart of their *raison d'être*. This, coupled with a commercial dynamic that has not wavered for years, means that these brands have taken up the banner of sustainability to protect their know-how. Brands have a strong desire to contribute to the collective good, they clearly understand the notion of companies' rights and duties and they encourage action. This was clearly seen in the most intense moments of the current pandemic.

This book takes a detailed look into a sector at the juxtaposi-tion between acceleration and disruption. Packed with testimo-nies, it gives numerous luxury industry players a chance to have their say, each of whom brings their current view of the sector's global activity, its development, and its future evolutions.

Luxury has many fruitful years still ahead of it. Its mission is to preserve, enrich and transmit. This three-part mission has never been so topical.

Laurent Boillot, CEO of Hennessy
and President of the Comité Colbert

"Nothing changes, everything changes"

This could be the new luxury paradigm. Like all sectors, it has been shaken by a dizzying earthquake which it has drawn inspiration from to gain new momentum. Always at the forefront, it is experiencing exciting, extraordinary times; a transformation which affects all its make-up – its meaning, values, links, and experience.

Luxury provides a field of expression where concepts feed off each other, where the short-lived contribute to a timeless narrative, where the metaverse enriches reality, where NFTs create uniqueness and where profitability works hand in hand with sustainable impact.

Its ability to constantly rethink itself has led it to put experience at the heart of its creations. This experience forms a bridge between the tangible and the intangible. Retail, far from being outdated, is rebuilding itself using the latest technologies and incorporating a virtual dimension into reality. Luxury is becoming the embodiment of the alliance between tradition and innovation. An alliance that means we can offer daring and unexpected customer journeys and a never-before-seen level of customization.

One of the potential success factors of luxury will be to cultivate this link between different worlds. Its entrepreneurial spirit positions it as a pioneer of a future where diversity is central. Its architecture enables it to create spaces of freedom where differing identities may express themselves.

Luxury clients want to dream bigger and better, yet their demand for commitment and transparency is just as high. The future will be built on luxury that places ethics at the heart of all it does. Its performance in the financial markets shows that the industry has the resources to build sustainable and virtuous ecosystems. France is no different. The privileged place held by French groups on an international scale testifies to the immortality of French luxury. It is an industry full of talent, a key contributor to our national economy, which has demonstrated its ability to transform adversity into growth opportunities. Its strength provides it with possibilities, but also responsibilities, in a world where reputation contributes to building trust.

More than ever, there are endless avenues for the development of luxury. Its new playgrounds for expression where content and shape are one, paint the contours of an unequaled creative space. Heir to a powerful history, its roots endow it with the privilege of being able to embrace these changes, harmonizing them in a rare concoction that only it knows the secret of.

The insights offered in this book are an invitation for the luxury sector to reflect on its future. Its authors give us a glimpse into the new geography of the sector by questioning the players and aspects concerned by this profound transformation. Thanks to this illustration and deciphering of the current and future trends, it sheds light on this new evolution.

Cyril Chapuy, President of L'Oréal Luxe

Introduction

C ovid and its consequences (lockdowns, shop closures, decrease in consumption of non-essential products) decimated national economies in 2020. Various economic sectors were impacted, including the aeronautical, tourism, hotel and catering and automotive industries.

At the heart of all these activities, the luxury sector was hit hard by this shutdown. But while European economies came to a screeching halt, it wasn't very long (March 2020) before China came out of lockdown. By mid-2020, the sector was in strong rebound. Thanks to its unparalleled creativity and agility, it was also able to quickly move into new areas. For many brands, the Covid crisis was actually a moment of reckoning where they had to increase their strength and energy, acting quickly to adopt new ways of selling and preserving their connection with their customers.

As the end of the pandemic appears to be within sight, the visions of the many luxury and fashion professionals we consulted show a very particular reading of the sector. Most agree that they are living through an exceptional period in the history of luxury, where challenges and opportunities are entwined. They want to act rather than wait and see what happens. Many brands in the sector are taking advantage of this historic moment to innovate, anticipate and equip themselves for the future. Others, struggling to keep up, with outdated positioning, will find it difficult to emerge from the crisis.

At the time of this book's publication, there are still many uncertainties. Brands will have to be working at all levels and investing in new areas of expression, action, involvement, and acquisition. Among the most pressing topics in luxury are the circular economy, gaming, NFTs and the metaverse, not to mention the development or conquest of key luxury markets such as India and China.

This book analyzes what the new normal of luxury is at the end of the crisis, how the sector is reorganizing itself, and what it needs to do to prepare and respond to the next crisis.

Part 1
The Dawn of a New Empire

The luxury sector is a sector experiencing many new types of accelerations and disruptions. Even if what was important in the past is still relevant, notably singularity, excellence, quality and rarity, many new qualities herald a new era for the sector at a global level, namely responsibility, commitment, transparency, increased creativity and finally, innovation. In a never-before experienced crisis, the stakes and opportunities are of vital importance for a sector that is now wondering about a new reason for being which goes beyond profit. Brands have used this hitherto unseen period to reflect on their role in society, demonstrating an unprecedented commitment, called for both by their customers and by the organizations themselves. They have developed their creativity by multiplying their expression and sales channels, and by investing in new areas. A new phenomenon emerged during the crisis, the "digitalization" of fashion.

1

An Empire Challenged by New Consumption Patterns

Changes in luxury consumption during the pandemic

The evolution of luxury consumption during the pandemic reveals common aspirations on three continents[1]. The study on luxury consumer trends[2] published in October 2020 highlights high expectations regarding the relevance of the offerings proposed and the importance of online sales. At the same time, the consumption of luxury products has never been such an essential pleasure. Wellness is the top concern in all three zones. Luxury contributes to this sense of wellbeing and is also associated with enhanced sensory appeal. Products offering a sensory experience were top purchases during the lockdowns, in particular, skincare, perfumes, wines, champagnes and spirits. In purchase desires, fashion and accessories are well placed, while jewelry and watches amount to less overall in Western countries.

---

1. For the sake of convenience, Oceania (excluding Australia) and Africa are not, for the time being and for the purposes of the survey, considered as significant players in the world of luxury.
2. Ipsos, WLT: annual barometer of luxury consumer trends, 2020 edition, "Nouvelles contraintes et nouvelles aspirations du luxe".

The study also highlights the importance of luxury consumption, regardless of the continent. For the Chinese, the added value of very high quality, authentic products improves their self-confidence. For Americans, they provide exceptional emotional experiences. For Europeans, they are above all, safe long-term investments. Purchasing luxury products is considered a privilege more than ever before. The wealthy and influential luxury clientele is aware that they are part of an elite.

VISION & PERSPECTIVE

Services and experiences

Elie SAAB Jr, CEO, Elie Saab

The pandemic has disrupted the natural evolutionary pace of luxury business. It accelerated the shift towards digital transformation directly impacting how we communicate and connect. The way the world has been evolving and the way it continues to grow, enhanced our services to include experiential journeys. Such services will only improve the more we bridge reality with the digital world. As we continue to combine the best of both worlds, we will be able to consistently build unforgettable creative experiences.

Elie Saab Jr. is CEO and Member of the Board of Directors of the Elie Saab Group. He is leading the group's transformation strategy, which includes an evolution of the brand's identity and the organization of its new global presence.

Wealthy Chinese

According to the survey, the majority of the affluent and influential Chinese population is confident in the country's economic situation – 50% of respondents are even very confident.

Luxury is becoming important in Chinese people's daily lives, who wish to purchase even more products than before the crisis. They, like many consumers in markets historically anchored in luxury consumption, have evolved in their relationship with luxury. Some of their expectations and motivations are similar to those of European and American consumers. While the older "baby boomers" maintain a traditional relationship with luxury products, the younger generations consume for the same reasons as the European and American Generation Z. They have studied abroad, travel more, and want to consume for "good" reasons. Consumers could quickly become disenchanted with the brands present in China if they are considered to be too oriented in a certain direction and non-authentic in their product and service offerings.

Wealthy Americans

The demanding American clientele, who have been particularly resilient despite being some of the most severely affected by the health crisis, have maintained a high level of confidence in their country's economic situation, despite being in the midst of the pandemic. Like in China, the period generated more interest in luxury products for everyday life. In a culture where luxury products were more associated with special occasions, the social and cultural evolution seen during the crisis is moving towards a more sensorial, everyday luxury for pleasure and enjoyment. There is an increased interest in beauty, luxury care products, wines and champagne, to the detriment of traditional categories such as watches and jewelry.

Even though Americans say they want to refocus on the basics, they are consuming more, especially digital services (apps, social networks, etc.). They expect immediate, easy satisfaction, but they also want to dream.

19

Wealthy Europeans

Wealthy Europeans were more impacted in their relationship to the luxury sector in the pandemic. New experiences such as treatments, spas and restaurants appeal to them more than before. They are a little less interested in the traditional categories of watches and jewelry, proving Patrick Thomas, former CEO of Hermès, right when he told Vogue Business:

"I don't like the word luxury because there are too many hypocrisies behind it. For me, a luxury product is one with another function beyond usage, which is linked to emotion. A bag is a bag. You can use a bag worth $50 or $5000. Why do you choose the expensive bag? Because it gives you more than usage, it gives you pleasure[3]."

While well-being is the dominant trend in Europe, the ethical dimension associated with luxury is growing. Expectations continue to rise for products to be cruelty-free and for companies to make ethical and ecological commitments. The French do not see luxury in the same way today. Most of them, according to the Cetelem Observatory[4], associate it mainly with products or experiences which are out of the ordinary. When describing luxury, they talk more about products like jewelry, clothing, and bags than about experiences such as spas, travel or hotels. According to the survey, while young people in general

---

3. Bella Webb, "Former Hermès CEO backs alternative leathers," *Vogue Business*, July 28, 2021.
4. Observatoire Cetelem, "Désir, rêve ou rejet: qu'est-ce que le luxe pour les Français?", survey conducted by Harris Interactive on October 6 and 7, 2020.

seem to be more attached to experiences, women seem to be more sensitive to the material aspect of luxury. Others see it in an immaterial way; as freedom, time for oneself, or the possibility to disconnect.

One thing is certain – luxury still fascinates people. In these difficult times, customers have seen it as a refuge, but also as a pleasure and an escape. Sales of goods dedicated to the home have exploded. Some brands, such as Fermob, were in heaven, with more than one million orders in the first months of lockdown. More established brands, such as Ligne Roset and Cinna, limited the damage by vastly accelerating sales online and outside France. Thanks to its strong export position (70% of sales), the Roset Group continued to receive orders. For Hermès, sales of decorative products exploded, even though this activity remains a side line for the great luxury fashion house, which offers exceptional pieces, combining, *"excellence and savoir-faire, a bold and elegant art of living"*.

Generations Y and Z, increased pressure on brands

More than ever, brands must respond to the new expectations and demands of their customers, while refreshing and inventing tomorrow's consumption for the new generations, who are more digital, more innovative, and more active. The luxury market is up against a rejuvenation of its clientele, which demands incomparable agility from brands.

Brands need to reinvent themselves, going further than the traditional issues of transforming and accelerating their organizations.

The different consumer generations

Baby boomers born between 1946 and 1965 – who were aged between 76 and 57 in 2022.

Generation X refers to people born between 1965 and 1980 – who were aged between 57 and 42 in 2022.

Generation Y or "millennials" were born between 1980 and 1997 – who were aged between 42 and 25 years old in 2022.

Generation Z refers to young people born in 1998 or later, i.e. 24 years old or younger in 2022.

The Alpha generation refers to children born between 2010 and 2025. They have been exposed to digital technology from an early age – Chinese children spend an average of four hours a day on smartphones and tablets. They are inheriting their parents' taste for luxury products and are already passive clients. One in seven people is currently a member of this generation, and more than 2.8 million new Generation Alpha members are born every week! At this rate, it is expected that there will be 2.2 billion multimodal users by 2025.

Henrys ("high earners not rich yet") have incomes ranging from $100,000 to $250,000 per year. They are addicted to e-commerce and capable of spending heavily on luxury experiences. They have very high demands of brands in terms of ethics and sustainable development.

While baby boomers and Gen Xers accounted for half of luxury customers and two thirds of total spending in 2018, they will only account for 45% of luxury purchases by 2025[5].

---

5. Claudia D'Arpizio, Federica Levato, Filippo Prete, Constance Gauet and Joëlle de Montgolfier, "Luxury Goods Worldwide Market Study, Fall-Winter 2018: The Future of Luxury: A Look into Tomorrow to Understand Today," *Bain & Company*, January 10, 2019.

Millennials (Y) and Generation Z will account for some 60% of global sales by 2026.

"Millennials now represent 60% of our clientele and, in China, 25% come from Generation Z," acknowledges Arnaud Carrez, Senior Vice President and Marketing and Communications Director at Cartier International[6]. More and more Ys and Zs are acquiring luxury personal products. Between 2016 and 2018, their share increased from 41% to 47% of the total number of buyers in the sector. By 2026, they will account for 60% of the total. However, their spending has not yet kept pace, rising from 28 to 33% of total consumer spending[7]. The first reason for this is a proportionally lower purchasing power than that of previous generations. The challenge for brands will be to retain this young clientele so that they increase their spending as their incomes increase.

Another explanation is that they focus their luxury purchases on more affordable items, such as accessories and shoes, rather than on watches and jewelry. A diversification strategy into more affordable sub-brands, specifically catering to the tastes of millennials and Generation Z, could then be a solution for the most prestigious groups.

These demands on brands and consumption habits are rapidly spreading to all age groups. Generations Y and Z are leading the way for older generation consumers. They are ushering in major changes in consumer behavior, in particular in luxury goods. These generations, while keen on technology, innovation and creativity, also want personalization and physical experiences.

---

6. Isabelle Musnik, interview with Arnaud Carrez, "Je crois profondément au "new retail" pour toutes les générations", *INfluencia*, January 5, 2021.
7. Bain & Company, *op. cit.*

The new president of De Beers Brands, Marc Jacheet, goes even further and talks about, *"co-creation and individualization that are a return to the roots of luxury. Each client will have their own product[8]."*

The Henrys – A segment yet to be conquered

Henrys (*"high earners not rich yet"*) – a term coined by Shawn Tully in 2003 in an article in *Fortune* magazine – are now on all luxury marketing professionals' radars. According to a Deloitte study, they are expected to quickly become the world's richest demographic group. Luxury brands have already begun to target them, cultivating their appreciation for authenticity, craftsmanship and heritage. For this highly connected generation, looking for products that combine luxury and new technologies, the object is certainly still an important social status symbol, but its production conditions have also become a strong purchasing criterion. *"We see the brightest long-term future for luxury players who take seriously their clients' desire for sustainable consumption,"* a Mazars study points out[9].

China's Generation Z, the motor powering new luxury

A monumental shift is taking place in the luxury sector in China, where the average luxury consumer is 28 years old, ten years younger than the average consumer in the rest of the world. It is estimated that 80% of affluent consumers in China are millennials and generation Z. These two generations, taken

---

8. Interview of Marc Jacheet by the authors.
9. Mazars, "Conscious, collaborative, connected: making over the luxury business model", study published in 2021.

from all income groups, will account for 65–70% of China's luxury goods market by 2025[10].

The Comité Colbert, which brings together 90 French luxury companies, has understood the importance of this phenomenon and in April 2020 launched an advertising campaign in China on the WeChat platform to seduce young people on social networks. *"We would like to share our passion, our tradition, our demand for quality and our love of beauty with them, because they are tomorrow's decision makers and it is often they who influence our choices,"* explained Jean-Marc Gallot, Chairman of the Comité Colbert International Commission and CEO of Veuve Clicquot in a press release.

These new luxury worshippers are very different from their European or American counterparts. *"You can't imagine the appetite for life these young people have, who have often studied abroad, speak English and yet are very proud of their country and repeat, "I want a happy life,"* explains Isabelle Capron, International Vice President at Icicle Shanghai Fashion Group and General Manager Paris[11]. Their access to luxury goods has only become possible in the last few decades. They have no long-standing loyalty to brands, and for them, luxury is more about expressing their culture, personality and status than it is about displaying their wealth. This generation has grown up surrounded by foreign brands, without differentiating between their origins, codes and hierarchies. Their first relationship with the brand is via its image, what it reflects about itself, and it is first played out on the Internet, not the stores. Luxury is transformed into a form of expression. They are more in search of authenticity and

---

10. Bain & Company, May 2021.
11. Interview of Isabelle Capron by the authors, May 2021.

personalization in their purchases and turn more to experiences they will share online than to one-off purchases. And the Covid crisis has only served to increase this.

The digitalization of brand relations was already well developed in China before the lockdown and helped cultivate a link with customers during the period – live-streaming sessions allowing people to test products compensating for the sensory experience absent from stores, talks organized with salespeople from luxury boutiques on WeChat, and the presence of brands online, even in games, such as Maserati's partnership with the game *Peace Elite* or Louis Vuitton's with *League of Legends*. These are all practices that are intensifying, and which are shaping new ways of relating to connected customers who consume online and demand that their digital journeys be fluid and intuitive.

An article published in *Jing Daily* titled "The 6 Big China Luxury Trends From 2020,"[12] provided an interesting insight into the behavior of young Chinese consumers. The journalist explains: *"Today's consumers do not wait to become wealthy before they make high-end purchases. Over 75.6% of the young consumers surveyed said they get support from parents to buy luxury goods, and plenty of them are also willing to take out loans to buy products that they cannot afford yet."*

These millennials are also the most connected, surfing on We Chat, Weibo, TikTok, and now The Little Red Book (an up-and-coming Shanghai application dedicated to e-commerce). Live-streaming is spreading at full speed. *"More than 200 brands participated in Singles' Day in 2020, including 65 for the first*

---

12. Nica San Juan, "The 6 Big China Luxury Trends From 2020," *Jing Daily*, November 23, 2020.

time,[13] says Sebastien Badault, then Alibaba's Managing Director for France. Cartier and Estée Lauder both sold over 1 billion yuan (€126 million) worth of goods[14]. On the day, Dior inaugurated a monthly installment payment system spread over twelve months allowing consumers to purchase a sweater for 15.18 yuan (€1.90) a day. Many luxury brands have also partnered with commercial live streamers, hosts who hold live teleshopping sessions. Viya now sells Piaget bracelets and Alexander McQueen sneakers. Austin Li, another well-known live streamer, was recruited by Coach.

Celebrities play a fundamental role in the aspirational lifestyle of Generation Z. Loyalty from KOLs ("key opinion leaders") is very important. They are considered to be both unattainable stars, but also to be close to people. Brands are using them more and more. Zenith thus achieved its best performance yet in 2021. According to its president Julien Tornare, its collaboration with Chinese singer/artist Eason Chan, initiated in 2018, strongly boosted sales. Many new buyers, who were not familiar with the brand, rushed to the stores or online to order the clothes worn by the singer.

There is a great temptation for companies to limit themselves to this type of campaign, but even though ambassadors are good one-off growth levers, they do not generate long-term growth. The objective is to get people to discover the brand. In China, where there is a real mass culture, individuals follow the group. The effect caused by the announcement of Zenith's collaboration with Eason Chan would not have had the same repercussions in Europe or the United States.

---

13. Julie Zaugg, "Le Single's day, la nouvelle vitrine chinoise pour le luxe", *Les Echos*, December 17, 2020.
14. Julie Zaugg, *ibid.*

Luxury under influence

The Covid crisis has set the use of social networks in stone, especially since they are now new instant sales channels. Instagram is the flagship social network of DNVBs (Digital Native Vertical Brands), which dedicated almost all of their communication and marketing strategy to it. A little over 10% of brands have more than 100,000 followers, with only one brand (@Sezane) having 2.4 million. According to a study conducted in May 2020 by Influence4You and HypeAuditor, DNVBs invest an average of €80,000 every year in social networks.

The presence of luxury brands on social networks is now essential and is part of their strategies and marketing plans. The influence of the ambassadors for fashion houses is constantly growing.

Many luxury companies have resisted adopting an influence strategy until recently, traditionally preferring to use celebrities to represent their brands. But the Covid crisis prevented brands from offering luxurious in-store customer experiences. Their desire to conquer the younger generation has forced them to work with real or virtual influencers. All the big names in the sector have surrounded themselves with specialists to design campaigns with influencers. Chanel and Coty have even created an influence management position.

So the big luxury companies aren't afraid to change the rules anymore, inviting young influencers to front row places in their fashion shows, even though their worlds may seem far from the image that people have of a luxury brand, and whose influence has had mixed results in the past. Prada, which had commissioned Charlie D'Amelio to post videos of its 2020 fall/winter fashion show in Milan, only obtained very mediocre results.

On the other hand, Dior called on the influencer Léna Mahfouf with her 3.5 million subscribers, gaining it 274,000 new subscribers in 2020. Jaguar signed an Instagram campaign in collaboration with influencers for the release of its 100% electric I-Pace model. It was a strategy that paid off for the brand, which gained 4.2 engagement rate points on social networks, giving itself a connected and modern image, while capturing a new audience.

Other strategies are being developed. For example, Dior and Chanel are keen on unboxing. This type of content can be adapted to YouTube, TikTok and Instagram, via stories or IGTV (mobile video sharing application). Chanel did this with the French-Belgian influencer Milkywaysblueyes, who was filmed opening a Chanel bag to the sound of Vivaldi's "four seasons". The TikTok application has become a real powerhouse that fashion needs to work with. More and more brands are using this platform to communicate. The #cheapestthing trend, which consists of acquiring a piece of luxury on a limited budget by ordering products as cheaply as possible from a luxury brand such as Chanel, Gucci, Prada or Hermes, is rapidly growing. A $27 Chanel cotton makeup remover pad became the number one object of desire on the platform thanks to a three-part video of American influencer Erin Smelcer, who unpacked her order and raved about the famous cotton pads. This was an unboxing that has been viewed more than 7 million times.

Companies need to choose their influencers well, as in some cases they have become their main ambassadors. Depending on the brand, strategies differ, with their own objectives and challenges. Balenciaga chooses more creative and image-oriented partnerships. Others, like Chloé or Céline, are more discreet about influencer marketing.

Tomorrow, brands may go further, as Laurent Boillot, president of Hennessy and President of the Comité Colbert explains, by working with DAOs (Decentralized Autonomous Organizations). *"That's the question everyone needs to ask themselves,"* he says[15]. These decentralized autonomous organizations, which can be similar to discussion groups (on Discord, Telegram, etc.), are communities of enthusiasts, for example of art or investment, who come together to do things and work and are governed by the members themselves. *"Are brands ready, rather than using influencers, to co-create and tell a story together?"* he asks.

A new promise: to give products a second life

Towards a circular luxury economy

Second-hand purchases have exploded since 2019. The year 2020 accelerated this and saw this type of purchase grow by almost 50%. The health crisis pushed people to question their consumption patterns and made one out of two French people want to consume more responsibly.

This commitment inevitably translates into their relationships with brands. Logistics were very complex during the health crisis. During the lockdowns, people sorted out, sold their clothes and bought other items. The Lithuanian platform Vinted, which continued to expand during the crisis, currently has 37 million users in eleven European countries.

Second-hand, back to luxury?

The very principle of second-hand works well with the unique nature of luxury products. Originally, luxury consisted of only a

---

15. Interview of Laurent Boillot by the authors.

few pieces of the same product. Similarly, second-hand offers only a selection of a few unique products. Second-hand works well for luxury because it combines two of its defining elements – durability and timelessness. Above all, second-hand is responding to an exploding demand, with a market of more than €130 billion. In the future, it is likely that the various countries, starting with those in Europe, will impose production quotas on all luxury goods players, leading to their total transformation. Second-hand will be as much a part of tomorrow's sales as new product sales are today.

All types of products and goods are exchanged today on e-commerce platforms. If we take the example of France, 17% of French people used the second-hand market in 2005. This increased to over 66% in 2021. The Le Bon Coin website has 29 million monthly visitors. Eight hundred thousand ads are posted every day. And luxury products can be found on it too. As early as 2016, the press was very excited about the site. Yachts, 600 m² villas, Rolexes and classic cars were up for sale on the site. We don't know if these exceptional properties found takers, but controlling this trend is important.

One of the pillars of the circular economy

Many brands are aware of this and now offer services to take back, recycle and resell their products to give them a second life. The exponential growth in second-hand purchases is mainly due to people looking for attractive prices and a desire to consume sensibly. Consumers have also become increasingly aware of where their clothing comes from, challenging the disposable fashion culture. Buying second-hand is no longer considered taboo; young consumers are even proud of it. Some studies estimate that the second-hand market will be 1.5 times larger than the fast fashion market by 2029. As many as 33 million Americans are buying second-hand clothing for the first time in the United States.

Keeping clothes as long as possible is a central strategy for a circular fashion economy. An analysis of the positive impact of e-commerce on the environment shows benefits everywhere. ThredUP, which receives thousands of items per day and has the capacity to process up to 100,000 items daily, diverts clothing from landfill and reuses it. They estimate that if every American bought a used item instead of a new one in 2020, it would save 3.6 million tons of CO_2 (66 million trees planted), 100 billion liters of water (1.25 billion showers), 200 million kilos of waste (18,700 full garbage trucks).

The millennials and Generation Z are particularly fond of vintage fashion. Nearly half of them buy second-hand clothing. According to data collected by Yubo, 44% of Zs say they regularly shop at thrift stores. Their Generation X elders have also been won over by this type of purchasing. This evolution is being driven both by an ever-growing commitment to the environment and by the growth of purchases on social networks and online communities, responding to a clear trend.

Like buyers, private sellers are often financially motivated by the opportunity to earn a few extra dollars or euros while cleaning out their closets at the same time. But the second-hand market is not just motivated by the commercial potential of reselling products. Consumers are increasingly looking for sustainability, prompting companies to design products that last. This trend means brands are positioning themselves selling responsible fashion, in a circular economy logic.

By building business models around second-hand offerings, companies can create new value for their customers and themselves. Resale companies can establish lock-in models, offering vouchers to be used in stores in exchange for used products. The longer the life cycle of the product, the more it can be resold. Another advantage is that buying back allows the brand to regain control of its old products, which would otherwise be sold on third-party platforms such as Le Bon Coin or Vinted, often resulting in brand dilution. Traditional companies are beginning to set up resale business models by launching pilot solutions to separate them from their core business.

An essential next step is circularity, which includes the design of reusable or upgradeable products, the recycling of materials and aesthetic renewal using new concepts. This will lead to a closer and more sustainable relationship between brands and their customers. The possibility of updating the products, or even transforming them into other items will lead to loyalty.

A first technique is to let the remains of a collection mature for several years, then to offer it as it is as vintage products to those nostalgic for an old fashion. For example, Raf Simons and Versace are putting their old classics back on the market and Dries Van Noten is putting vintage pieces on sale in Los Angeles.

VISION & PERSPECTIVE

"The time is ripe for changing messages and searching for deep resonance."

Marc JACHEET, CEO, De Beers Brands

The Covid-19 crisis has had a dual effect on the luxury industry, seeing an acceleration of changes which had already been largely implemented and the emergence of new trends; some of which could become fully integrated into business structures. Personalization is increasing. Brands are all racing to collaborate on increasingly limited series, which are great for improving their image and exclusivity. In the future, they will be called on to co-create and personalize products with their customers, which is essentially a return to the roots of luxury with each customer having their own products. Digitalization is the order of the day for all companies, but few are completely "omni-

$\rightarrow$

33

→
channel" for the time being. Customers expect fluidity between the different information, purchase, delivery or repair channels. Brands need to hugely transform their technical infrastructures and train their teams. Continually offering new products, which had been underway for years, has come to a sudden halt. Many companies previously focused on entry-level prices with few new ultra-luxury products. During the Covid crisis, high net worth clients quickly reinvested in the latter.

Beyond these changes, several trends revealed by the Covid crisis have now become central. Due to the successive lockdowns and limited travel, the global discourse of major brands is evolving towards a more local approach. The time is ripe for changing messages and searching for deep resonance. Due to more awareness of the challenges linked to sustainable development, many brands have embarked on in-depth transformations: ecodesign of products, High Environmental Quality stores, "carbon positive" impact, etc. But few offer alternative, more ecological and sustainable distribution models. There are two trends which companies should closely follow – rental and resale.

Over the last ten years, several factors have driven the growth of luxury goods: the explosion of demand in China, the birth of digital technology, the ultra-fast changing of collections and the development of customer experiences.

It's time to consume "less but better". Luxury products could become items that are repaired and cared for throughout their lives.

Marc Jacheet began his career in marketing positions at Unilever and then Danone in Europe and the United States. He was Marketing Director at Moët & Chandon and then Director of Communications for Louis Vuitton in Europe. He was most recently President EMEA of Tiffany & Co. after serving as Managing Director France and President Asia Pacific in Singapore.

Upcycling

Upcycling, which consists in transforming a product to give it a second life (the product is reinvented by diverting it from its original use), has always existed, but it was not necessarily labeled as such. The most famous example is the "Petit H" collection by Hermès. New products are developed by multidisciplinary teams from leather, silk scraps or broken or imperfect crystal and goldsmithery objects.

The famous Dutch design duo Viktor & Rolf presented a couture collection made entirely of old stocks of lace ribbons, pieces of dresses, parts of sweatshirts and other remnants of previous designs, which seemed to have been assembled at random. The mannequins wore second-hand jewelry and shoes made of recycled plastic.

Louis Vuitton also transformed unsold "LV Trainer" sneakers into "LV Trainer Upcycling" sneakers. Prada uses recycled nylon for its Re-Nylon line. John Galliano, who is Creative Director at Maison Margiela, created the Recicla line. Fabric is cut, collars are lengthened and a label states the garment's previous origin and date. The same happens at Miu Miu who, after a capsule collection of 80 dresses from around the world, gave new life to used denim in collaboration with Levi's. A Marni collection was made from blankets and curtains painted with abstract graffiti.

Companies such as the Reiner Upcycling platform are championing the fight against waste and overturning these luxury codes by bringing a new generation of designers and brands to the forefront. In the U.S., the retail platform The RealRealReal has signed agreements with Stella McCartney, Burberry, Balenciaga, Dries Van Noten, Jacquemus and Gucci to create an upcycled line called "ReCollection01" using their unsold or defective pieces.

It is an initiative that goes beyond classic upcycling, its goal being to give the new items more value than the original ones.

The pandemic has acted as a catalyst, and upcycling has now become a grassroots movement that speaks to new generations, even if it is often still a marginal project whose impacts and limits are not yet fully understood.

"We are following what is happening," said Antoine Arnault at LVMH Climate Week in December 2020. It is an economy that exists and that is growing in importance. But it's still a little early for us."

The rise of e-commerce platforms

The rise of Internet resale

The e-commerce platform Monnier Frères, which brings together some 90 luxury brands including Balenciaga and Isabel Marant, spotted this phenomenon. It launched a second-hand service in 2021, in partnership with startup company Reflaunt.

"This service is a continuation of what we offer. Our aim was to respond to the increasingly strong expectations of our consumers with regard to impact to the environment,[16]" explained Diaa Elyaacoubi, who manages Monnier Frères, to *Challenges*. For the platform, which draws 65% of its traffic from millennials and Generation Zers, the introduction of this second-hand service was a no-brainer.

Across the Atlantic, the Rebag, Poshmark and HEWI (HardlyEverWornIt) platforms are growing rapidly. Collector

---

16. Valérie Xandry, "La seconde main: un nouvel eldorado du luxe?", *Challenges*, June 2, 2021.

Square, a specialist in online sales of second-hand luxury items, increased its sales by 45% in 2020.

Etsy, a U.S. platform for creative crafts (jewelry, leather goods, home decor), acquired British second-hand fashion platform Depop for $1.6 billion in early 2021, which is particularly popular with Generation Z. This example demonstrates the potential of this new niche. In 2020 Depop recorded 100% growth. The fragmented second-hand sector is expected to see an increase in concentration of applications and platforms.

While several luxury brands, including Chanel, prefer to keep their distance from The RealReal, others have joined forces with the site specializing in second-hand luxury goods, which, with its 17 million users, is one of the sector heavyweights, to encourage the resale of their own products, including, in October 2020, Gucci. With this new partner, the luxury second-hand platform is gaining in notoriety and credibility. *"Together we're shining a global spotlight on resale that we hope will encourage all consumers to support the circular economy and join us in reducing fashion's carbon footprint,"* Julie Wainwright, founder and CEO of The RealReal said in a statement. The platform has created a site dedicated to the resale of Gucci products – therealreal.com/gucci. Gucci continues to experience strong growth in demand, posting +19% in 2020. It is also the most requested masculine brand on the site for the third year in a row. By promoting the resale of its products, Gucci is extending their lifespan according to The RealReal, which claims that the brand's clothing deliveries to its site have *"saved 230 tons of carbon dioxide and more than 10 million liters of water to date, if we consider the environmental costs generated during the manufacturing of these items[17]"*.

---

17. Dominique Muret, "Gucci s'associe au site de seconde main TheRealReal", *Fashion Network*, October 7, 2020.

The Kering Group also confirmed its interest in the resale market by acquiring a 5% stake in Vestiaire Collective, the leader in second-hand fashion, in March 2021, now valued at over €1 billion. Founded in 2008, the French unicorn saw its transaction volumes grow by 100% in 2020 and recorded a 90% growth in the number of its members over one year (11 million). François-Henri Pinault, CEO of the Kering group, explained why in a press release:

"Second-hand luxury is now a real, deep-rooted trend, especially among younger consumers. Rather than ignore it, we want to seize this opportunity to continue to improve the services we offer our customers and to steer the future of our industry toward more innovative and sustainable practices. This is a natural fit with our entrepreneurial culture, our pioneering sustainable development strategy and our modern vision of luxury." Grégory Boutté, Chief Client and Digital Officer at Kering, agrees,

"Our innovation strategy aims to invest in brands and technologies for the next generation of consumers, focusing on breakthrough business models that will help us to better serve our customers and further improve our performance. Kering's investment in Vestiaire Collective fully meets these two key challenges."

Towards an integrated resale model

At first reluctant, brands are also beginning to create their own resale channels, such as Isabel Marant Vintage or Maje location. In the fall of 2021, Gucci announced the creation of Gucci Vault, a site dedicated to the sale of archive pieces and available in Europe, the United States and Japan. The idea is to sell vintage Gucci pieces, collected by the house's archivists from individuals and collectors around the world, which are reconditioned and sometimes also customized by designer Alessandro Michele.

It includes a selection of the brand's iconic bags from the 1960s to the 1980s, suitcases, scarves, as well as designer tableware.

The fashion house also offers a selection of pieces designed by emerging designers. "*Gucci Vault is a time machine, archive, library, laboratory and a meeting place,*" the brand explains in a press release.

"Weston Vintage": An example to follow

The French high-end shoe company J.M. Weston has always encouraged its customers to extend their shoes' lives – its restoration workshop in Limoges already reassembles and repairs 10,000 pairs every year. It wanted to go even further in the circular economy process. In January 2020, the company launched the "Weston Vintage" project in its store on rue Saint-Honoré. Customers can return Westons they no longer wear. An expert checks that the pair of shoes is repairable. If it is, the customer is given a voucher with a minimum value of €150. The shoes are sent back to Limoges for repair and are then available for sale in the collection and in Weston Vintage boutiques (Champs-Elysées, Saint-Honoré in Paris and Aoyama in Tokyo). If the shoes cannot be repaired, the customer is offered a treatment in the store. Is the project a good idea? "*It's a tribute to the collections that have built the history of the company. It also makes J.M. Weston reflect on production and consumption – that they are responsible,*" said Olivier Saillard, Artistic, Image and Culture Director of J.M. Weston[18].

The objective is also to recruit new customers, which explains such an aggressive pricing strategy, especially from a younger

18. Quoted by Laëtitia Blin, "J.M. Weston lance une gamme vintage de seconde main," *Leather Fashion Design*, November 6, 2019.

segment. J.M. Weston also caters to Japanese customers who are very fond of vintage products. But the brand also faces many challenges. The authentication of its products is a real issue and it is thinking of implementing a system using new technologies available (RFID, blockchain). Another challenge is that the prices charged by Weston Vintage are low compared to the product's real value. The perceived value of the product can send a negative message. Just as some watch brands, the most exemplary being Rolex, go up in value for certain models upon purchase, so should Weston shoes. The factory is also committed to restoring their shoes, with particular attention paid to the interior of the shoe.

VISION & PERSPECTIVE

"Luxury must offer a 1001 lives to its products."

Marc DURIE, President, J.M. Weston

The notion of eternity has always been closely linked to the world of luxury companies. This is seen in the time spent by the artisans to create materials and products, the intrinsic quality of products which are supposed to be able to resist the passage of time and the long-term vision of investments made to build a long-lasting brand.

A new frontier has recently been created for luxury, resulting from an increased awareness of the scarcity of our resources and more responsible consumption of them. The notion of eternity and time, coupled with environmental awareness, is beginning to lead luxury companies to refashion a product's history–from its creation to its first owner–but also the 1001 lives that will follow.

These successive histories will gradually shape the product and give it back the unique character that was at the very source of the notion of luxury, where products were originally elitist, completely handcrafted and unique. The extraordinary

→

→
development of the luxury industry in the last 30 years has caused it to lose much this notion of scarcity that is the very essence of its existence.

This passage of time on the product, and the story told by the different owners should allow brands to get back to their rare magical roots.

Marc Durie, a graduate of the EM Lyon business school, has held important positions in luxury goods companies such as Louis Vuitton, J. Mendel, Yves Saint Laurent and Louboutin.

His duties included merchandizing (LV), directing the global marketing strategy and presiding over the Asia-Pacific region (YSL).

Finally, Weston, like many other luxury brands, competes with multi-brand resale platforms such as TheRealReal or Vestiaire Collective, which sometimes offer more attractive buyback prices.

At the same time, many brands have been reluctant to develop their own sales platforms. They are more aware of the stakes in terms of image and business. Many branded products are not checked or authenticated on the various platforms, making it easy for many counterfeit items to be listed. There are many reasons for brands to act quickly and not to give up space to platforms whose objective is very different – to do business and not to be guarantors of the image of the brands they resell.

The second-hand jewelry and watch sector is also very active. In June 2018, Richemont acquired Watchfinder, a specialist in the retail of pre-owned watches.

In July 2018, MB&F opened a section on its website called "MB&F Certified Pre-Owned," dedicated to selling rare pre-owned pieces. Cartier also founded the "Cartier Care" program for its watches, which offers rental services and buy-back offers. Zenith has launched the "Zenith Icons" collection, offering an assortment of rare and highly coveted watches that have been acquired, restored and certified by the manufacturer.

Panerai and Vacheron Constantin, subsidiaries of the Richemont Group, are also offering a new trade-in service in partnership with Watchfinder. In its stores, a Panerai watch can be obtained, after being verified by Watchfinder's experts, in exchange for a luxury watch – first and foremost from Richemont such as Cartier, IWC, Jaeger le Coultre, A. Lange & Sohne or Vacheron Constantin. For Vacheron Constantin, exchanges can only be made within the brand's range. By entering the second-hand market, watchmaking companies are following their objective of preserving their models and their heritage. Another key benefit of reselling is improving companies' lifetime relationships with their customers, offering essential services to upgrade their products and benefit from the latest technologies.

Another example is the Rolex Submariner, known as the "Kermit" or the "Hulk". Sold at €9,050, it can be resold for over €18,000 the same day on the site Chrono24, and even reach more than €25,000 a few months later. Some observers caution, however, that the market for pre-owned luxury watches has experienced many financial bubbles. The pattern is well known – a model becomes rare, collectors rush to buy it, making the price of the watch rise, sellers flood the market and the bubble bursts.

Second life: a new revolution for department stores

The retail sector has understood the importance of the movement, especially the department stores, which suffered greatly from the health crisis, which deprived them of their international clientele.

In May 2021, Selfridges, already home to second-hand and rental clothing stands, launched "Project Earth," a new five-year plan to become more attractive to younger consumers whose purchases are more heavily influenced by ethical and environmental principles. Selfridges director Anne Pitcher tells the *Guardian* she is seeing an evolution that goes far beyond simply moving from physical to online shopping:

"Consumers will shop with businesses that they trust, that they know care, businesses that choose doing the right thing over making money, and businesses who are transparent in the way they do business[19]." For example, the plan encourages the use of sustainable materials, such as organic cotton or nylon made from marine waste. By 2025, Selfridges even wants to exclusively use materials from sustainable sources. All plastic packaging will be recyclable, reusable or compostable. On the second-hand platform Resellfridges, customers can buy vintage clothing and offer their own items for sale in exchange for vouchers. In collaboration with the specialist Hurr Collective, the British department store is also launching a rental service where you can rent items for 4 to 20 days. Selfridges is also changing people's perception of second-hand clothing by placing them in a luxury section and providing customers with a high-end experience.

In France, after the launch of their Go for Good label in 2018, which highlights products that have a reduced impact on the environment, Galeries Lafayette has continued its commitment to new lifestyles with the inauguration of a 5,600-square-meter Parisian venue dedicated to circulatory fashion at Paris Haussmann (Re) Store Galeries Lafayette in the fall of 2021, combining vintage, responsible brands and services where customers can drop off

---

19. Sarah Butler, "Selfridges launches Project Earth to connect with its ethical consumers," *The Guardian*, August 17, 2020.

and recycle old clothes. *"Thirty percent of French people bought second-hand items in the last 12 months, and this booming market is transforming the fashion sector long-term and becoming part of our customers' everyday life."* Says Nicolas Houzé, CEO of Galeries Lafayette and BHV. *"As a leading department store that aims to make responsible retailing accessible to all, it was appropriate for us to provide a credible and desirable offering and concept and include a complete ecosystem of products and services, because second-hand fashion has its rightful place in both our physical and online stores[20]."*

Seven partners specializing in second-hand goods have taken up residence on the (Re)Store floor, some of them exclusively, including Monogram, a specialist in items from luxury fashion houses and cutting-edge labels; Relique, which sells clothing and decorations inspired by the 1970s; Personal Seller Paris, the first personal selling service for private individuals; and Imparfaite, a marketplace specializing in sales of vintage clothing and accessories, bringing together over 2,000 partners. The floor also offers a space for brands committed to more responsible fashion. The brands use upcycling, reuse of offcuts, natural, organic or recycled materials and limited series. Patine, Salut Beauté, Barje, Maison Flore and Patagonia are among the partner brands. In addition to textiles (Re)Store also offers a concept store-style drugstore with refillable cosmetics, ultra-concentrated detergent, water bottles and Marseille soap. The store also offers services to complement the product offering. Customers can bring back items to resell them through the venue's partners. It is also possible to bring back textiles, shoes, perfume bottles or make-up packaging

---

20. Galerie Lafayette Group, "The Galeries Lafayette group inaugurates Le (Re)Store Galeries Lafayette and reviews progress made in responsible fashion," Group website, September 14, 2021.

for recycling, which customers then earn loyalty points for. It is a way for companies to create a link with customers by thinking outside the commercial box.

Luxury is torn between priorities that are not pressing for decision makers, and there is always a wait-and-see attitude towards certain positions. Second life or new life illustrates this well. Brands are still often reluctant to take the plunge. There are still many obstacles for them. As brands grow, it is difficult for them to think about second life business models. Focused on the short term, they are afraid of cannibalization and think that a catalog of "second life" products won't bring additional sales and, on the contrary, would have a negative impact on sales and margins. They are wrong, though, because these are different customers and different experiences. In addition, the ability to tell the story of a piece of jewelry, a bag or a piece of clothing worn by several people or generations without revealing the identity of former customers makes storytelling even more exciting.

VISION & PERSPECTIVE

"We are joining a global conversation that no longer distinguishes between high and low culture."

Guillaume Houzé, Image and Communication Director, Member of the Board of Directors, Galeries Lafayette

I remember the image of Kylian Mbappé on the pitch at the 2018 World Cup wearing a pair of Nike Off-Whites signed by Virgil Abloh, Louis Vuitton Artistic Director. I think this is a good illustration that fashion and luxury today (and even more so tomorrow) feeds (and will feed) more than just a market. The sector's small industrial revolution is being primarily carried out as a cultural revolution.

→

→

For several years now, hybridization has been changing our industries' preconceived ideas. Creators show us how much our social and cultural models must adapt to the great challenges of our time. In a post-Internet or post-truth world, notions of authority and legitimacy are being challenged.

And it is precisely these concepts that fashion and luxury have used to flourish in recent decades. I would say that we are gaining vitality and relevance because we are joining a global conversation that no longer distinguishes between high and low culture.

Guillaume Houzé joined the family group in 2008. He has developed a program of events and sponsorship focused on industrial and artistic creation. He is President of the group's corporate foundation – Lafayette Anticipations – as well as President of Andam (National Association for the Development of Fashion Arts).

Luxury product rental, responsible and reasonable consumption

Rental is also growing, especially among the younger generations, and now forms part of the post-pandemic redeployment of spending. It also participates in the grassroots movement of responsible consumption and circularity. The user pays less to satisfy their desire for enjoyment, appearance and change. The producer initiates and cultivates a relationship with the consumer, and promotes future purchases. Seven out of ten French people say they are interested in the long-term rental of at least one product or piece of equipment and one out of two would choose long-term rental of clothing for special occasions and holidays[21].

---

21. Sofinscope, July 2021.

For the moment, the rental of luxury goods represents only a small portion of the second-hand market – about one tenth of its turnover[22] – but it is growing rapidly.

Rental of luxury items and transactions between individuals, particularly in fashion, are two rapidly growing trends that are gradually affecting all personal luxury items. Transactions between individuals are booming. The market had a turnover of more than 100 billion dollars in 2019, according to the British firm Deloitte. But the health crisis has had a major impact on the sector. For example, the American website Rent the Runway, launched in 2009, has closed five of its stores, including its Manhattan flagship store. Among the reasons for the closures is the decline in events such as weddings, cocktail parties and meetings which can justify rental, but also logistical constraints increased by the additional disinfection required.

With Panoply, Chic by Choice, Rent the Runway, By Rotation, you can rent by the item or through a subscription. Vivrelle, a specialist in fashion accessory rentals, recently made significant sales. There are considerable growth prospects for rental for different lengths of time, with the possibility of exchange. Many brands will undoubtedly occupy this niche, in line with reasonable and sustainable consumption. Ralph Lauren is already developing its own rental service. For $125 per month, subscribers select a set of clothing from the Lauren mid-range collection. The clothes are sent in batches of four. The service includes delivery, return and upkeep of the clothes. This is a test run, for possible extension to another range. Kering also decided to test renting bags from major brands in 2021, by taking a stake in the Cocoon platform.

---

22. Victor Gosselin, "La location, marché d'avenir pour la mode?", *Time to Disrupt*, December 26, 2020.

Other brands refuse to offer such services for the moment. Their credo is that there is a fusion between the luxury product, clothing or accessory and the personality of the customer who has chosen it. The subtle mix cannot be repeated and especially not in the short time of a rental. This argument is consistent with the image of the luxury product as something exceptional. In total, rental revenues could, according to Bain, account for 10% of total revenue by 2030.

Ultra-luxury in Covid times

While some companies such as Accor are expanding into the ultra-luxury segment, the Covid crisis, unlike the financial crisis of 2008, has not had an impact on this segment. The number of "ultra-rich" people with a net worth of more than $50 million has not fallen according to Credit Suisse. Only 120 individuals have fallen out of this category of 176,000 people, half of whom are American.

As for billionaires, they have not been affected the crisis. They increased from 2,095 in 2019 to 2,755 in 2020. 660 new billionaires made it into the *Forbes* business magazine's famous annual ranking for 2021. As the magazine summarizes, since March 2020, "the world on average gained a new billionaire every 17 hours[23]." The cumulative wealth of these 2,755 billionaires is now 13,100 billion dollars against "only" 8,000 in 2020. In the overall ranking, the United States and China are the most represented countries: "*The United States is still in the lead, with 724 billionaires, followed by China (including Hong Kong and Macau) with 698 billionaires*," says the American magazine.

---

23. Chase Peterson-Withorn, "Nearly 500 people became billionaires during the pandemic year," *Forbes*, April 6, 2021.

Like Ferrari, several brands have been able to resist the crisis. Rolls Royce, which at the start of the pandemic lost 20 to 25% in sales volume, has rebounded strongly since the last quarter of 2020:+49% over the year. This has never before been seen in the history of the brand, which was founded in 1904. *"Demand remains very strong, and not just from Asia, but from the United States and Europe too. There is currently a promising global situation and I think that it is the same for all of the luxury sector. There is lots of money waiting to be spent,"* CEO Torsten Müller-Ötvös told AFP, when he announced the launch of a car for the ultra-rich in May 2021; the most expensive car in the world at €23.5 million, the "Boat Tail", whose rear mirrors a yacht. *"Customers come to us with an idea in mind, which is exactly what happened a hundred years ago [...]. This back-to-basics goes back to the "Sweptail" in 2017, when we launched the first modern-day Coachbuild unit project. [...] It caught the attention of some customers who wanted something similar, but even more spectacular,"* he explained. The price wasn't revealed, *"We never talk about price in agreements with our customers."* But the rumors that the Sweptail cost $13 million were probably pretty close to the truth, knowing that *"the Boat Tail is much more refined."*

Richard Mille is the most luxurious watch brand in the world, loved by billionaires, Russian oligarchs, wealthy Indians, Emirati princes and star footballers. It is the quintessence of ultra-luxury positioning. Its first watch, the RM 001 Tourbillon, dates back to 2001. From the outset, Richard Mille has produced watches using exceptional technology and an original look recognizable to everyone with the mechanism on show. The brand benefits from prestigious ambassadors, sponsors high-end sports events and severely limits the number of its stores to carefully selected global metropolises. It has also been forward-thinking, having implemented a solution for guaranteed second-hand acquisitions as early as 2015, with a network of ten authorized dealers.

Jacob & Co. jewelry and watches are worn by showbiz stars. For many hip-hop artists, a trip to Jacob & Co. is synonymous with success. Jacob & Co. watches offer one-of-a-kind items, some selling for over $18 million.

The pandemic did not stop the jeweler from innovating. In 2020 he launched a fantastic communications campaign by creating the most luxurious mask in the world, "The Diamond Face Mask", composed of more than 3,000 diamonds and in 2021 with Alec Monopoly, a renowned artist from New York, who became famous for his ironic paintings inspired by a certain board game based on transactions, he launched nine limited edition Monopoly watches priced at $600,000 each.

Philipp Plein, a self-made provocateur, has built an empire on evening wear jogging suits, skull and crossbones T-shirts, diamond-encrusted skulls and studded sneakers; luxury clothing, which is, of course, extremely expensive, fashioned in a "street couture" spirit, where the "ugly", far from being banished, is welcomed. The German has no limits and is proud of it.

In the midst of the storm, the ultra-luxury sector has nevertheless experienced some downturns. Apart from Ferrari and Rolls Royce, the luxury car segment has stalled, with a 10% decline according to Bain. Private airplane flights also dropped by 30% in the midst of the crisis, as did visits to luxury hotels, which, according to the same source, lost 60% of their revenue. The crisis has clearly had an impact on the wealthiest proportion of the population's consumption, who have redirected their spending, particularly into segments such as the home. Hermès Maison, for example, had never before experienced such an explosion in sales.

2

The Emergence of a New Normal

T he unprecedented Covid crisis has led organizations to quickly react and reorganize themselves. The luxury sector had never found itself at such a standstill before. Having gone through two years of crisis, brands have been able to adapt and take stock of the "new normal".

Generalized digitalization of brands

The luxury sector had cautiously developed its presence on the Internet in the 2010s. Product information, information about the brand and its history had long been the main, if not exclusive, purpose of websites. The pandemic swept away any reluctance by companies. Digital technology, which was considered a threat by the most prestigious luxury companies, has become something unavoidable and is right at the heart of the sector's transformation. For luxury brands, the main challenge is to accompany their customers through a multitude of new contact points and to offer a multi-channel strategy.

"The responsibility of brands to create lead to progress in luxury."

Henrik WENDERS, Senior Vice President, Audi

Luxury is entering the most exciting era of a true win-win situation for luxury. We will win more luxurious experiences thanks to digitalization and greater personalization thanks to artificial intelligence, which enables brands to give experiences at the right time at the right location, which feel tailor-made. The second win is that the audience, which is able to appreciate luxurious moments and ecosystems are realizing the race that humankind must win: the race to save the planet's resources before it is too late. Indeed, the audience, which is consuming luxurious moments have a prestigious role to play in the future of luxury because as they are the ones who are deciding and defining trends. Luxury customers today are interested in solutions to slow purchase and not fast purchase. By consuming with low impact, this is the key, the interest in quality is further increased, which is a win for luxury brands. In summary, the future of luxury will be progressive, and consumers will appreciate in a progressive way, both in the online and offline standpoint.

Luxury brands need to find solutions that meet customers' needs for luxury moments and experiences, but that enable them to do so responsibly. This new era of progressive luxury will be here for the decade, so let's catch the train and apply a progressive way to enjoy luxury. Let's apply solutions to the most educated society on planet earth, leverage the know-how and solutions to create a world that we want to live in.

Henrik Wenders spent part of his career at BMW, first as Head of International Advertising, then as Head of Brand Management for Mini in Europe, and later Vice President of Product Management for BMWi. He has been Senior Vice President of the Audi brand since 2020.

In Burberry's "social retail store" in Shenzhen, China, omnichannel has been integrated into the shopping experience: customers are rewarded with a social currency for their online engagement on the brand's WeChat mini-program, which is redeemable against free food at the store's café. Some brands have developed a 100% digital offering, like DressX and The Fabricant, which have entered the digital fashion market. DressX is reinventing consumption for an audience seeking constant novelty and something to wear online.

Fashion weeks have returned to their pre-Covid timetable, but several brands, including the leading ones, have taken advantage of the crisis to revolutionize them. While these fashion weeks in the major capitals used to involve lavishly creative shows, travel all over the world and direct contact with the media and buyers, the health crisis has sparked shows in new digital formats and prompted brands to reject the traditional four collections per year. Saint Laurent presented a spectacular online collection in the middle of the desert with a final statement, *"I wish you were here"*. After the Moroccan dunes, the house presented its women's ready-to-wear collection for the fall/winter 2021–2022 season in a fashion show filmed in Iceland.

Thanks to the agility of digital technology, creators can be more in control of their schedules. Shows are more innovative and more accessible and brands reach more people. Louis Vuitton broadcast its September 2021 fashion show live on the Internet from the Louvre, getting 10 million views compared to 1 million the year before. The new normal of luxury has a new fundamental dimension – digital technology. Many brands have developed ways to combine digital with physical. Augmented reality offers experiences that are impossible in-store. For example, Too Faced offered virtual makeup tutorials and Louis Vuitton used its logo to trigger a "virtual installation" featuring an image of its iconic suitcases. Digital technology enables companies to be permanently connected to their customers, even when physical sales aren't possible. Brands have continued to offer their services in spite of the crisis, such as Louis Vuitton, which has equipped all of its salespeople with software that gives them access to the entire stock inventory in their area. Deployed worldwide, these new strategies add a new aspect to market conquest.

The brand as a new media type

Bottega Veneta's announcement in early 2021 that it would withdraw from all social networks had a huge impact. The double-digit sales growth in the last quarter of 2020 had allowed it to differentiate itself, at least for a limited period. The brand's long-term policy on social networks will bring many lessons. Which substitutes to digital forums can be used to keep a community of customers alive and expand it? The brand's decision was not made on a whim by its artistic director Daniel Lee, who has since left Bottega Veneta. It was a strategic decision. François-Henri Pinault, CEO of Kering, which the brand belongs to, explained that he wanted to make a different use of social networks, and provide influencers with the material they needed to talk about the brand. Bottega Veneta has not actually left the Internet. Firstly, because it has kept its accounts on social media in Asia (Japan, Korea and China). Not losing its presence on this continent and particularly in China means that this is where the customers are and therefore its priority market. To celebrate the Chinese New Year in January 2021, the Italian company installed a giant digital screen on a part of the Great Wall of China for six days, featuring its logo with the words "Happy New Year" in Mandarin. Then, a few months later, in April 2021, it launched its first digital magazine, *Issue*, presented as an immersive and intimate experience, which will be published at each collection launch.

Digital magazines like Bottega Veneta's or podcasts are all ways for brands to regain some power, because they control their content and their environment, unlike on social networks. However, the major fashion brands are increasingly getting to grips with digital media. The Internet is no longer only used to inform, present and conclude sales online. Their creative minds have also started to use this new media in their creations.

In an environment where more and more brands are launching their own podcasts, the luxury sector is following the trend. According to a Havas/CSA study, there are now more than 3.4 million podcast fans in France, the majority of whom are in the highest professional categories. 58% of listeners are under 35 years old. Brands such as Chanel, Gucci, Dior, Balmain, Cartier and Guerlain use podcasts in different ways to express their values, or to start a dialogue with customers, experts or celebrities. Since the pandemic, podcasts have dramatically increased in number. There is definitely a "market" out there for them.

LVMH has developed an in-house digital radio station on its Shero platform for sharing articles, videos and podcasts dedicated to career development within the group. Videos of internal events increased in 2020: fashion shows, documentaries such as *Woman*, testimonies on *Echo Day*, showcases such as "LVMH's Diversity and Inclusion Policy" and internal promotion of the Life 360 plan.

In the spring of 2021, Guerlain launched a new beauty experience – Olfactory Creations, available exclusively on Clubhouse. It featured an intimate conversation with Guerlain's master perfumer, Thierry Wasser, and *Harper's Bazaar US* beauty director and blogger Jessica Matlin. The 40-minute discussion focused on the art of high perfumery, as told by the fifth-generation Guerlain perfumer. Through this live chat, Guerlain offered a much more active experience than on other social platforms.

Balmain has launched L'Atelier Balmain Podcast, a series exploring the key themes and history of the 75-year-old company to understand how the ideas of its artistic director, Olivier Rousteing and his team build on this legacy, and it then launched its miniseries *Fracture* in September 2021, with five episodes available on VOD on the UK Channel 4 website, as well as on the brand's website.

"I'm so proud to announce that we have been working on creating a new Balmain series with Channel 4 called Fracture. *It's a new exciting project and I'm so glad to go beyond fashion and start working in a new world for me. I can't wait for you to see our new series."* Olivier Rousteing announced on Instagram. Through the show, Internet users can discover the brand's new fall/winter collection. The aim is to have other seasons of the series in the future. This is the first time that a brand of this kind has created this type of audiovisual production. For Txampi Diz, Balmain's CMO, the brand is entering a new phase in the development of a strategy initiated several years ago, which aims to replace traditional communication with entertainment content developed and distributed in-house: *"Brands, fashion houses, are becoming media. We need to act as media. The key for that is storytelling, it is content."* To build up the universe around the show and especially to encourage the creation of traffic to its e-commerce site, Balmain is also setting up a dedicated Instagram account, Le Rêve Motel; the name of one of the main sets on the series. It offers additional content and will be an area for interaction between fans and the brand.

YSL Beauté went one step further in its media presence. The brand launched a documentary in September 2021 called "Push the Boundaries" *"to highlight those who have dared going beyond expectations and norms"*. The movement is embodied in three inspiring young women. Each episode reveals the daily life and unusual journey of these talented women. Dancer and choreographer BadGyalCassie, DJ Chloé and gamer Jasmine tell how they rebelled and fought to make a place for themselves, each in their own way.

And to celebrate this new era, YSL opened a new venue in Shanghai in July 2021. The four-level "Push the Boundaries". Beauty Zone is a life-size video game-like space dedicated to discovery, experimentation and passion. Inside, a new universe opens up, where live performances, dance challenges, master-classes and drone battles take place – all broadcast live on 360° screens and the brand's social networks. Each level lets visitors live out their passions, without forgetting to enjoy beauty expe-riences. There is a dedicated space for game girls. Dancers can push themselves with TikTok challenges, or test products while dancing. Guided by the YSL Beauty Zone App, visitors have access to exclusive shopping opportunities and can create unique content. For Stephan Bezy, YSL Beauté's International General Manager, *"the YSL Beauty Zone is a post-Covid concept imagi-ned to help people bring their ideas to fruition, to collaborate and to learn from each other. It offers our influencers a platform to improve their visibility, to allow them to reveal their talents and express themselves freely. The Beauty Zone is a place of disco-very designed to encourage an exchange of ideas, allow visitors to meet, act and create links. By adding a live-streaming element to the elevator walls and our social media, we've concocted the perfect recipe to bring unique, cutting-edge events to life[24]."*

After video games, TV series or live-streaming, brands are also launching their own TV channels to reveal, in addition to simple runway shows or collections, real creative universes and

---

24. AFP-Relaxnews, "Telfar lance sa propre chaîne de télévision," *Fashion Network*, September 14, 2021.

stay in permanent contact, whether there is a pandemic or not, with their community. At New York Fashion Week in September 2021, Telfar Clemens, founder of the Telfar brand, announced the launch of his brand's television channel, Telfar TV. This innovative concept will showcase a variety of talents from different backgrounds including music, Telfar Clemens' other passion. The designer, who launched his brand in 2005, wants to reclaim the content surrounding his label and offer his customers items that they can purchase directly–without having to deal with stock outs caused by automated purchasing of hundreds of pieces at a time. The channel can be streamed on a dedicated site and is also available for download on Apple TV or Roku. Among its highlights, Telfar TV will offer random QR codes for brand fans and customers to access new products online. It is a way to encourage loyalty from those who don't always have access to limited edition collections or collaborations.

Something else which appeared in the Covid pandemic in 2020 was the Clubhouse social network, an audio platform for peer-to-peer discussion. Several brands have invested in this new network. Knowledgeable customers can converse with experts in different themed lounges. Breitling is developing its aeronautical roots by organizing meetings on aviation. Versace launched part of its "Medusa Power" campaign there. Stars such as Virgil Abloh and Naomi Campbell act as influencers. However, Clubhouse has come up against significant user disaffection with their return to "normal" life.

The explosion of e-commerce platforms

Covid and the closure of stores led to an explosion of purchases on the Internet and e-commerce has taken hold. Online sales for luxury brands rose sharply in 2020. Prada has tripled its sales.

"The pandemic has accelerated our digital evolution, reinforcing our omnichannel strategy," commented the Italian brand at the presentation of its annual results. Its e-commerce is supported by a global logistics platform. *"The online customer experience is becoming more and more immersive,"* Prada adds. In the third quarter, Kering recorded a 102% jump in online sales, driven by the United States and Asia-Pacific. *"In the first nine months of the year, e-commerce accounted for 12.5% of own sales,"* the group said.

According to figures reported by L'Oréal for all of its activities, e-commerce accounted for 26.8% of sales in the first quarter of 2021. For the same period, Gucci generated 14% of its retail sales online, up from 9% in the first half of 2020.

At LVMH a strong acceleration in online sales in 2020 partially offset the effect on sales of the closure of the group's stores for several months. *"LVMH showed remarkable resilience against the unprecedented health crisis the world experienced in 2020 [...] Our Maisons have shown great agility and creative energy in continuing to bring to life our customers' dreams through a unique digital experience thereby further strengthening their desirability."* commented Bernard Arnault, its CEO, during the presentation of its 2020 fourth quarter results. In addition to Vuitton, which has a strong digital presence, the perfumes and cosmetics business, particularly in Asia, has seen a strong growth in online sales. Sephora is also at the forefront of this area, with online sales reaching historic levels in all of its markets, and the development of services such as click & collect and live shopping.

The online sale of luxury goods has significantly accelerated. It accounted for 12% of the market in 2019. It reached 22% in 2021 and is expected to rise to 29% of total sales in 2025[25]. For

---

25. Bain & Company, "Luxury Goods Worldwide Market Study, Fall 2021", study, 20th edition, November 2021.

many years, the luxury industry resisted the temptation of online sales. Brands developed their own tools at first. Platforms specializing in luxury were a second step. Then big multi-brand platforms such as Farfetch, Net-a-Porter, Matchesfashion.com and Mytheresa became essential.

Brands are using Farfetch and its global expansion to open up new markets, especially in China. With the health crisis, they have had to step up their investments in this area, as the young Chinese generations are constantly connected to social networks.

In November 2020, the luxury group Richemont (owner of Cartier, among others) and the Chinese giant Alibaba announced that they were injecting $1.1 billion into Farfetch and its new Chinese marketplace. The installation of Farfetch on Alibaba's Tmall Luxury Pavilion has offered unparalleled visibility to its 3,500 brands, which are now accessible to the 760 million users of its Chinese ally. Two platforms specialized in luxury goods are breaking into the market in China – Alibaba's Tmall Luxury Pavilion and JD.com.

Created in 2018, Tmall Luxury Pavilion brought together more than 200 luxury brands around the world in 2021. The platform offers personalized experiences with augmented reality, magazines, games and live-streaming events hosted by the brands themselves. In addition, Tmall has a Luxury Soho outlet store, aimed at Generation Zers, offering promotions, vintage products and capsule collections.

Moschino joined Tmall in 2018. At a roundtable discussion during the New York Retail Show in January 2021, attended by Stefano Secchi, Managing Director of the Italian brand, Christina Fontana, Head of Fashion and Luxury at Alibaba's luxury division, Tmall explained *"Tmall allows brands to distribute their content in the form of programs to targeted audiences in China...*

It is up to brands to entertain, engage customers and increase their loyalty." It is a successful partnership–Moschino is said to have doubled its revenue generated on Tmall Luxury Pavilion in 2020.

Hermès completed its site's e-commerce activities by moving to Tmall Luxury Pavilion for perfumes and cosmetics. Cartier has also successfully used this platform. Live stream demonstrations reach an audience of nearly one million Chinese Internet users. Cartier's results on this platform are judged to be the best of all luxury houses. Gucci is also a flagship of Luxury Pavilion, like Balenciaga and Kenzo.

In early 2021, Louis Vuitton, which had been the first luxury brand to partner with Little Red Book (Xiaohongshu), also known as Red, China's most popular social and commerce platform created in 2013, chose to establish itself on the Chinese site JD.com, which has annual traffic of 472 million users. Clicks on the French brand's products featured on the platform will lead to its official WeChat program where the transaction can be concluded.

A fierce battle is being waged between the popular platforms among Chinese consumers. Montreal-based platform Ssense raised $4.1 billion to expand its footprint in Asia-Pacific. The origin of this financing was the Chinese fund Sequoia Capital China, which has also taken a majority stake in the French brand AMI and more recently in the South Korean designer We11Done. Ssense offers a selection of brands oriented towards the under 40s. Gucci, Balenciaga and Prada are among its best-sellers.

Amazon, the e-commerce giant until now shunned by fashion, launched a luxury space in September 2021 to make a place for itself alongside the major platforms in the sector.

Today, these platforms are developing in a different direction by launching their own brand. After Mr. Porter and 8 by Yoox, it's the turn of a new brand to see the light of day on a luxury online sales platform, the women's ready-to-wear line There Was One (TWO), launched in October 2021 on the Farfetch site, in partnership with New Guards Group (NGG), which was acquired by the site in August 2019, and which includes Palm Angels, Marcelo Burlon, Opening Ceremony and Heron Preston among others, and which manages the production and distribution of Off-White.

Brands have realized the importance of e-commerce. They have also been able to revisit their strategies and know that these different platforms, apart from generating valuable revenues, capture useful data about their customers. But the popularization of these platforms, with an increasing number of brands present – from entry-level to the most exclusive brands – can act as a repellent. It is likely that in the near future, a large number of luxury brands will reserve their sales to their own e-commerce sites, leaving the less exclusive brands to existing platforms.

Finally, e-commerce should not reduce the number of customers visiting stores. According to a survey conducted in early 2021 in the United States by Ifop, upper-class women prefer to shop for high-end products in the brand's boutiques. This direct link is just as important as having a website.

VISION & PERSPECTIVE

"A more customer-oriented vision of luxury"

Pauline DOLLÉ-LABBÉ, Chief Marketing Officer, 24S (groupe LVMH)

We are at a turning point for consumer society.

I forecast three trends for luxury.

It will certainly be more responsible with brands that are increasingly actively involved. Tomorrow's consumers are today's

→

→

younger generations and they are looking for transparency, inclusiveness and responsibility. Luxury brands have already understood this and have set a movement in motion that will only become more pronounced, to play an active role in ecological change and also to defend more and more social, cultural and political causes. They will unite communities around values that go beyond their initial value proposition.

Tomorrow's luxury will increasingly focus on services and experiences, with growing importance placed on entertainment. Consumers will be looking less for material possessions and more for fluidity and extreme ease of use. This is where brands will be able to compete in terms of services – notably thanks to digital technology – but also in terms of wonder and experience, sources of unique, exclusive and memorable emotions.

Finally, driven by the power of digital technology, the luxury industry will be increasingly required to make a shift from a traditional product-centric and retail-centric focus to a much more client-centric focus. Customer knowledge, ultra-personalization, tailor-made services, omnichannel presence to match customers' wishes and satisfaction measurement are already a must in many industries and will impose a profound transformation on luxury companies' cultures and organizations.

The challenge will be to deal with these profound changes by constantly innovating and reinventing, while cultivating the luxury industry's magic and age-old skills that will forever fascinate customers.

Pauline Dollé-Labbé began her career at Club Med Paris and then in Singapore where she deployed the expansion strategy in Asia as well as the brand's upmarket positioning. Previously, she was Marketing Director at FNAC, and joined 24S (LVMH) as Chief Marketing Officer in 2018.

Livestream shopping

Live shopping, an online sales technique that lets social network users buy products presented in a live video straight away, is becoming a new trendy shopping technique. This trend, which originated in China and is said to have accounted for more than 1 billion yuan of spending ($154 billion) in 2020, was popularized by e-commerce giant Alibaba with its annual Singles Day shopping festival.

More than a short-lived fashion fad, live shopping, and more broadly the concept of "shoppertainment" (online shopping while having fun), is gaining in popularity[26]. According to Frost & Sullivan, its global turnover should reach 413 billion dollars in 2022 – a godsend for brands faced with consumers who are still reluctant to come and stroll around stores! This concept has many advantages: developing brands' notoriety, expanding their catchment area to an international level, personalizing offerings and saving on their marketing budget by accessing an existing community of subscribers. The trend is still in its infancy in France, but an Altavia ShopperMind/ Opinionway study published in March 2021, shows that French people's interest, particularly young women's, in live shopping is promising.

How can this strong interest be explained? In addition to the fact that it is a mode of purchase that is considered innovative, it also has the benefits of being both practical and easy to access. It also adds the feel of it being an "event" which increases its appeal.

---

26. See Robin Coulet's article, "*Live shopping*: la prochaine revolution *retail*", *Journal du Net*, October 9, 2020.

According to the same study, live shopping inspires confidence in the young women surveyed. It adapts to their needs, saves them time and helps improve their image of the salesperson. Finally, it is a distribution method that appeals to socialites, especially generation Zers. Consumers can have the same experience as in a physical store, with the advantage of getting the opinion of an influencer. They also see the reactions of other consumers and don't have to go anywhere. For example, the Chinese influencer known as "Lipstick Brother 1" sold 15,000 tubes of lipstick in just 15 minutes in a live shopping event on Taobao!

The Italian fashion house Dolce & Gabbana unveiled its "Virtual Boutique Experience" in Osaka, Japan in September 2020. Its promise is a site dedicated to virtual shopping in the company's iconic boutiques, all from the comfort of your home. It has been a real success for the brand, which has since rolled out this experience in France.

Many American and European brands (Kim Kardashian Perfumes, Lancôme, Louis Vuitton) have seized upon the live shopping opportunity to access the Chinese market, but in France its development is still timid. During the lockdowns, forced to close their stores, Galeries Lafayette reacted quickly to maintain their customer experience by offering "Exclusive Live Shopping", a unique shopping experience that connects the consumer at home with an advisor physically present in store. The shopper can then make purchases over the video. The offering includes 120 luxury and premium fashion brands and cosmetics (Balenciaga, Jacquemus, Maje, Bonton, Dior, Sisley, Diptyque, Fresh or Nars among others). The purchases are then available either by click & collect or home delivery. *"In one month, 1,000 live videos were produced, with a transformation rate two to three times higher than what is usually done in e-commerce. And above all, we saw real customer satisfaction thanks to the advice given by personal shoppers,"* explains Antso Rakotoson, Head of Innovation and Omnichannel Experience[27].

In February 2021, Lancôme launched an immersive shopping session during its "Lancôme Happiness Nights", an event dedicated to brand content and retail filmed live from its flagship at 52 Avenue des Champs-Elysées.

In March 2021, Monnier Frères held its first ever session in France – a Coach bag sale with two French influencers chatting over a cup of tea. In one hour, the online seller recorded a higher than 20% engagement rate, 26,600 likes, 1,350 comments and 5,500 unique viewers[28]. For the multi-brand online retailer of luxury women's accessories, the goal is to eventually offer a fully fledged direct shopping channel.

Emotion at the heart of in-store experiences

The store is no longer just a place to make purchases but has also become a theater. The "Gucci Wooster" boutique, located in a listed building from the second half of the 19th century in New York, is one of the most striking examples, with its projection room, 3D equipment, customization and relaxation areas, conferences and mini-concerts. This demand meets the expectations of new luxury consumers: 68% of millennials demand integrated, multi-channel experiences, and 62% of 18–26-year-olds would rather spend $10,000 on an experience, compared to 38% on a product[6].

---

27. Presentation at the "Hubtalk" on November 23, 2020, "Comment le e-commerce répond aux challenges luxe, beauté, mode?", HUB Institute Digital Business.
28. According to the brand.

Today, there are many challenges to be overcome to attract customers to stores. Consumer habits have permanently evolved. After an initial retail model that has been at the heart of the success and growth of many brands in luxury as well as in fashion, the time has come for reinvention of points of sale.

Players such as Dover Street Market (a division of Comme des Garçons that accounts for just over a third of the group's sales) with new approaches to retailing, are at the forefront of inventing tomorrow's points of sale, just as they did more than 15 years ago. The temple of "Made in London" fashion, created some 15 years ago by Japanese Rei Kawakubo (the cult stylist of Comme des Garçons) and her husband Adrian Joffe, which now has six addresses around the world (London, Tokyo, New York, Los Angeles, Beijing and Singapore), is increasing its presence in Paris. After a first concept entirely dedicated to perfume – the Dover Street Parfums Market which opened in October 2019 in the Marais – the brand opened a second Parisian fashion hot spot in early 2021 – the Dover Street Little Market – within the Comme des Garçons flagship at 54, rue du Faubourg Saint-Honoré, dedicated to a modern selection of emerging designers.

The next step is the opening of a Dover Street Market in the prestigious 3,500-square-meter Hôtel de Coulanges located in the heart of the Marais in 2022. "Structure 35–37," as it has been named, promises to be much more than a boutique selling streetwear and luxury brands, but also a culture venue and a promoter of urban renewal and social well-being. *"It's a new way of doing business, of which retail is only a part,"* said Adrian Joffe in an interview with *WWD*[29], listing a multitude of possibilities, such as hosting concerts, poetry readings and lectures, exhibitions, fashion shows, literary and art events, renting space

---

29. Disko Agency Study, 2018.

for filming and temporary residencies for creators. He continues, *"I want to develop the Dover Street Market idea and ethos beyond a physical store and because, coincidentally, the building we have secured is part of a Paris-wide project, it seemed a good idea to take the already existing idea of all the DSM's to create a community of creative and visionary people, all with something to say, and expand that idea beyond just the physical store."* And he adds, *"Maybe the retail space will be part of the event, rather than the event being part of the retail space."*

The pace of openings has picked up again, and it is no longer possible to count the new flagships, department stores and new concepts. Louis Vuitton's Tokyo store has been completely revamped with a facade entirely covered in glass with a holographic effect. Inside, a four-story wall shows a painting by Kimiko Fujimura, a painter known for his seascape paintings. On the top floor of the boutique, there is a private lounge for VIP clients and the LV café, run by one of the world's best chefs, Yosuke Suga, marking his second gastronomic collaboration with Louis Vuitton.

Other examples are La Samaritaine which has finally reopened in Paris, Hermès multiplying its points of sale (in 2021 it opened three new flagship stores in Tokyo, Macao and Harrods in London), the Chinese brand, ICICLE opening its second store in Paris, Louis Vuitton opening a new flagship in Osaka, Brunello Cucinelli arriving in London, Versace adding two new addresses in Paris and London, new Burberry stores in Shanghai, Paris and London and Montblanc setting up its "multi-sensory" flagship boutique in New York. *"Tomorrow luxury customer experiences will still happen in store, where customers will get the real brand experience,"* Michael David, Digital Omnichannel Officer at LVMH said at a round table organized at Vivatech in June 2021, *"but the outlines of new digital storytelling need to be redrawn."*

Premium brands already used their boutiques as a showcase for their brand. With the new social retail concept, the customer takes a more active part in discovering luxury stores. Burberry's new concept store opened in August 2020 in Shenzhen, China, with a new ultra-connected format. Tencent has developed a variation of its WeChat in the form of an application that can be downloaded for free in stores. It guides customers through the sales areas. The 538-square-meter store has been reorganized into ten themed areas, which offer exclusive content to discover the collections and supply product information.

There is also a custom mini game. To boost click-through and further incentivize customers, the app offers rewards. The more customers use the application and browse the digital content, the more points they accumulate, giving them rewards. This will quickly increase the engagement rate. The application installed in the store also aims to provide a tailored shopping experience. Everything revolves around customization. And the three fitting rooms are no exception to the rule. Burberry has committed to offering an immersive experience. Each fitting room has a playlist and its own distinctive design by Riccardo Tisci, the brand's artistic director. When preparing for their visit, customers can reserve their choice of fitting room. They can also make an appointment with one of the store's personal shoppers. Burberry has also created a complete interactive digital replica of its Ginza store in Tokyo[30]. Digital visitors can move around the virtual store and buy items displayed as icons. It is possible to have audio and video conversations with salespeople present in the points of sale and probably with a person present in the virtual store soon. The two worlds, both physical and virtual will be exactly the same.

---

30. "La marque Burberry mise tous azimuts sur les innovations digitales", *La Revue du digital*, June 22, 2021.

Department store challenges

Department stores face two major challenges. The explosion of e-commerce has reduced their direct sales and the interruption to international tourism has left their aisles deserted. Their recovery depends, first of all, on them developing a digital offering that is more complete and more secure than e-commerce platforms currently offer. Alexandre Liot, director of Galeries Lafayette Paris Haussmann, reveals that the store has made strong progress on its omnichannel strategy, rising from *"2% in 2019 to 25% of its turnover today"*. It is a welcome breakthrough after months of closure, successive restrictions due to the health crisis and the absence of tourists, knowing that the latter account for 60% of the department store's turnover. "We want Galeries Lafayette to be a place filled with emotion. Our mission is to put pleasure back at the heart of fashion," explained Guillaume Gellusseau, Chief Marketing & Communication Officer for Galeries Lafayette/BHV Marais at the presentation of the Galeries' transformation in September 2021. And Alexandre Liot agrees, "The department store of old is dead. It's now a place where you don't just come to buy, but to discover."

Parisian department stores want to become a destination. This means more restaurants – the surface area of cafés and restaurants has increased by more than 20% at Galeries Lafayette since 2019 and, in the new Samaritaine, 12 dining venues each with exclusive concepts have been opened – but also exhibitions, events, the development of services such as yoga classes, shoe repair spaces or personal sales consultants. La Samaritaine hosts a beauty studio, a spa, and a private area, "l'Appartement", where you can organize your own private shopping session in the middle of works of art.

Le Bon Marché and Selfridges: living spaces focusing on emotion

The best example is Le Bon Marché, owned by the LVMH group. Le Bon Marché has managed to return to its original vocation, which is to be a place of discovery, life and innovation. Art takes pride of place. Since 1989, Le Bon Marché has been acquiring paintings and sculptures. The "Collection Rive Gauche" is completed by pieces of 20th and 21st century decorative furniture exhibited throughout the store. This is a reflection of the brand's desire to be close to and exchange with artists and creators. This artistic expression, whether it be exhibitions or the Rive Gauche collection, is designed to arouse emotion and wonder. All year long, Le Bon Marché invites artists and creators to use its spaces. Visual arts, fashion, design or music are exhibited during events and carte blanche is given to artists like the famous Chinese artist Ai Weiwei. The "Porte-Bonheurs" exhibition was organized in 2021, with a spectacular installation of 20,000 multicolored fabric flowers designed by Thebe Magugu, winner of the 2019 LVMH Prize and handmade by 120 women through the humanitarian association Dessine l'Espoir. People go to Le Bon Marché to browse, buy new services and have new experiences. Le Bon Marché has established itself among Parisian customers by going back to the original mid-19th century department store concept. Department stores used to be places people went to discover the new wonders of what was to become available to all in the future. Le Bon Marché is considered to be the world's first department store.

Selfridges, the famous London luxury store on Oxford Street, has a reputation for offering its customers amazing experiences, from indoor cycling classes, a skateboarding track, a space dedicated to virtual reality, a real cinema and, as of September 2021, wedding organization.

The evolution of retail to focus on experience and services

These examples are the forerunners to retail's evolution towards a focus on experience and services. Services, the cornerstone of brand ecosystems, like giving products a second life, should eventually represent up to 70% of stores' sales according to some. This evolution is a logical continuation of the acceleration linked to Covid, which has made more reluctant customers switch to online shopping, reserving store visits for when they want to revel in wonder or have new experiences.

Brands also want to improve their services for their online customers. Hermès offers a number of tools to satisfy its customers: distance selling by phone or video, in-store appointment scheduling, a customized concierge service for home deliveries, product reservations from the website, etc.

In the UK, Rag & Bone has launched the RbDelivered service, which offers items carefully selected by stylists based on customer preferences and delivered to the customer's home. The brand has set up virtual appointments where you can pay by phone and then meet the sales staff in front of the store to collect your purchases in person. Several brands such as Prada have launched collections which can be picked up in store and have implemented contactless payment.

At Breitling, appointments in the boutique are now made in advance and personalized. Using the customer's web browsing in the hundred days before their visit, the company sends a PDF file to the store sales staff so that they can prepare the appointment made by the customer online. This way, salespeople know which watches they are most likely to like, but also the customer's language thanks to their browsing history. This is possible thanks to the connection between the store and website CRM. In-store appointment scheduling has been extended to the websites of the brand's 1,800 official dealers around the world.

In Milan, Sergio Rossi launched a special Covid pop-up store in 2020 which allowed shopping by appointment only. Infrared sensors were set up to take customers' temperatures, while a five-meter slide was set up to deliver customer purchases from the warehouse above.

Social media at the heart of the empire

Social media is one of the main levers of influence. A 2020 study by Facebook and the Ipsos polling institute on the behavior of luxury consumers indicated that a third say they go to social networks to discover and look for product recommendations. So brands need to be present on social networks. All social media platforms are used for storytelling, product demonstrations, influencers: Instagram for sharing photos and videos, announcing events, showing behind the scenes and publishing stories; Snapchat for briefly sharing photos, videos, chats and professional stories; TikTok for short videos set to music; Pinterest, Facebook, YouTube, WeChat and Weibo in China, etc.

Today, more than 93% of luxury brands have a presence on Instagram and their ever-growing follower count continues to rise to dizzying heights. Chanel is the most followed brand with 48.2 million subscribers, ahead of Gucci with 46.9 million; Louis Vuitton with 46.9 million; Dior with 38.9 million; Prada with 28.2 million and Dolce & Gabbana with 27.3 million[31].

TikTok, used by one billion monthly active users worldwide (15 million in France) and which targets a young audience (60%

---

31. As of January 7, 2022

of users are aged 13 to 24), is attracting more and more luxury brands. The network also announced several partnerships for the launch of its own "Month-long digital fashion event" in the fall of 2020. Balmain was the first label to create its account there in 2019. The most popular brand on the platform is Gucci, according to the *Vogue Business* ranking. When, in August 2020, the influencer Morgan Presley made a fashion parody by explaining in voiceover and video how to blend into the Gucci universe, the house exploited the concept by using this TikTok creation to launch the #GucciModelChallenge, which garnered over 184 million views, in which users posted looks inspired by the brand's aesthetic.

At Céline, "The Dancing Kid" fashion show was broadcast live on TikTok. The collection was inspired by the teen idol Noen Eubanks, photographed by Hedi Slimane. The show's music was the long version of a TikTok anthem composed by the rapper Tiagz, himself a tiktokker, and cut up into fifteen second grabs on the fashion house's account. Finally, the models are none other than the platform's stars. This is a perfect example of what a brand can do on TikTok. The social network took another step forward by launching TikTok Shopping in August 2021 in the United States, Canada and the United Kingdom, a new feature allowing sellers to add their online stores directly to their profiles. Dior is still the leader in terms of digital audience and presence on most social networks, particularly on the Chinese platform WeChat.

Luxury brands are fixated by engagement rates (a formula which counts the number of likes relative to the number of followers, which indicate the effectiveness of social network posts). Most brands have managers responsible for maximizing their presence on Instagram, YouTube, Twitter, Facebook, Snapchat or WeChat. Chanel now has its own Instagram team.

Brands are turning their fans into customers and competing with each other by creating their own channels or programs. Louis Vuitton, Gucci and Dior have launched their own channels, which have more than a million subscribers. Each publication gets millions of views and reactions from Internet users. In July, Louis Vuitton posted a video on its TikTok account with the K-pop group BTS which generated over 15 million views. In a more classic move, in June 2021, Hermès launched yoga exercise tutorials on its WeChat Mini program to promote its latest accessories (belts, scarves, leather goods, hats).

But beyond working on a brand's image, social networks are becoming new sales channels. Big names like Cartier, Louis Vuitton and Bulgari market and sell products on WeChat. Modeling the Chinese app, Facebook launched Facebook Shops in May 2020, its new tool to make it easy for merchants to create online stores and for customers to explore the world of brands in more detail and, in some cases, make purchases, without ever having to leave the social network.

However, since the pandemic, luxury has opened to other spaces of expression and hyper-localized communication: outdoor advertising, pop-up stores, Parisian strolls along the Seine, etc. An example is Bottega Veneta, which has left social media behind and set up shop on the roof of a warehouse just a stone's throw from Los Angeles International Airport, where it displays its collections, which are only visible during take-off and landing. Or Louis Vuitton which exhibited its works at a bookstall on the Quai Malaquais in Paris.

Once again, the luxury sector is demonstrating its ability to break away from the "norm" by investing in new areas of expression and engagement with increasingly versatile customers.

Augmented reality, the future of luxury

Augmented and virtual reality offer new, playful perspectives for the luxury sector, modernizing it, offering new means of engagement and attracting new audiences. They work in the relationship between brands and their customers, in their stores but also directly online. They are also a pathway to the metaverse, which is closely related to virtual and augmented reality technologies.

Burberry invites Burberry.com and Burberry app users to modify their Pocket Bag with the different visuals presented on-screen. Users can then take a snapshot of their version to post on social networks. The Pocket Bag can also be set up and viewed in the future client's environment.

According to a recent report[32], the virtual fitting room market is booming and is expected to achieve an annual growth of 25.2% between 2021 and 2028 to reach $15.43 billion by 2028 (up from $2.44 billion in 2019). In its *Global Powers of Luxury Goods 2020* report, Deloitte states that when shopping online, the time a customer spends on a brand's products increases by more than 70% with augmented reality experiences compared to traditional browsing.

Since the beginning of spring 2020, for example, U.S. startup Obsess, founded by Neha Singh, has seen a 300% increase in incoming inquiries compared to the previous year. Its clients include Tommy Hilfiger, Ulta Beauty, Carmen Sol, Charlotte Tilbury and Dior, who it worked with on the virtual version of its Champs-Élysées boutique. The store offers shoppers in France a 360-degree 3D online shopping experience. Users can virtually

---

32. Fortune Business Insights, "Virtual Fitting Room Market, Size, Share and COVID-19 Impact Analysis, 2020–2027," report, August 2021.

browse the collection of perfumes, soaps, lotions and candles, then zoom in on items and purchase them on the site[33].

Estée Lauder, which saw double-digit online sales growth in the second quarter of 2021, has created a software platform to more quickly market augmented reality services for its 25 beauty brands, allowing consumers to "try on" makeup virtually. The Virtual Try On (VTO) AR platform helps consumers see what lipsticks, mascaras, foundations, eye shadows and other beauty products would look like on them. This is a contactless trial using the connected device of their choice.

Virtual testing of beauty products is a growing trend. Several L'Oréal brands use this technology on their online Instagram Shops. The group acquired Canadian startup ModiFace in 2018 and its Lancôme, NYX Professional Makeup, Urban Decay and Maybelline brands will be available for virtual try on, as well as on Facebook's Spark AR.

Gaming, a sensational entry into luxury

The gaming industry[34] has grown at an unprecedented rate in recent years and the global health crisis has further accelerated its momentum. With an average annual growth rate of 8.7% from 2019 to 2021, the market is now worth $180 billion[35] with 3.2 billion players, including nearly 40 million French people, i.e. nearly one in two people worldwide. With the advent of the metaverse (fictional virtual world), gaming is now a must for

---

33. *Ibid.*
34. Yves Hanania and Nathalie Rémy, "Le jeu vidéo: un secteur lucratif pour les géants de la mode", *INfluencia*, November 30, 2021.
35. Source: "Video Game Industry Statistics, Trends and Data in 2022," *wepc. com*, January 18, 2022.

fashion and luxury brands and it's not surprising to see the most innovative among them widely experimenting.

Luxury and fashion take on gaming

The gaming world has become a media form in its own right, with a diverse international audience that includes 49% women and 64% young adults. On average, gamers spend 6.33 hours a week playing games, but we should also count their exposure to the many different streams (live videos on platforms like Twitch) and competitions. The esports trend is growing and growing. These local, national or international video game competitions are attracting more and more fans and the sector has exploded since 2010, with some events gathering more than 100 million viewers. Real ecosystems are being created around video games, from developers to streaming platforms like YouTube, Twitch, Facebook Gaming (the three main platforms). All of these players and services are opportunities for brands, seduced by the interactivity and high level of player engagement, to connect with their current and future customers.

Fashion and luxury brands have quickly understood the importance of integrating the world of video games into their media strategies, collaborating with development studios to offer exclusive content, placing their products in different games, working with influencers from the games universe or by sponsoring esports teams or competitions. The movement started in 2012 with Prada, which used characters from the Final Fantasy game as models to promote its collection. Louis Vuitton has opted for sponsorship, partnering with League of Legends, one of the most followed games in the world. The brand created its own collection of clothing, as well as "in-game" products for the famous video game's World Cup. This collaboration enabled the brand to appear on several social platforms such as WeChat,

Xiaohongshu (the Chinese Instagram, also called Little Red Book), Douyin (Chinese version of TikTok) and Bilibili (Chinese video platform).

BMW is also following suit with its "United in Rivalry" program, which brings together five international esports teams. This program aims to promote the esports discipline and bring the digital and racing worlds together around shared values.

Burberry, one of the luxury group digital communication leaders, is using the world of video games as a new medium for broadcasting and communication. It was the first luxury house to go on Twitch to broadcast its spring/summer 2021 fashion show. During the lockdowns, brands like Valentino, Marc Jacobs and Gillette collaborated with Animal Crossing so that players could interact with their now-digitized products.

The luxury brands then flooded to the digital worlds by developing technological products marketed on video game platforms. *"Customizing their avatars is one of the main reasons gamers spend money in games,"* reported Facebook IQ, in its annual report[36]. Gucci also has a strong presence in the world of video games, with collaborations with Fnatic, a famous European esports team, Animal Crossing, Tennis Clash, Pokémon Go and Roblox, an American gaming platform that had 202 million users as of April 2021. Its exhibition, "Archetypes" at the Gucci Garden in Florence was transposed into digital form. Thanks to specially developed features, gamers could browse an interactive gallery and customize their avatars with clothing by Alessandro Michele, the brand's creative director. In addition, they could purchase clothing and original accessories. On the day it went live, the application received more than one million visits. With

---

36. Facebook Gaming and Facebook IQ, "Marketing et jeux vidéos. Perspectives 2021," report, January 2021.

half of Roblox users under the age of thirteen, Gucci is introducing its world and aesthetic to potential future customers.

More and more brands have been inspired by the world of video games to develop specific real-life products and collections. For example, in 2020, Longchamp partnered with The Pokémon Company to launch a brand new collection, both in-store and in the Pokémon Go game.

"We've always liked to break the codes a bit and surprise. For me, the idea was to bring together two completely different worlds, and to show that we can totally bring together the world of video games with the world of fashion and our know-how," Sophie Delafontaine, Longchamp's artistic director explained to AFP. *"We've done a lot with art, design, architecture. Gaming is a new form of exploration and creativity"* with *"very strong imagination and a wealth of graphics"*, she added.

Burberry also embarked on a collaboration with China's most popular video game, Honor Of Kings, on which the 100 million daily users spent $2.6 billion in 2020. But China canceled the collaboration following the brand's comments about Uyghurs.

The reason behind such partnerships is that the video game industry is a lucrative sector that fashion giants do not want to miss out on. Beyond the financial stakes, gaming offers brand-new grounds for expression and engagement in an imaginary world where the limits of creativity and storytelling are endless.

Brands producing their own games

More recently, brands have also started to create their own games. Hermès pioneered the concept with the mobile game *H-Pitchhh*, released for its annual show jumping competition. Others have followed suit. Gucci launched Gucci Arcade. Burberry created B Bounce, Ratberry and B Surf, which celebrates the "TB Summer Monogram" collection.

Louis Vuitton has extended its reach with its own game Louis, the Game, which celebrates the brand's 200th anniversary and allows players to find out about the house's creator through an adventure game.

Balenciaga went even further by presenting its fall/winter 2021–2022 collection through a complex game called *Afterworld: The Age of Tomorrow*, which explores the limits of a dystopian world. It invented an entire universe. Users scroll through it to view new items. Propelled to the year 2031, the player, dressed entirely in Balenciaga, aims to become the master of both worlds. On the way, they discover the collection's 50 looks, which were also presented to 330 guests via a virtual reality headset in the first lockdown. It was a first in the luxury world. A further step was taken by the brand in the video game Blankos Block Party. This multiplayer game allows players to activate Blankos, figurines that become real virtual characters which can be edited and acquired as NFT (Non-Fungible Tokens), unique 100% digital goods. The brand sees these innovations as an opportunity for gamers to adopt its aesthetic codes and acquire new products. NFTs then become an element of personalization. Players can adopt a brand's aesthetic by matching their avatar's outfits with those on sale.

Such partnerships exist because the video game industry is a lucrative business sector. With 8% growth in 2021, the market is now worth $175.8 billion, and the community consists of 2.96 billion gamers. This is a figure that the pandemic should have boosted for the months to come as well. For the world of fashion, the financial stakes are real.

Younger generations are particularly sensitive to social networks and therefore to their online reputation. They build an identity, a personality. The virtual worlds offered by the world of online games are places where young people can express themselves without limits. They are an opportunity for brands to play a role in society with young people who are dependent on the image they want to project on social networks.

The dawn of virtual luxury

Fashion is currently going through a deep transition due to economic and ecological issues. There is a real boom in virtual fashion with brands investing more and more in cyberspace, with innovative 3D digital design methods, virtual filters to try on Dior and Chanel accessories, 3D models for Burberry or Mugler, video game-like fashion shows for Christian Louboutin or Balenciaga, the NFT collection for Dolce & Gabbana.

Fashion 2.0 naturally speaks to the younger generations and comes at a time when buying motivations are changing. Gucci has already successfully sold virtual clothing in a test run. Entirely at ease digitally, millennials are a perfect target for this new, more sustainable industry model, wearing clothes that could never physically exist. It is a perfect fit for Instagram and other social networks.

This is contactless cyber fashion where clothes are available for all sexes, genders and sizes, allowing young people to build an identity through the most amazingly creative accessible digital wardrobes. The world of digital fashion holds real potential for the big fashion houses to transform the sector's economy with the creation of several digital fashion houses.

The movement is still in its infancy, but it is a clear new trend that is here to stay. In 2018, The Fabricant, the world's first digital fashion house, arrived on the market. "*In 2019 the brand's first virtual dress called "Iridescence" was auctioned for \$9,500. Since then, their line of future streetwear continues to seduce a clientele in love with these 100% virtual pieces.*" Kerry Murphy and Amber Slooten, the brand founders, explained in an interview with *Numéro* that virtual fashion and real life fashion can coexist: "*Virtual fashion does not necessarily exclude physical fashion. It is simply a new step. A necessary step for brands that want to embark on true digital transformation, strategic change and build long-term resilience. Young consumers instinctively understand virtual fashion. So now it's up to the brands to do the work to stay relevant and allow their audience to experience fashion in a way that fits into their new lifestyle[37].*"

Today many virtual fashion brands whose pieces exist only in digital format are emerging, such as Tribute Brand or XR Couture. It is a fashion for the future that plays on environmental concerns. "It is *estimated that more than half of all fast fashion is discarded within a year of its purchase. Digital-only clothing significantly reduces the impact of fashion on the planet's resources and on nature. Digital fashion production generates ten times less CO_2 emissions in its life cycle (0.7g of CO_2) compared to a physical garment (8g of CO_2). Digital fashion will never end up in landfills, will never generate plastic waste and will never contribute to water pollution. Given the amount of pollution the fashion industry is responsible for, pioneering a digital fashion sector can only have a positive impact on the industry as a whole*," state Kerry Murphy and Amber Slooten.

With digital fashion, what about the shopping experience, though? Daria Shapovalova and Natalia Modenova created an

---

37. Léa Zetlaoui, "Mode virtuelle: The Fabricant, pionnier de la mode virtuelle", *Numéro*, February 22, 2021.

e-shop dedicated to 100% virtual clothing in 2019. *"While in real life these outfits can run into the tens of thousands of dollars, DressX offers models for no more than $200, digitally added to a photo of their customers."*

A flash in the pan or a lasting trend? In a world where sustainability is the new paradigm, isn't the virtual industry also a big polluter? What is the future for this type of product? *"We all live a digital life and express ourselves through different virtual reality channels. Our expectations are to be able to express ourselves without limits thanks to sustainable and democratic fashion. Virtual fashion places no physical limits on creativity. It creates an interactive sensory narrative that can be accessed anytime, anywhere. We are all members of different digital communities, we believe that digital fashion definitely has mainstream potential. For everyone in the fashion industry today, the question isn't, "Will 3D live up to what we can create in real life?" anymore. It's more like, "Will our new everyday reality be able to match the extraordinary capacity of 3D"* answer the founders of DressX[38]. *"Today, this market is evolving at a very fast pace, probably because of Covid-19. Whether it's physical brands or regular customers, everyone wants in! Of course, we wondered why anyone would pay for something that doesn't exist, but that question is becoming less and less important now. We think it's similar to what cryptocurrencies were originally. So, there will be more and more virtual fashion brands with different goals and aesthetics, just like in the physical fashion system,"* add Gala MarijaVrbanic and Filip Vajda, founders of the young label Tribute Brand, launched in 2020[39].

---

38. *Op. cit.*
39. Léa Zetlaoui, "Mode virtuelle: Tribute Brand, la première marque de vêtements 100 % virtuels", *Numéro*, February 22, 2021.

Interestingly, brands are starting to follow suit. The shoe manufacturer Christian Louboutin was the first to make virtual versions of its shoes on the Korean application Zepeto (200 million users) with reproductions of recent models. For the occasion, a 3D modeling studio scanned each shoe from every angle to capture every detail. To buy a pair of Louboutin pumps, you had to pay 30 diamonds (the currency on Zepeto), the equivalent of €2, compared to at least €500 in real life. More recently, Dior's beauty branch partnered with Zepeto to launch a collection of digital makeup, aimed at Generation Z (with nine looks in the collection).

"We're seeing a lot of interest in virtual fashion from traditional fashion brands, and we have several existing collaborations to date, for example with Buffalo London x The Fabricant and with Gary James McQueen, which will launch in April. We are also working on other future partnerships," Daria Shapovalova, cofounder of DressX, told *Numéro* magazine in February 2021[40].

Gucci, meanwhile, has designed "Virtual 25", its first pair of virtual sneakers. This fictitious sneaker, available for the tiny price of €12.99 on the Gucci application, can be tried on online or exported to video game platforms such as Roblox, to customize the avatar. Gucci's Chief Marketing Officer, Robert Triefus, told *Fast Company*[41], *"The virtual world is creating its own economy. The worlds of fashion and gaming are colliding. We're approaching gaming with a sense of experimentation, because this will put us in a good position to be ahead of the trends when they become ingrained."*

---

40. Léa Zetlaoui, "Mode virtuelle: DressX, le premier e-shop de couture virtuelle", *Numéro*, February 22, 2021.
41. Elizabeth Segran, "Would you spend $10,000 on a virtual dress? Gucci is betting on it," *Fast Company*, September 8, 2020.

How far will this shift to a metaverse go? Will customers embrace this growing digital omnipresence in their daily lives? How will brands adapt to this in the long run? More importantly, how will they prepare and invest?

The world of virtual clothing is certainly one of the solutions for fashion to solve one of its greatest challenges – reducing its ecological impact. Be that as it may, it isn't the future of fashion. Consumers in the physical world will continue to want real clothes. The emperor can't go around naked. In the meantime, virtual fashion is well underway and it is a safe bet that all these new technologies will once again lead to an incredible acceleration of the meeting of the virtual world with the real world.

3

Management of the Empire

D espite its supposed "invulnerability", the luxury sector cannot go through the current succession of crises and revolutions, including digitalization, without modifying its production and distribution methods.

The luxury industry has come out strengthened despite its apprehension towards the current issues. The pandemic has called into question brands' positioning and made them question their reasons for existence. They have taken advantage of this opportunity to take the measure of both accelerations and ruptures. The question of the post-Covid era has rapidly arisen. Were we going to see a revolution? Would the crisis call into question the very foundations of luxury? What was the world going to be like afterwards? The notion of a "new normal" soon made its appearance. In the luxury sector, it has been characterized by innovations in all areas of brand management. Brand management didn't simply take the downstream revolution into account. The entire value chain is evolving to differing extents depending on the company.

Upstream revolutions: digital technology, a booster for luxury production

The supply chain is very complex in the fashion and luxury industry. There are many players including small and ultra-specialized suppliers, and many production sites for the same product.

For example, Australian leather tanned in Italy with assembly units in different countries, in addition to a multitude of sales channels.

Risks to the supply chain

The Covid-19 crisis has made logistical difficulties worse, *"We have been impacted at all levels. We have decided to close our factories, which has had an impact on our suppliers, as they have not been able to deliver for two months"*, said representatives of major French luxury groups[42].

There were multiple challenges: supplier delays and order cancellations, closure of manufacturing sites and stores or accu-mulation or shortage of stocks in some points of sale. At the same time, the growth of e-commerce made it necessary to supplement existing channels with new supply loops.

In general, legal and regulatory constraints are increasing and can change abruptly. For example, customs duties in the United States under the Republican presidency, non-tariff barriers and intellectual property legislation for champagne in Russia.

---

42. Adra, Buy Your Way and le Médiateur des entreprises, "Impacts présents et futurs de la Covid-19 sur les chaînes d'approvisionnement et les pratiques d'achats", study, June 2020.

Increased agility thanks to digital technology

The best possible evolution of the supply chain should focus on the sustainability of supplies environmentally and ethically. The physical and economic constraints of logistics became a priority during the Covid-19 health crisis. *"Risk management is extremely important for a purchasing department: supplier risk management, closure risk, copyright risk, irresponsible practices, communication risk, social risk[43]."*

The challenges of the post-Covid world are no less daunting. Consumers are becoming increasingly versatile. It is essential for companies to be reactive to keep up with new trends. The number of collections is increasing, including limited capsule collections, and this has led to a further acceleration in the digitalization of the entire supply chain[44]. The technological tidal wave of digitalization even challenges the manufacturing and design of products. Several sectors are seeing digital innovations flourish – fashion, jewelry and leather goods in particular. "See Now, Buy Now" (a practice whereby it becomes possible to buy a new creation a few hours or days after its presentation at a fashion show) seems to be attracting more and more brands, such as Gucci or Burberry, as a complement or replacement for the classic "See Now, Buy Later".

Other supply crises could occur. Supply chains must be doubled or tripled to avoid such risks. According to Chanel and Louis Vuitton, *"we took advantage of our almost daily*

---

43. *Ibid.*
44. Shen, Bin & Minner, Stefan & Chan, Hauling & Brun and Alessandro, "Logistics and Supply Chain Management in the Luxury Industry," *Transportation Research Part E: Logistics and Transportation Review*, Elsevier, vol. 143, C, September 2020.

conversations with our suppliers to ask them about the identity and situation of their own suppliers, right down to the bottom[4]. This increased our awareness that we know too little about the players behind each supplier. We don't always know. This reinforced our need to have an accurate macro view of our entire supply chain[45]." With environmental pressure, "reshoring" –a return to local industrial production -may be necessary to better control production and limit companies' carbon footprints[46].

According to the Gartner Group, firms need to analyze all of their supplies segment by segment. The total cost of inputs must include not only the purchase price but also the costs of replacement and the risk involved in each contract.[47] Digitalization must therefore be extended to the entire value chain: procurement of materials, relations with subcontractors, order processing, organization of production, stocks and transport. All luxury goods companies are automating their manufacturing processes. The major brands must therefore help with this evolution and connect their subcontractors, whether they be bottle makers, packers, logisticians, etc. to the market.

Supply chain agility is now a major focus of brand management. Its planning used to be at best done weekly. It must be done on a daily basis to counter disruptions. The goal is for the brand manager to be in perfect communication with production, raw material supplies and manufacturing schedules. They need to know the status of stocks as well as their position in the distribution chain between the sales channels and the stores in real time, and evolution of demand on an almost hour-by-hour basis.

---

45. Adra, Buy Your Way and le Médiateur des entreprises, *op. cit.*
46. Paolo Barbagallo, sedAptagroup, September 2021.
47. *Les Echos*, September 5, 2021.

After the major industrial firms, such as automotive and aeronautics, ERP[48] software packages are proving their usefulness in the luxury and fashion worlds, replacing dedicated specialized applications. Stock solutions such as SAP, JD Edwards Enterprise One or Oracle Cloud ERP are being challenged by fashion and luxury-oriented software packages such as Aims360, ApparelMagic, S2K Enterprise or Cantel Apparel. Sephora and Tapestry use SAP, Sarenza uses Sage. The total computerization of the value chain is essential for luxury houses of all sizes, from SMEs to large groups. This is a major yet essential organizational challenge.

The fashion agenda called into question

"How the Covid pandemic has turned the fashion world upside down", was the headline of *Les Echos* on April 16, 2021: "*Digital shows accessible to all, physical shows in Asia, questioning of the official fashion week calendars, the health crisis is reshuffling the cards of the fashion agenda*[49]." Digital technology and the pandemic crisis have exploded the traditional fashion calendar in terms of collections and fashion weeks. Brands have taken advantage of this upheaval to make decisions that they had been hesitating to make for many years.

The frequency of launches

The lockdowns and their consequences – digital shows – have led to a growing popularity for two fashion collections per year.

---

48. Enterprise Resource Planning.
49. Frédéric Martin-Bernard, "Comment la pandémie de la Covid a bouleversé la planète mode", *Les Echos*, April 16, 2021.

In France, under the aegis of the Fédération de la haute couture et de la mode, a traditional calendar had been adopted, with two collections per year presented a few months before they went on sale. The major fashion houses have also brought the cruise collections offered since the 1920s to summer and cruise passengers of the time up to date. These collections are an additional mid-season product line, which the designers have to dream up. They particularly target markets in the Middle East, Southeast Asia, Brazil and the southern and western United States.

Several British or North American houses such as Burberry, Tom Ford or Vetements, have tried to put an end to the frantic succession of creations by proposing that the collections presented be immediately available in stores. French haute couture brands, including Dior, Chanel and Hermès, rejected the new calendar, arguing that it would stifle creativity.

The magic of fashion shows and online fashion weeks

Another important evolution began from 2020 and the beginning of 2021. The lockdowns and the suspension of international flights have upset fashion shows and fashion weeks, which transferred to online versions.

Fashion weeks used to be lavishly staged creative challenges, like Alexander McQueen's performances or "Lagerfeld-style" shows like Chanel's Ground Control. Because of the travel bans, direct exchanges between creatives, media and buyers disappeared. Most of the fashion week shows in New York, London, Milan and Paris took place online. This gave rise to major film, art and digital innovations. Prestigious locations like the Rodin Museum or the Hall of Mirrors of the Palace of Versailles have been used again, with the major difference being the lack of public. Breathtaking locations were used, such as the Moroccan dunes filmed for the Saint Laurent spring/summer 2021 fashion show. Saint Laurent offered the entire world (and no longer just a happy few at the Parisian, New York or Milanese fashion shows) a show of a rare beauty. Karl Lagerfeld, known for the grandeur of his fashion shows, could not have competed today!

Covid has thus made it possible for brands to explore new possibilities, presenting collections inviting both travel and escape. In the same vein, many brands increased their agility and creativity to share and present their new collections, sometimes without the success they expected. Novel events, such as Coperni's March 2021 "drive-in" show, which guests watched from their cars, made their mark. The models moved between the luxury electric cars parked at Bercy Arena. The guests, brought in in these vehicles, watched the show from the safety of their cars. It was a new fashion week format for a time when no fashion shows were allowed with audiences. For its Spring/Summer 2022 collection presented in Milan, Moncler broke down boundaries by presenting Mondogenius, a digital experience that took global communities on a journey through five cities (Milan, New York, Shanghai, Seoul and Tokyo), sharing the creative visions of 11 designers, in a show hosted by singer Alicia Keys. The show was broadcast on a dedicated microsite as well as over 30 platforms, including social networks, e-shops, websites and selected media channels, giving all types of audiences the opportunity to access this extraordinary journey.

Many thought that the magic would disappear without physical shows. However, the opposite happened. Brands competed with each other in terms of creativity and inventiveness and raised the level of these shows to such an extent that we might wonder whether the extremely high quality of the videos and the multitude of digital tools might actually challenge traditional fashion events. Some fashion houses and designers have taken advantage of this pause to reflect and have decided not to follow the frantic pace of the fashion show calendar. Hedi Slimane, artistic director of Céline, who, even before the pandemic, considered fashion week to be "obsolete", said in an interview with the newspaper *Le Monde* in January 2020, *"A special occasion and scarcity seem more essential to me today than the obligatory hour of style.*[50]*"* Others have chosen to accelerate the transition to digital by innovating, for example with the help of augmented reality.

But most designers refuse to consider a future without traditional fashion shows. Giorgio Armani confided to the newspaper *Le Monde, "I don't think the solution is to rely entirely on digital. […] Fashion Week is a fundamental social occasion for the sector […]. It needs to remain a network that brings together the great and the small and offers all the opportunity to present their work at the same time. I am therefore convinced that Fashion Week, as such, must be preserved. The virtual show may be a tool, but it is not the future*[51]*."*

Finally, after a year of virtual fashion shows, physical fashion shows made a comeback in historical or impressive places. Dior organized its Cruise 2022 fashion show in June 2021 in the ancient Olympic stadium in Athens. In September 2021, LaQuan Smith unveiled its Spring/Summer 2022 collection atop the iconic Empire State Building in Manhattan.

On October 1, 2021, Valentino models walked the runway at the Carreau du Temple in Paris for its Spring/Summer 2022 collection and invited the global Clubhouse community to the front row.

---

50. Elvire von Bardeleben, "Hedi Slimane: 'Il n'y a rien de plus difficile que la simplicité'", *Le Monde*, January 17, 2020.
51. Elvine von Bandeleben, "Giorgio Armani: 'Le défilé virtuel n'est pas l'avenir'", *Le Monde*, February 25, 2021.

This is proof that a hybrid future, meeting everyone's expectations, seems to be taking shape in the fashion industry today, offering more creativity as well as more opportunities for expression and engagement with customers. It is the best of both worlds.

Professionalization of collaborations

The concept of collaborations, initially reserved for a few rare brands, took off in 2004 with the collaboration between Karl Lagerfeld and H&M. H&M's capsule collections, designed by designers such as Karl Lagerfeld, Lanvin or Sonia Rykiel, as well as those of Uniqlo with Inès de la Fressange, have met with great "popular" success, making luxury available to all.

Chanel, Gucci, Versace, Prada, Off-White and many other brands have created collaborations. They are limited in terms of both volume and time duration, and can be part of the brand's aesthetic or, on the contrary, move completely away from it. These successful associations offer regular opportunities to shine spotlights on luxury brands. The limited editions are then carried on or abandoned depending on sales. A media personality can also be associated with the collection, to inspire it, co-design it or to be its the iconic client.

Since 2017, with the capsule launched by Louis Vuitton and Supreme, partnerships have also extended to outdoor and streetwear. This mix has given a new creative breath to luxury. The "unmissable" opportunity of the capsule collection can be doubled by sales in a pop-up store, often event-driven, installed in a department store–a very useful place to complete the communication on the Net–, a hotel or a busy street; if possible one specialized in luxury. After the partnerships between Jordan Brand and Dior (five million people are said to have logged on to the Dior Air Jordan online mini-site launched in April 2020) or between Adidas and Prada in 2020, in 2021, it was the striking duo of Gucci and The North Face who collaborated to present a brand new collection combining Gucci's originality and style with The North Face's seventies-accented utilitarian aspect, respecting the eco-friendly commitments dear to both brands, in terms of environmentally sustainable activities.

Off-White has chosen a more artistic path by imagining a capsule (branded cap, shoulder bag, hoodie, t-shirt) for the Metropolitan Museum of Art in New York in September 2021. To launch the collection, the museum partnered with Instagram for a live shopping event organized the previous weekend. The idea? To allow users to purchase limited edition pieces directly from the Instagram Store, during a live stream session cohosted by Virgil Abloh, founder of Off-White, and Eva Chen, influencer, author and director of fashion partnerships for Instagram.

Collaborations have multiplied in the wake of the pandemic. Brands have found it to be an opportunity to regain momentum, by joining forces with a brand with similar DNA and values. Customers find it an additional differentiation element, adding to the exceptional nature and exclusivity of their choices. Collaborations are also increasingly made in the form of partnerships with influencers. To celebrate model Devon Lee Carlson's 27th birthday, Marc Jacobs partnered with the It-girl to create a selection of pieces that represented her signature world. There are many benefits for brands. The Fusalp × Chloé collaboration has enabled the former to increase its presence in China and the latter to benefit from the reputation and technicality of Fusalp's revived products.

Other forms of collaboration are possible. To promote the new models in its Panamera range, Porsche has teamed up with fashion icon Olivier Rousteing, creative director of Balmain, to create videos on a theme called "Drive Defined," which is meant to describe the inner strength that drives the designer, just like the brand's drivers. The short episodes of the series created for the occasion were published on the various Porsche social media accounts and on the creator's Instagram. Porsche and Balmain decided to go beyond simple event sponsorship or an (expected) exclusive model designed by Olivier Rousteing to bring a touch of glamour and style to the brand and femininity to the car brand's legendary design. It is a great example of the transformative power of brands. This is a long-term collaboration between Porsche and Olivier Rousteing and should give rise to other projects.

The explosion of capsule collections

An older practice updated by the use of digital technology; capsule collections, which today are released in succession and punctuate brands' calendars, allow them to put new life and creativity into their collections, to innovate, test new models in boutiques or in fleeting pop-up stores. They are sometimes snatched up and highly anticipated.

For example, to celebrate the 100th anniversary of its iconic N° 5 perfume, Chanel launched a capsule collection of 17 beauty products in July 2021, designed in a pop art spirit, using the house's traditional color codes, namely black and white. Each was made in the form of everyday objects. The shower gel is presented in a paint pot, the body cream in a gouache tube, the bath pebbles in a tea canister, and the emulsion in a detergent refill. *"This concept highlights the fact that an industrial product with very functional packaging can be transformed into a unique and desirable object by appropriating the identity codes of No. 5, without losing its fundamental features, namely its functionality,"* said Thomas du Prè de Saint Maur, Head of Global Creative Resources for Chanel Fragrances and Beauty, in a press release. Chanel also opened pop-up stores in several cities. On its website it was possible to follow the manufacturing chain of the beauty products.

Another example is when Louis Vuitton and its artistic director installed a pop-up store in Paris in January 2021 dedicated solely to exhibiting LV Trainer sneakers and accessories created by Virgil Abloh since 2019.

Dom Pérignon partnered with Lady Gaga in the fall of 2021 to produce two limited edition boxes and an exclusive item. The champagne house offered these bottles for sale on a digital pop-up for "Non-Fungible Tokens". Each box, sold in cryptocurrency (ether), included a real bottle delivered to the customer's home as well as a numbered 3D NFT version to keep. A 100% virtual pop-up was designed to discover the collection, in which 100 bottles were offered for sale as a preview in NFT version.

Playing the artistic card, Saint Laurent imagined a capsule collection entirely dedicated to the American painter Jean-Michel Basquiat in July 2021. On the program were T-shirts, hoodies, backpacks, tote bags and fanny packs, but also other lifestyle products such as a skateboard, phone covers and a selection of books.

The watch industry has also been seduced by the concept of the capsule collection. Chanel presented its capsule collection Chanel Electro in September 2021, whose graphic codes are borrowed from Electro culture. The collection included four models and a limited edition run of just 1,244 watches.

All of these capsule collections bring luxury or fashion brands increased media exposure, the chance to reach a new clientele, constantly reinvent themselves or test new business models, but also to boost their images. But there is one possible risk – that this weakens the desirability of a prestigious company when it becomes a too well-known brand and is (over)exposed. This is a risk which may have to be managed in the future with the increasingly frantic pace which collections are now subject to. However, collaboration strategies have been refined and brands are aligning their goals. These strategies are good marketing tactics, with, for some collaborations, shared image or distribution strategies. Some collaborations are undertaken with a very specific target in sight, which is often to increase their presence in a certain market, such as China.

From diversification to brand ecosystems

With the health crisis, brands are looking to shake things up. Before, certain product categories had been discarded because they were too far removed from the brand's main offering and its values, but today brands are more open to new sources of revenue. Only a few rare companies nowadays haven't capitalized on their image and reputation to add new products. This diversification increases their visibility and brings products to the market that might bring them new customers. The luxury industry is growing, leading to significant benefits for brands. These companies are not only increasing their scope of action and income, but also enriching their universes with newly boosted product and service offerings. By offering experiences, they expand their core audience and develop real communities and in turn true brand ecosystems.

An example of this is Longchamp's diversification. Today, Longchamp can envisage real diversification in several areas: broadening its product range, opening up towards the travel sector, offering innovative products breaking away from their classic leather goods. Perhaps even a Longchamp café? There are so many opportunities to consider for its future in terms of new

99

segments and expression. A line of perfumes has been launched, which had never been envisaged before. Once again, beyond the obvious revenues that such a range could represent, it would strengthen the brand's link with its customers, as Longchamp remains a brand whose clientele is mainly female.

VISION & PERSPECTIVE

"The challenge of luxury is to reveal itself while continuing to make people dream

Jean CASSEGRAIN, CEO, Longchamp

The luxury of the future, like the luxury of the past, will be based on the relationship of trust between a brand and its customers.

This trust is the key to the value of all brands, but customers' demands on luxury brands are rightly even higher – for product quality and service excellence. What is changing is that trust is now conditional on an additional requirement – social and environmental responsibility. Customers expect more from luxury brands and it is important not to disappoint them. How are the products made? Where do they come from, are skills transmitted, how does the brand work to move the company in the right direction? To deserve the trust that its customers, but also its employees and partners place in it, a brand must act with sincerity and transparency.

In a world that cultivates mystery to better amaze customers, this is the challenge of tomorrow's luxury: to combine commitment and transparency, to reveal itself, while continuing to make people dream.

A graduate of ESCP Europe, Jean Cassegrain joined Longchamp in 1991. In 2020, he succeeded his father as CEO of Longchamp and his two sons Adrien and Hector Cassegrain joined the family business.

Bang & Olufsen, a forward-thinking brand

Since its first product was launched in 1926, Bang & Olufsen has been a forward-thinking brand, participating in the history of design and technology and focusing on aesthetics, material, and acoustics to deliver excellent quality products. It is one of the few brands that can imagine the intelligent home of tomorrow, whose challenges are greater connectivity and the use of artificial intelligence, spearheaded today by home automation. The brand is launching more and more products to boost sales, such as the Beosound Level, a portable, sustainable speaker made of natural and recycled materials – at a time when planned obsolescence is often the order of the day in the sector – or the Beovision Contour 55, a high-end television set. The Danish brand wants to rejuvenate its customer base with entry-level products such as headphones. It has also developed a policy of collaboration with other luxury brands: Saint Laurent (headphones, speakers) and more recently Berluti (speakers, headphones, TV sets) to design limited edition items. *"For nearly a century, Bang & Olufsen has been pushing the boundaries of audio technology and the company continues to sit at the forefront of acoustic innovation. Together with Berluti, we are bringing the best of artisanship to the fore with our expertise in sound and design, and Berluti's knowledge in leather craftsmanship to create a truly remarkable collection,"* said Christoffer Poulsen, SVP of Product Management & Brand Partnering at Bang & Olufsen, at its launch in June 2021.

Diversification in the hotel business

Over the past twenty years, the hotel industry has become fertile ground for diversification of luxury brands. The latest announcement being that of German car manufacturer Porsche, which signed a partnership with Deutsche Hospitality, a German hotel company in October 2021 with the goal of opening Porsche Design-stamped hotels "in the near future".

But it is mainly the fashion and jewelry brands that have largely invested in the hotel industry. In 2000, Versace opened the Palazzo Versace in Brisbane, and then one in Dubai in 2015. In the wake of the launch of its Armani Casa products, Armani has invested in hotels in Milan and Dubai. Baccarat opened its first hotel in New York City in 2015 in partnership with Starwood Capital, which has been a real success. Since its opening, the hotel has become a flagship address in the city, illustrating the interest brands have in pursuing this type of diversification.

Chopard, best known for its two flagship divisions, watch-making, and jewelry, took over the Union hôtelière parisienne, owner of the Hôtel de Vendôme in Paris. The Swiss brand is also expanding into perfumery and other accessories.

But it is Bulgari which is the best-case study in diversification. *"Bulgari is an authentic universe that goes far beyond a brand characterized by a single product type. Bulgari is a global luxury brand active in five areas: jewelry, watches, accessories, perfumes and hotels. The idea of globality translates into a "brand experience" that implements transversal synergies between the different product types[52]"*, explained its president Jean-Christophe Babin to *Décideurs* magazine in August 2018. The Italian jeweler, acquired by LVMH for €3.7 billion in 2011, successfully began its diversification in 1992 with its first perfume, called "Eau parfumée au Thé vert". Then came scarves and fashion accessories, pens, leather goods, glasses, tableware, crystal, porcelain, cutlery, and cosmetics. In 2001, Bulgari joined

---

52. Hervé Bornes, "Bulgari est un authentique univers qui va bien au-delà d'une marque," *Décideurs Magazine*, August 27, 2018.

forces with Marriott International to create Bulgari Hotels & Resorts. The first establishment was opened in Milan in 2004, the next in Bali in 2006, and then the next in London in 2012.

With Bulgari, LVMH is taking its first step into the luxury experience sector. Bulgari Hotels & Resorts now has seven hotels worldwide (London, Milan, Dubai, Bali, Beijing, Shanghai and Paris), with five more openings planned: Rome, Moscow, Tokyo in 2022, Miami Beach in 2024 and Los Angeles in 2025. However, this activity remains modest for the group as a whole. Its revenues are consolidated under the "other activities" heading, which includes many other areas[53]. It doesn't matter because this activity contributes to other things. *"Our hotels have never responded to an economic logic. We don't build them just for the money they bring in; otherwise there would be more than seven, but to extend the image of our brand,"* says Silvio Ursini, Bulgari's Executive Vice President in Charge of Hotels[54].

A second, more important step was taken in December 2018, with the purchase of the Belmond Group and the some 40 "exceptional hotels" it owns (the Cipriani in Venice, the Copacabana Palace in Rio de Janeiro, and the Grand Hotel Europe in St. Petersburg), as well as other assets, since the group also operates legendary trains such as the Venice Simplon-Orient-Express, or cruises such as the Belmond Afloat in France. This acquisition is consistent with the group's long-term strategy to offer consumers a full range of high-end experiences. *"The acquisition of Belmond, which perfectly complements our Cheval Blanc houses and Bulgari's hotel activities, will significantly strengthen the*

---

53. "Other activities" in the 2020 consolidated financial statements of LVMH include: the press – *Les Echos-Investir*, Le *Parisien* and *Aujourd'hui en France* –, Royal Van Lent-Feadship, La Samaritaine, Belmond and Pâtisserie Cova.
54. *Le Figaro*, November 25, 2021.

presence of the LVMH group in the world of exceptional hotels," explained Bernard Arnault, CEO of LVMH, in a press release.

By mid-2021, LVMH owned five Cheval Blanc hotels, and it has just opened a sixth in the French West Indies[55]. The Cheval Blanc Paris, opposite the Pont Neuf in the former premises of the Samaritaine, which opened in September 2021, is the jewel in its crown. This evolution towards the group's hotel business acknowledges the importance that clients place on luxury experiences.

Expanding audience and community

The primary purpose of diversification is, of course, to expand the customer base. Moët & Chandon has been able to develop more modern, accessible ranges, even going so far as to create a new dedicated brand; Chandon. Its communication has adopted new codes with a tone that differentiates it from conventional communication. With #LiveLifeUnplanned or #EnjoyTheSpark, Chandon has adopted a decidedly millennial tone, addressing a younger consumer community.

Devialet, which became famous among music lovers by launching a range of amplifiers in 2010 whose prices range from €5,000 to €28,000, has become the high-end reference. The French gem has set itself a major challenge – to up-scale, reaching a much wider audience in a very competitive niche, without losing its image or spoiling its brand. In October 2018 it decided to market a new model, the Phantom Reactor, the "baby" of its flagship product Phantom, at an accessible price of only €990. The objective is to increase sales from 50,000 units per year to several hundred thousand. The company has also rethought its

---

55. Cheval Blanc Paris, Courchevel, Saint-Tropez, Saint-Barth, Randheli (Maldives).

distribution channels, to be both in physical stores (from 460 to 100 outlets) and online. *"Amazon is now our second commercial partner,"* explained Franck Lebouchard, company CEO, who has also signed partnerships with major digital players such as Sky in the UK and Free in France.

Devialet has demonstrated that it is possible to create a luxury brand by adopting a strategy driven by innovation and resolutely focused on product excellence. The brand has been able to seduce the most demanding customers. With its Phantom listening rooms, called "Immersive Rooms", Devialet puts customer experience at the heart of its development. The "Immersive Rooms" are above all points of sale, located in shopping centers, train stations and airports throughout the world, or at prestigious partners such as Barneys New York since 2007. Devialet has also signed a partnership with the French equipment manufacturer Faurecia to equip some Audi cars with an audio system using Devialet technology.

VISION & PERSPECTIVE

"The evocative power of luxury"

François RUAULT, Chief Sales and Marketing Officer, Devialet

Luxury remains a reflection of an extraordinary desire, but the components of this pleasure are richer—no pun intended—than they have ever been.

The choice of a luxury product is based on its materials and design, and, in the case of a technology product, on its performance and the quality of the user interface (UI) for a maximized experience (UX).

Today, another choice factor for luxury products is increasingly based on sustainable development. It concerns the sourcing of materials, whether products can be recycled or

→

$\rightarrow$
repaired, if the brand contributes to local employment, inclusion and has an exemplary fiscal record. Luxury must also be more restrained, only revealing itself at a second glance.

A brand's mission, values and reputation are the essential underpinnings of its appeal. If a brand has all these facets, then its evocative power can be both local and universal.

François Ruault worked at Apple, Inc., then at Microsoft and HoloLens. Today, he is Chief Sales and Marketing Officer of Devialet.

The importance of technology in luxury

Luxury has always been at the forefront of trends and has a strong innovative dimension. The sector doesn't avoid high technology; far from it. It is one of its driving forces. The use of the metaverse and the explosion of NFTs and gaming in the luxury world all illustrate this.

New technologies invest in the products themselves. New or smart materials and 3D printing are new tools for designers. A first test was carried out with flat screens inserted in a Louis Vuitton bag. Will we begin to see close collaborations between luxury brands and high technology to develop completely new products?

The alliance between brands of equivalent prestige, such as Apple and Hermès, is still in its infancy. After the double band bracelet for the Apple Watch designed in 1998 by Martin Margiela, several objects using the Apple "Find My" application were marketed in spring 2021 as Apple AirTag Hermes: keychains, bag accessories, luggage tags and address tags. Montblanc proposed its Augmented Paper connected pen as well as a connected watch and a high-tech headset.

It is certain that breakthrough innovations will come out in other areas, such as in materials, manufacturing processes and distribution, creating new opportunities. In luxury products, they will open the way to new creative fields. Intelligent coatings are already being developed that change color according to temperature, pressure or light[56]. Whatever happens though, technology will never replace the hands of high-level artisans. Their leadership and involvement are essential.

Most cosmetics and fragrance brands already invest heavily in applied research to define their formulas, test them and put them into production.

For example, LVMH has two research centers in Cosmetic Valley – LVMH Research, founded in 1981, and Helios, a technology platform founded in 2013. Today, these two centers include 425 researchers. Their expenditure amounted to €139 million in 2020. R&D concentrates on cosmetics and perfumes[57].

LVMH has clearly understood that it must identify innovative start-ups that will provide solutions and products to help its brands perform. In this spirit, the group opened La Maison des Startups in 2018, an acceleration program at Station F, the largest startup incubator in the world. The group explains, *"The House of Startups aims to accelerate collaboration between LVMH Maisons and startups to design innovative products and services for the luxury industry. It is one of the pillars of the group's innovation policy."* Each year, around 50 international startups are welcomed there[58].

---

56. Smart materials from OliKrom.
57. LVMH, universal registration document, 2020 fiscal year.
58. Capucine Cousin, "LVMH s'invite au sein de l'incubateur Station F", *Challenges*, April 10, 2018.

LVMH intends to capitalize on the innovations created by these startups. The best way to stimulate innovation is with an international competition. The fifth LVMH Innovation Award 2021 focused on five key areas of the luxury future: operations and manufacturing excellence; employee experience and sustainability; omnichannel and retail experience; data and artificial intelligence; media and brand awareness. The prize was one year of personalized support and a place in La Maison des Startups.

Among the fields covered were connected objects, e-commerce and virtual reality. Many of these young companies are now working on concrete solutions. Orbis, a startup that is revolutionizing corporate communication through the use of holograms, was part of the program's first year and has since launched its first collaboration with Zenith. Other projects have also been with LVMH Maisons such as Guerlain and Kenzo Parfums.

L'Oréal has been the exclusive sponsor of the beauty startup accelerator, part of Station F, since January 2018. It receives up to 20 high-potential startups each year and helps them accelerate their development by providing strategic sponsorship and operational support. *"Our partnership with Station F is strategic to help us meet, collaborate with and support the next generation of beauty entrepreneurs. We are pleased to provide resident startups with access to a qualified network and a comprehensive mentoring program across the group's brands, laboratories, and sales teams to accelerate their development,"* explained Lubomira Rochet, L'Oréal's Digital Director at the time, in a press release.

Kering has created a research laboratory, Material Innovation Lab, for textiles[59]. But the luxury sector's involvement in research

---

59. Kering, "Sustainability progress report 2017–2020," report, 2021.

must go even further. The sector is contributing to current French "deep tech", with the support of Bpifrance. In the next few years, breakthrough innovations will appear in all fields thanks to scientific advances.

The intangible represents a new essential field for luxury. According to *La Fabrique de l'utopie*, "*Luxury in 2074 is now a way of being.*" Technology will largely condition its emergence.

VISION & PERSPECTIVE

"Technology, the enemy of the luxury sector?"

Gregory CARPENTER, Senior Academic Advisor
Kellogg School of Management

For centuries, luxury goods have been prized for their beauty, extraordinary craftsmanship, and rarity. Luxury brands connect us with the brand's heritage and remind us of threatened traditions and vanishing skills. With that special combination of qualities, luxury goods elevate the lives of consumers, making even the most mundane object or experience a moment capable of bring rare pleasure.

Today, consumers appear obsessed with technology and innovation rather than tradition and elegance. Innovation has eclipsed heritage and tradition. For years, competing in separate markets, technology and luxury firms now compete directly, such as in the watch market. Will technology render luxury brands as simply interesting historical curiosities? Perhaps.

But another, intriguing future appears more encouraging. By having great tradition and heritage, luxury brands can invite consumers to play a part in the story of their brand and its rich legacy. Rather than conserving their heritage, luxury brands and their devoted fans can co-author the next chapters of their epic dramas. Becoming more democratic and more unpredictable, luxury brands can draw on the past

→

⟶
to invent the future in ways that even the most sophisticated tech firm has yet to imagine.

Gregory Carpenter is Professor of Marketing Strategy at Northwestern University's Kellogg School of Management. He teaches an elective in the MBA program, Marketing Luxury, created and co-taught with Yves Hanania.

3D printing, intelligent materials: A new era of creation

The beginning of 21st century is seeing the rapid spread of 3D printing. In the case of luxury goods, this technology makes it possible to manufacture the object directly in the store in front of the customer, according to their personal choices.

High fashion designers have already taken the plunge and are producing 3D printed pieces. Their goal is to unleash creativity and to offer creations that are ever more innovative in terms of design or material. In fashion, this technique is already used to create designs by biomimicry. For its spring-summer 2019 collection, Balenciaga presented jackets and coats designed with modern molding techniques and 3D scanning using a scanner using models' measurements. Dutch designer Iris van Herpen is now positioning herself as an ambassador for 3D printing in the luxury and high fashion sector.

The world's leading jewelry group, Hong Kong's Chow Tai Fook Jewellery Group, is designing stores where customers will be able to watch their jewelry being made by a human/machine duo, with the best 3D technology and artisans. In the automotive industry, Bugatti is the first manufacturer to use 3D printing to produce custom-made brake aids in titanium. Mercedes, and

Porsche Classic, have also embarked on the 3D printing of certain parts for vintage vehicles, thus considerably reducing costs.

At the same time, advances in nanotechnology are making it possible to create new, better performing materials. In 2018, Prada relaunched its classic line Prada Linea Rossa. A line, the brand insists, *"that combines high fashion and high performance"*, with new generation materials including fabrics *"incorporating nanotechnologies with excellent conduction capabilities, promoting body temperature regulation; graphene, a substance derived from graphite; a new generation of quilting, composed of graphene and recycled polyester; Gore-Tex Pro, a water-repellent microfiber; PrimaLoft quilting; and highly abrasion-resistant 3L nylon, the world's thinnest material."*

Current projects will enable the body to be directly coated with materials applied by controlled spraying, so that the clothes are perfectly adapted to the customer's body. The future also belongs to connected clothing with health data sensors. These new types of garments could also provide innovative services such as temperature regulation, therapeutic compression of certain areas of the human body, or even serve as exoskeletons.

The essential role of personalization

Personalization isn't anything new. For many years, it has been the hobbyhorse of many luxury companies and fashion houses and it is used by all segments of the sector. Fred launched Atelier Fred in France, but also in Hong Kong, Japan and Korea. Accompanied by a dedicated consultant, the customer composes their bracelet step by step, from the material to the color, among more than 100,000 possible combinations. Finally, an engraving service can be used to sign their creation. This personalization gives the customer the possibility of creating a jewel that matches them.

But the best examples can be found in the perfumery sector. Personalized perfumes and cosmetics are currently being widely developed. Guerlain allows buyers to create their own fragrances and establish their own unique personal scent profile based on information they provide in advance on an iPad.

It will also be possible to create custom-made cosmetics in store, matching each client's skin in the future thanks to digital technology. The startup Oto Systems has developed a unique industrial system under the brand name Eponyma, which automatically produces personalized creams. Its founder is convinced of its merits, *"Today, with technology advances, we are able to analyze a certain number of skin features from a connected mirror, or even a smartphone or a tablet […] All these elements would make it possible to refine the composition of products and their uses in real time. Digital is extraordinary opportunity for brands in the cosmetics industry to go deeper and analyze data in a more relevant way than ever before"*[60].

Another example of personalization is in perfumery. Maxime Garcia Janin has launched Sillages Paris, the *"first customizable, online, accessible high-end perfumery house created by and for millennials"*. *"I wanted everyone to be able to create a perfume for themselves, one that truly resembles them, with the beautiful, natural and sustainable ingredients of high-end perfumes,"* he explains. The principle is simple – thanks to an algorithm, the user selects six ingredients from a list proposed by four creative perfumers: Amélie Jacquin (Givaudan), Alex Lee (Mane), Mylène Alran (Robertet) and Sébastien Plan. Customers then order their perfume, test it at home and can send it back free of

---

60. "Clés de demain," interview with Florent Pascal, "Les jeunes générations sont à l'affût de la moindre nouvelle tendance en cosmétique," *Le Monde*, December 10, 2018.

charge for a full refund if it isn't suitable. It is an original and interesting personalization initiative, anticipating the possible future for the perfumery sector.

Today, personalization offers brands many benefits, starting with a luxury in-store experience, with the possibility of increasingly and better personalizing products. In street fashion, the Golden Goose LAB sneaker brand is a good example of this movement to bring customers who are more likely than ever to buy online back into stores. In Milan, the store puts customization at the forefront, with "Sneakers Makers", on-site artisans available to interact with customers and help them "co-create" their shoes by adding designs, messages, charms, laces or crystals. A "Dream Wall"; an interactive kiosk with a screen, lets customers digitally design unique items. Cameras record the process to provide customers with souvenir videos they can keep or post online, facilitating the brand's marketing. *"Don't be perfect, Be Younique,"* the brand suggests. This concept, which puts co-creation at the heart of the experience, is being rolled out worldwide. It is a start towards getting customers to fall back in love with points of sale–essential for bringing customers back into stores.

4

Luxury, on a Mission to Promote Sustainable Development

In 2022, issues such as climate change, environmental pollution, resource depletion and biodiversity loss are widely shared fears. The luxury sector is taking these new constraints into account through the actions of its managers, employees, financial community, and consumers.

In the coming decades, it will not only be a question of not damaging nature. Are these projects linked to sustainable development just a trend or are they about profoundly correcting production methods?

In 2019, we emphasized that the sector could and should take on the role of a standard bearer for sustainable development. Three years later, it can be said that the major groups have made progress towards more virtuous practices. However, there are many challenges and there is still a long way to go. Too many companies in the sector are struggling to make sustainability a priority, even though the circular economy is firmly now on the agenda.

The driving role of the major luxury groups

Since the early 2000s, luxury groups have understood the need to manage and reduce their impact on the environment. Most of them engage in such approaches. Many measures are already in place to reduce manufacturing and marketing waste.

LVMH, a group that does not have the luxury of waiting

Reducing the environmental footprint of all its products throughout their life cycle was one of LVMH's commitments for 2020[61]. The group is aiming for a 10% improvement in key environmental performance indicators for all of its industrial, administrative and boutique sites.

LVMH's recognition of its environmental responsibility resulted in the creation of its Environmental Department in 1992; the signing of an Environmental Charter in 2001; the launch of the LIFE program (LVMH Initiatives For the Environment) in 2012; and the establishment of an internal carbon fund in 2015. At the same time, the Group's raw material supplies are being reviewed to ensure full compliance with the highest environmental standards by 2025.

In July 2019 LVMH and Stella McCartney announced the signing of an agreement that would aim to *"accelerate the global development of the Stella McCartney House, while remaining faithful to its long-standing commitment to sustainable and ethical fashion."* LMVH's Chair and CEO explained, *"Stella was the first to put environmental and ethical issues on the front*

---

61. LVMH, 2018 report.

stage, very early on, and she built her house around these issues. It emphasizes LVMH Groups' commitment to sustainability. LVMH was the first large company in France to create a sustainability department, more than 25 years ago, and Stella will help us further increase awareness on these important topics." Stella McCartney's vision isn't just limited to high-end fashion, but also to collaborations with the sportswear sector, which she sees as a potential vehicle for new materials and new attitudes towards the environment. Her objective is to increase the awareness of an ever-wider audience.

The many concrete actions in favor of the environment undertaken by LVMH have borne their fruit. The group's CO_2 emissions decreased by 15% in 2020 compared to 2019, energy consumption by 11%, water consumption by 20%, and final packaging weight by 22%. These improvements however, are mainly due to the 17% decrease in sales in 2020 compared to 2019. LVMH ramped things up in 2020, defining what "new luxury" is for all of its houses. It is a question of contributing to a new alliance between Man and Nature.

The LIFE 360 banner brings together all of the group's actions to help the environment. The two pillars of the program are the fight against climate change and protection of biodiversity. Reducing the group's carbon footprint is a priority objective. While the proportion of renewable energy used in its sites and stores is currently at 40%, it is expected to reach 100% by 2026. A 55% reduction in greenhouse gas emissions is targeted for 2030 in raw materials and transportation. Biodiversity protection is the second pillar. It is in the best interest of the group's companies so as to make their products successful.

As a partner in the UNESCO Mab (*"Man and the Biosphere"*) program, LVMH has taken the imperative need to protect the natural raw materials used in its products on board – flowers for its perfumes, grapes for its wines and spirits, cotton for its fashion, leather for its leather goods and stones for its jewelry. The biodiversity program therefore has four pillars: measuring the biodiversity footprint, reducing the impact of its activities on ecosystems, promoting animal welfare and regenerating ecosystems.

As an example, the Ruinart champagne house is launching a pilot project of regenerative agriculture in the mountains of Reims. Vitiforestry has been implemented on 40 hectares, where vines will be uprooted in favor of 25,000 shrub plants. The expected gains are soil improvement, promotion of biodiversity, landscape harmonization and protection against weathering. In 2026, 100% of the strategic raw materials used by LVMH must be certified as preserving ecosystems and water resources.

The fight against waste also contributes to sustainable development and is the subject of remarkable initiatives. Surplus raw materials ordered for the production of LVMH items will be offered for sale by the startup Nona Source. The B2B platform will offer to reuse the unused fabric and leather stocks from all of the group's houses. It will be open to independent designers, to all LVMH group companies, as well as to their competitors. Its shipments are limited to Europe. LVMH has action indicators for all of its houses. The group's commitment is demonstrated by the regular publication of their results.

As a further step, LVMH strengthened its partnership with Central Saint Martins fashion school in spring 2021. This partnership, called Maison/0, aims to develop students' inventiveness concerning the concept of the alliance between nature and creativity. On the menu: scholarships, R&D on innovative materials, study paths focused on biodiversity protection and regenerative agriculture, projects on new creative practices for sustainable innovation and innovation competitions. The objective is to permeate sustainability within the heart of creativity.

Finally, LVMH will create a global research and innovation center for sustainable luxury in Saclay in 2024–2025. Its 300 future employees and researchers will work alongside the some 20,000 professors and researchers at the top-level university institutes and R&D organizations in Paris-Saclay. The new LVMH center will bring the number of employees committed to sustainable development to approximately 1,000.

Guerlain is particularly aware of the vital role played by bees in the pollination of the flowers and plants which it draws its active ingredients from. It also markets a line of products whose active ingredients come from pollen. The company sponsors a series of programs dedicated to bee preservation: sponsorship of the association for the conservation of the black Breton bees of Ouessant, partnership with the French Observatory of Apidology, creation of the international "Bee School", a partnership with UNESCO to encourage and support entrepreneurship in the field of beekeeping.

Kering, a commitment model?

Kering is also very ambitious, as indicated in its 2025 strategy for sustainable development[62]. This large-scale project consists, first of all, of reinventing its business model. The group is also committed to the entire luxury sector, showing its willingness to share its new knowledge and know-how with its competitors.

Kering pursues the main objectives of sustainable development, in particular the reduction and sustainability of raw materials used, the adoption of sustainable designs and the reduction

---

62. Kering, "Sustainability progress report 2017–2020", *op. cit.*

of the environmental impact of its activities. The group intends to increase the quality of its collaboration with its employees and stakeholders. It is about creating entirely new business models. The main innovation developed by Kering is the EP&L (Environmental Profit & Loss) method, a monetary accounting of the impacts of its activities on the environment. It is based on two pillars. The first is the collection and measurement of all of the environmental impacts of the entire value chain of its luxury products. The second is the monetization of environmental damage[63].

This very ambitious method displays the company's activity in two different lights: the first traditional, in terms of accounting and finance; the other, innovative, relating to the environmental footprint of its business. As a result of this effort, Kering is now considered the seventh most sustainable company in the world in the "Global 100 2020" ranking by *Corporate Knights*, and the first in the "textile, clothing and accessories" sector.

"Our ambition by 2025 is to reduce our environmental footprint by 40% and make our supply chain 100% transparent and responsible. This includes further improving the traceability of our raw materials and increasing the production of materials from responsible and monitored sources. We are also very determined when it comes to animal welfare," explains Marie-Claire Daveu, Kering's Chief Sustainability Officer and Head of International Institutional Affairs[64].

"Our environmental profit and loss account, which was set up almost ten years ago, enables us to measure the impact of our companies' activities on the entire supply and production chain. Thanks to this tool, we know that Kering has already reduced it

---

63. The value of each damage is equal to the direct or indirect costs or gains that it generates on people's wellbeing.
64. Kering, press release, *Le Figaro Partners*, May 2021.

by 29% between 2015 and 2019 and is therefore well on its way to reaching its target of 40% by 2025."

The group wants to halt the reduction of biodiversity, the disappearance of endangered species and promote systemic change in procurement. Its Regenerative Fund for Nature aims, in collaboration with the NGO Conservation International, to convert one million hectares to regenerative agriculture by 2025. Its innovation laboratory focuses on the research, evaluation, and selection of new materials.

Hermès and L'Oréal Luxe, a rigorous approach

Hermès set up a Sustainable Development Committee in 2007, supported by ad hoc management and an ethics charter. The strategic framework, entitled "All artisans of our sustainable development", defines several pillars: the transmission of knowledge and responsibility towards its ecosystem.

The brand recognizes that its sustainability is based on the availability of quality materials that must be protected, and that environmental protection must also be one of its objectives. In its annual report, Hermès provides detailed information on the effective reduction of its industrial waste, as well as the reduction of its water and energy consumption.

L'Oréal reported a triple A score from the CDP[65] for the sixth year in a row in 2021 for its sustainability, for reducing its carbon emissions, water management and protecting forests

---

65. CDP for Carbon Disclosure Project until 2012, now CDP Disclosure Insight Action. The CDP is a British not-for-profit charity that assesses the performance of 7,000 companies and 620 communities on climate change, water and forest protection. The French members of the CDP are AXA, BNP Paribas, Caisse des Dépôts, Edmond de Rothschild Asset Management and Ostrum Asset Management.

in the supply chain. We can only applaud the transparency and exemplary nature of its many brands.

VISION & PERSPECTIVE

"Enhanced beauty, exclusive yet inclusive luxury"

Jean-Claude LE GRAND, Chief Human Relations Officer, L'Oréal Group

Does luxury have a future in a world of mass consumption where values are changing? Yes, if we define luxury as the desire to push the limits of what is possible.

On the other hand, luxury codes will change in the light of two major developments: the growing influence of technology, and social and societal responsibility, the latter having been irreversibly strengthened during the major crisis we have just experienced.

From beauty to beauty tech: towards a more global approach

If in the past, luxury in beauty referred to ingredient rarity, original textures or precious bottles, the beauty of the future will be primarily technology-based, allowing access to increasingly exclusive services and products. In this emerging world, Beauty tech is a new model to be pursued.

Data, artificial intelligence, augmented reality and the whole range of new technologies are opening up the field of possibilities in terms of diagnosis, customized products and experiences.

The future of luxury? Exclusive yes, but always more inclusive…

Today more than ever, the second trend that is redefining luxury codes is the responsibility and ability of brands to be "inclusive". Consumers are looking for meaning, for brands with strong values, increasingly committed to inclusion, diversity and differences.

→

→

Thus, without distorting the inspiring and exclusive status of luxury, environmental safety, health, diversity and inclusion will increasingly be luxury prerequisites. From the selection of materials to the production manner, including the choice of partners and stakeholders, the entire value chain will be dictated by these fundamental principles.

We are convinced that work on these issues is long term, progressive, continuous work, because a profound transformation needs to be initiated for inclusion to be a reality and luxury, in its aspirational role, will not be able to avoid this imperative.

Luxury will be inclusive, or it will no longer continue to exist!

Jean-Claude Le Grand, Chief Human Relations Officer of the L'Oréal group, has spent his entire career in human relations. Since 1996, he has alternated between operational and strategic positions (international recruitment, talent development, etc.). In 2006, he created and directed the Diversity and Inclusion Department.

New production models

The long-term sustainability of luxury goods is conditioned by the implementation of new production models. The materials used and the manufacturing processes, whether artisanal or industrial are essential.

New materials for luxury products

First target: packaging

Luxury goods must resolutely embrace the materials revolution. According to The Canadian study As You Sow, 6.3 billion tons of plastics were put in landfill between 1950 and 2015.

There is no way to effectively reprocess the enormous tonnages produced each year. The only solution is to prohibit their use. The economic stakes are high: these packages represent considerable sources of revenue for the petrochemical industries. Drastic measures are needed. Canada set a first example in 2021. Plastics are now classified as toxic substances.

As an alternative, wood pulp that dissolves in water can be used for skin care products. Algae-based bioplastics are replacing plastic bags. Organic packages containing seeds which can be planted enable regeneration.

In the area of pricey champagnes, Ruinart is innovating with its "second skin" case made of fully recyclable paper. Veuve Clicquot, in collaboration with K-Way, offers a coolbag using the colors, materials and zipper of the famous raincoat. It is when this case is recycled that sustainability comes into play.

The fact remains that packaging in the luxury industry is part of the overall experience of consuming luxury products. For example, watchmakers sell their watches in cases that are veritable jewel cases.

Second target: textiles and leathers

Recent research shows that bacteria can be used to stain material as a substitute for certain chemicals.

Towards sustainable leather

The use of leather by the luxury sector does not seem to deserve all the criticism it receives. Cattle leather is a "recovered" material from animals slaughtered for meat consumption[66].

---

66. Interview by the authors with Laurent Grosgogeat, Executive Vice President Cerutti 1881, November 2021.

The quality of the hides used by luxury houses requires that the animals be treated well throughout their lives right up until the end. Fashion and leather goods companies are working to reduce animal suffering through various professional organizations, issuing labels such as WelFur. Mushroom leather is used in fashion and sportswear. Stella McCartney has developed a range of clothing using this type of leather, developed with her partner Bolt Threads. The designer made a radical decision. Animal leather and fur have been banned from her collections since the creation of her brand and replaced with recycled polyester and synthetic fur.

Gucci has announced the use of a new material, Demetra, which is entirely vegan and made from plant-based materials, to replace leather. Leather tanning is another process with a strong environmental impact. Luxury brands are participating in a private international organization, the Leather Working Group, founded in 2005, whose mission is to develop an auditing protocol for leather producers. The aim is to encourage them to use physical and chemical methods that are compatible with environmental protection. The use of chromium and heavy metals in their manufacture must be banned in the long term. LVMH reported in 2018 that 48% of the leather purchased by its houses comes from LWG-certified tanneries.

Hermès uses mycelium from mushrooms for a version of its Victoria bag. Wooden fibers, once spun, can be used for weaving, as experimented by H&M. Another way is to use fabrics impregnated with algae, so that the garment has the same photosynthetic function of absorbing carbon dioxide and releasing oxygen as a plant. Designer Phillip Lim designed a green sequin dress made of seaweed fabric. The same fabric can be used to make a high-quality waterproof coat.

Issey Miyake has been working on a fiber made from recycled PET (polyethylene terephthalate) since 2010, a plastic material derived from petroleum and used in particular for containers and plastic packaging. This recycling means a reduction of 80% of CO_2 emissions compared to what producing the initial material expended.

Reducing the impact on the biosphere is a central issue for the fashion and luxury industries. Material recycling is a major solution to achieve this goal. Today, we must go beyond this already virtuous practice with circularity, which is undoubtedly an essential path for the future of all luxury products. Recycling precious stones and metals is common in the jewelry industry. Recycling precious textiles, furs and leathers is becoming increasingly widespread in fashion, as is reusing plastics. This is a road that many designers are taking.

Major group commitment: a long way to go

In 2022 luxury companies have made multiple public commitments to increase their production sustainability.

The changes made over the past two decades are beginning to bear fruit. However, the sector is not immune to the growing environmental demands of the public and its employees. It needs to step up its efforts as a strategic priority. No matter what, increased reforms in the luxury sector will be scrutinized by financial analysts, as CSR is now becoming a performance criterion that complements accounting data.

> ## "The main challenge is to incorporate accountability into the business model"
>
> ### Cédric Prouvé, Group President International, Estée Lauder Group
>
> The future of luxury will no longer be defined in terms of value, price or material abundance, but in terms of new dimensions that are difficult to quantify: the freedom to take time, pleasure, elegance, sublime art, "inspired" design, "unique" experiences, ultimate wellbeing but also the preservation of nature.
>
> Brands can meet these new expectations, while taking a sustainable development approach to achieve the "zero carbon" objective. The main challenge will be to combine accountability with a business model. The pandemic has only accentuated this movement and the world's leading luxury companies are on the move.
>
> *Cédric Prouvé is responsible for all Estée Lauder Group sales and profits in all markets outside North America and for all of the activities of its sales subsidiaries.*

Initiatives to follow

As we have seen, many initiatives are being taken to develop materials to replace leather for example, or to produce new fibers that can outperform some natural products.

The main target of the critics is the most used vegetable fiber in the world – cotton. Its traditional cultivation is the most polluting on the planet, and it uses a significant amount of pesticides, which is why organic cotton, grown according to other more environmentally-friendly standards, is so popular. Several other textile fibers of animal origin used for high fashion or luxury clothing are also targeted.

There is growing concern about cashmere production, which is mainly done in Mongolia and China. Goat farms are driving the local economy towards monoproduction and the land is under threat of desertification. Stella McCartney already stated that cashmere was responsible for a considerable part of the environmental impact of all of its production in 2014. Thus, 28% of the EP&L (Environmental Profit & Loss) impact of the brand was due to cashmere, which accounted for only 0.1% of the total materials used in its manufacturing. Other fibers of animal origin have been blamed for the mistreatment of animals: Australian wool, angora, 90% of which comes from China, and vicuña, from small llamas living in the Andes.

Several companies including Hermès, wishing to go further than simply reducing their direct carbon footprint, created the Livelihoods Carbon Fund[67] at the end of 2011 to implement actions and instruments to repair the environment. As of June 2012, the fund possessed €25 million, invested in five major reforestation projects in sensitive areas of Africa and Asia[68]. At the end of its first six years of operation, Livelihoods has planted 130 million trees, contributing not only to the absorption of CO_2 but also to improving the protection of vulnerable populations against cyclones and droughts and protecting biodiversity.

In the area of climate change and pollution mitigation, synergies will also result from joint initiatives with companies in the sector.

---

67. The founders of this fund (in December 2011) were Crédit Agricole, Schneider Electric, CDC Climat, joined in early 2012 by La Poste, in June 2012 by Hermès, and then other companies, including Danone.
68. Livelihoods Funds, July 4, 2012.

Large-scale operations can be imagined, such as the collection of floating plastic waste aggregates in the Mediterranean, their recycling and reprocessing into new materials which can be then used in different sectors of activity. Carrying this out under the flag of French or Italian luxury would lead to considerable gains in efficiency and image.

Traceability of raw materials, an imperative

The fashion industry is primarily concerned with tracing its raw materials, which it uses in large quantities. Cotton, used in huge volumes, must be identified in terms of geographical origin and crop types. Water-saving agronomic practices must be promoted. Implantation of a bioluminescent pigment in the fiber will make it possible to trace the cotton's origin.

Blockchain will also be able to guarantee the origin of personal luxury goods. The Arianee Project aims to build standards for the certification of valuable objects, offering digital guarantees of authenticity and security.

In this respect, Cartier, Prada and LVMH are launching joint initiatives concerning the supply chain, traceability and the fight against counterfeiting. With Aura technology, the three brands will implement a passport attached to the product, for the whole of its lifespan. The QRCode is a first solution developed by the Yoox Net-A-Porter group for the traceability of the 5,000 mid- and high-end fashion brands it distributes. This solution has every chance of flourishing, given the weight of this e-commerce platform; world leader belonging to the Richemont group since 2018.

Traceability is also of crucial interest to luxury houses. Counterfeiting is a great scourge for the economy as a whole.

Counterfeit transactions amount to several hundred billion dollars per year. Luxury goods account for more than half of this.

For each of its watches, Hublot gives a digital e-guarantee written in an *Aura* blockchain. This guarantee covers the materials used to build it and follows it from the factory to the customer. This "Hublot e-warranty" will also serve as a vehicle for new services.

The French luxury and fashion industry has identified the traceability of the materials it uses as a priority. It is a question of responding to the demand for transparency demanded of manufacturers, clients, brands and distributors.

"Distributed" registers will be established, using blockchain technology, listing the main manufacturing stages, data flows, existing certification tools and proposing computer protocols for recording transactions. The project's ambition is immense, especially since it will mobilize multiple stakeholders in many countries. The €200,000 budgeted for leather marking alone appears insufficient. The entire industry will have to find considerable funding.

The importance of certification standards in the jewelry industry

The luxury jewelry groups emphasize that the majority of their diamond and gold purchases are made from intermediaries certified under the Responsible Jewellery Council Code of Practices (RJC COP).

The RJC is a private international organization, whose members include more than 1,100 companies involved in the entire jewelry raw materials supply chain. In particular, the code addresses human rights, labor rights, environmental impact, mining techniques used and product declaration. RJC members are committed to accepting independent audits on each of these issues. In 2017, the gold acquired by a group like LVMH was 75% RJC COP certified and its diamonds 98.5%.

Other solutions are possible. Young brands are offering jewelry made from materials that come from identified sources or that are recycled according to current standards. As an example of these new trends, the French brand Jem (*"Jewellery ethically minded"*) offers, *"a positive alternative to uncontrolled artisanal mining activities, to the current impacts of industrial mining, to the delocalization of the jewelry industry and its know-how, to the lack of transparency, as well as to the non-traceability of the supply chain."* Jem is the first company in France to commit to solely buying gold from the Fairmined network. It believes that artisanal gold mining should be encouraged and linked directly to jewelers around the world, with the aim of providing a livelihood for the 15 million miners working in the poorest countries. To do this, the label organizes small-scale communities and provides them with environmentally friendly management structures and techniques. Remarkably, Jem has had a successful major crowd-funding campaign, a sign that its approach addresses a growing public concern about jewelry sourcing.

Cartier has committed to using recycled gold. It is currently using 95% and soon 100% recycled gold. This policy reduces the environmental impact of its manufacture by a factor of 10. Synthetic diamonds could be a promising new area to develop. With identical atomic structures to natural stones, they are manufactured in a laboratory using the HPHT (High-Pressure High Temperature) technique or by the CVP (Chemical Vapor Deposition) technique, which is less energy consuming. The stones are 4C graded by independent gemological institutes.

131

The Parisian company, DFLY offers a line of jewelry using only synthetic diamonds. Heloïse et Abélard specializes in upcycling gold and diamonds, which are given a new aesthetic life. For Cartier, the symbolic value of the diamond comes from its naturalness and its origins in time – more than a million years old – which gives it a dimension of eternity.

Vegan luxury?

A growing number of people around the world are speaking out against the poor treatment of animals. The iconic organization Peta (People for the Ethical Treatment of Animals) is now endorsed by 6.5 million people. Luxury brands support the actions of the international organization IWTO (International Wool Textile Organisation), which strives to provide answers to consumer concerns. Other organizations, such as L214, Fourrure-Torture or the Brigitte Bardot Foundation, are fighting the same fight. By lobbying public opinion and politicians, they are trying to put an end to all forms of animal cruelty, from their lives in intensive farming to the time they are slaughtered.

The non-governmental organization UEBT (Union for Ethical Biotrade) sets standards for ethical sourcing of ingredients to protect biodiversity. It provides certification to members who respect the conservation and sustainable use of biodiversity, the sharing of profits and socio-economic sustainability, and the respect of laws and stakeholders' rights. Guerlain became a member of the UEBT in May 2021. Its objective is to have all its sectors certified by 2026.

The CDP (Carbon Disclosure Project), which has expanded its scope to become the Global Disclosure System, is an NGO that questions companies about their environmental performance.

"Succeeding with responsible marketing" (an Ademe – the French Environment and Energy Management Agency – platform designed in partnership with the Union des marques, Prodimarques and Adetem) proposes another method. The aim is to demonstrate that brands that are truly committed to sustainable development are more successful overall. The commercial and environmental success stories certified by Ademe receive wide publicity, favorable both to the companies lauded and to sustainability[69].

Another solution would be the creation of an international Luxury Stewardship Council (LSC) organization, like the FSC (Forest Stewardship Council), which brings together all stakeholders – industry, consumers, public authorities and NGOs. This type of organization would be able to monitor the development of new manufacturing processes, the ramp-up of new practices, and to label sectors.

The need for a global indicator

As respectable as they are, something needs to be done about the multitude of certifications. It needs to be easier for customers to find out about a brand's performance. All of the groups' different actions need to be translated into an indicator proving their global, undisputed image.

Business of Fashion, the site broadcasting news from the fashion and luxury world, has developed a method to measure the real global situation of fashion groups. There are three core sectors: high street, sportswear and luxury. The 15 largest groups are scrutinized. There are six main categories of measurement, comprising of a total of 338 metrics: transparency of information,

---

69. Amelle Nebia, "La plateforme "réussir avec un marketing responsable" orchestrée par David Garbous", *CBNews*, October 5, 2021.

reduction of greenhouse gas emissions, reduction of water and chemical consumption, savings of raw materials through recycling and regeneration, worker's rights in the company, reduction of waste. The overall result for the fashion industry – a score of 36 out of 100 – shows the gap that still exists between statements and achievements.

In the luxury sector, results are mixed. Kering received a score of 49 out of 100. Its strong points (above 50) are transparency, water and chemical consumption reduction, savings in raw materials. VH Corp (Tommy Hilfiger and Calvin Klein) scored 41 of 100. Its strong point is reduction of its emissions. Hermès scored 32, with a good performance in terms of transparency. LVMH scored 30 out of 100 and Richemont 14. *Business of Fashion's* method will certainly be refined as its analysis campaigns continue.

The indispensable cooperation of luxury groups

François-Henri Pinault, CEO of Kering, was tasked in 2019 by French President Emmanuel Macron with mobilizing the fashion industry to adopt good practices and reduce its environmental impact[70]. The "Fashion Pact" was presented at the G7 in Biarritz at the end of August 2019, and at the UN climate summit in September of the same year.

60 companies, representing over 200 brands (retailers, manufacturers, producers) in fashion (Zara, H&M, Sandro, Maje and Claudie Pierlot), sportswear (Nike and Adidas) and luxury goods

---

70. Juliette Garnier, "Emmanuel Macron charge François-Henri Pinault de mobiliser la mode autour de l'environnement," *Le Monde,* May 15, 2019.

(Kering, Chanel and Hermès) committed to eliminating single-use plastic packaging by 2030, to using 100% renewable energy by that date and to achieving zero net CO_2 emissions by 2050. A first assessment of this "Fashion Pact" took place in October 2021, at the Fashion Summit in Copenhagen.

In addition, Cartier, on behalf of the Richemont Group, and Kering have launched the "Watch & Jewellery Initiative 2030", a cooperation with the Responsible Jewellery Council. Its goal is to welcome watch and jewelry brands from all over the world, willing to commit to a set of ambitious goals in three areas: building climate resilience, preserving resources, and fostering inclusiveness.

"As the watch and jewellery sector relies on the earth's precious resources and people's know-how around the world within its value chains, the imperative to act together in creating a more positive impact has become ever clearer. We are thrilled to join efforts towards a more sustainable industry together with Kering, in partnership with the Responsible Jewellery Council, and to invite other industry actors to join this initiative. More than ever, we remain committed to share our common vision of a future where all Maisons, their suppliers and business partners are empowered to collaborate on projects that deliver positive impact on the planet and its people," said Cyrille Vigneron, President and CEO of Cartier, in a press release.

The challenges of sustainable development are numerous and complex for the luxury sector. The "Fashion Pact" and the "Watch & Jewellery Initiative 2030" are important first initiatives, but there is still progress to be made in many areas such as materials, manufacturing processes, logistics and distribution channels. Moreover, luxury covers new fields such as wellness, virtual reality or the metaverse. Cooperations are possible to build new baselines upstream of creation. European groups have everything to gain when faced with global competition by developing new coalitions – for example in environmental protection or high tech – with the establishment of official labels authenticating their specific features.

5

Social and Corporate Responsibility at a Crossroads

ndividual companies are being called upon to define their missions and explain their contribution to general public interest. Politicians, trade unions, associations and non-governmental organizations are all demanding this. The sustainability of production and distribution, and even of consumption, has become a requirement dictated by climate change. Consumers and employees are the two main drivers of this evolution.

The luxury sector is in the eye of the storm. It is faced with exhaustion due to material consumption, growth in the demand for digital services and increasing consumer guilt. The promotion of ethical values is essential if it wants to be in line with public thinking and maintain its success in the long run.

Luxury groups at the service of society

Luxury brands are taking their social responsibility into account by drawing up innovative human resources management policies giving them enviable places in the lists of good companies to work for. There is significant room for improvement, both for the wellbeing of employees and for the companies themselves.

An unprecedented role in mobilization against the pandemic

As early as the first lockdown of France in March 2020, there were severe shortages of products essential to stopping the spread of Covid-19: hand gels, masks, gowns, resuscitation equipment. Several luxury houses worked to fill the supply gap. Parfums Christian Dior, Guerlain, Parfums Givenchy and Bulgari in Italy produced several tons of hand gel.

Despite the shortage of workers and the strict protocols for employee safety, 16 Louis Vuitton workshops around France manufactured 500,000 masks and 11,000 protective gowns for French hospitals. Givenchy and Dior manufactured masks for the general public. The group imported 40 million surgical and FFP2 masks and acquired resuscitation and testing equipment.

Brands didn't just react during the lockdowns. Many continue to help in the fight against Covid. Bulgari created the "Bulgari Virus Free Fund", an NGO to finance work on infectious diseases. In particular, the fund will support Oxford University's Jenner Institute and the Lazzaro Spallanzani Institute of Infectious Diseases in Rome.

Long-term initiatives

The Kering Foundation – Stop Violence, Improve Women's Lives is an outstanding example of a company's commitment to society. Created in 2009 and chaired by François-Henri Pinault, it supports projects led by local NGOs, accompanies social entre-preneurs and organizes awareness campaigns.

Among its various campaigns are the fight against domestic and sexual violence, including female genital mutilation. Special programs focus on supporting women refugees and raising awareness to change behavior. A digital application making the filing of complaints easier and a company for the economic and social integration of asylum seekers have also been created. A project for discussion groups on violent male behavior is underway. The total amount of grants awarded was just over €1 million over three years (2015–2017), the largest being the mobilization of the group's 40,000 employees. Their awareness of women's issues is complemented by their work for the organizations involved in the foundation's actions.

The LVMH group considers philanthropy to be one of its responsibilities. Its patronage benefits the Robert Debré Hospital (AP-HP) in particular, and research on hereditary genetic diseases. LVMH has also allocated €100 million to the reconstruction of Notre-Dame. The Arnault family donated the same amount.

LVMH has joined forces with Cafés Joyeux to contribute to improvement of disabled people's lives. The association reintegrates disabled people with Down's syndrome or autistic people, by giving them work in its eight establishments.

Luxury houses are making other demands of themselves and developing projects with a significant social impact. Cartier has been 100% funding its Cartier Philanthropy foundation since 2013. Since its inception, aid mobilized for women and children in the world's poorest countries amounts to €65 million.

"Authenticity and tradition, the two pillars of luxury"

Shannon WASHBURN, CEO, Shinola

The perception of what makes an item luxury vs. being a mainstream product has been changing as people demand more from brands, regardless of whether they are spending $50 or $50,000. They want a product built to last with a rich, genuine story behind it. I see this philosophy playing out at the Shinola Hotels. The pursuit of luxury often is the pursuit of authenticity more than simply the pursuit of exclusivity; the pursuit of a meaningful experience equates to more than just acquiring something that costs a lot of money. In a nutshell, luxury is far more about quality than it is quantity.

Luxury brands, like other brands, have a responsibility to not simply just sell their products. They have shown their resilience and powers of adaptation to the Covid-19 crisis. They are committed to their employees and their customers.

As far as Shinola is concerned, our motivation has always been about being locally based and working with the people and resources of the city of Detroit. Based on the ideas of our founder Tom Kartsotis, *"we wanted to create a modern American brand, reintroduce the idea of national production on a scale that shapes a corporate culture, bringing a community together around products that last"*.

Shannon Washburn is the CEO of Shinola, overseeing all aspects of the business since 2019. Prior to becoming president in early 2018, Shannon spent six years working with the watch and jewelry product development and design teams. Prior to Shinola, Shannon was a buyer for Dillard's before her 14-year tenure at Fossil.

The place of employees in luxury companies

It is well known that the working conditions in a company -regardless of the sector–play an important role in the degree of employee involvement. Remote working, which has become more prevalent during the health crisis, has further increased their demands. This concerns all areas. Luxury companies are trying to provide solutions.

At the heart of LVMH's specific annual report on the implementation of its corporate social responsibility is respect for individuals. The different pillars are constant attention to working conditions, prevention of discrimination and respect for individuality, development of talent and know-how, and local social involvement. The annual report gives an overview of the actions carried out with insights into various missions. As proclaimed in its business report, the values of LVMH are creativity and innovation, excellence, and entrepreneurship. All LVMH managers and employees strongly believe: "*It is our talents that make the difference*"[71]. In 2009, the LVMH group adopted a code of conduct for all its companies, with rules that each employee must follow when performing their duties and responsibilities, with particular emphasis on "*the integrity required of all*". The six main principles to be respected are acting responsibly and in a spirit of solidarity, providing a fulfilling work environment and valuing talent, committing to the preservation of the environment, earning the trust of customers, earning the trust of shareholders, and achieving and promoting integrity in the conduct of business[72].

---

71. Talents, business report, LVMH 2017.
72. Social responsibility, 2017 report, LVMH 2018.

One of the objectives is to promote equal pay for men and women, female leadership and the recognition of multiple talents. The Bloomberg Gender Equality Index audits companies' performance in this area. LVMH has developed its own internal inclusion index. It is about gender equality and initiatives taken in favor of the LGBT community. Policies are being implemented to increase the number of women on management committees and boards of directors. Similarly, ethnic diversity is a key objective in recruitment and promotions. It is inseparable from the design of products and services that serve to include social groups that were previously excluded from the world of luxury. Diversity is positive in terms of creativity. The LVMH Heart Fund, launched in 2021 with an endowment of €30 million, is a program to support its employees who find themselves in sudden serious personal situations. It is aimed at its 150,000 employees worldwide.

"Value" sharing on the agenda

Employee shareholding is now on the agenda. The commitment of employees and their loyalty to a company make it a modern management tool, aiding a company's overall performance. Less well known is the fact that employee shareholding also represents a means of increasing their pay over time. The Equalis 2021 index, which measures the valuation of 42 unlisted companies (mainly small and medium-sized enterprises) shows an increase of 27% over one year and even 177% over five years.

All LVMH Group companies with more than 50 employees have a profit sharing, incentive or savings plan, and the total cost in 2020 amounted to €310.9 million for the group as a whole, an increase of 10.4% compared to 2018. This amount represented approximately 10% of the dividends paid in the same year. With regard to employee shareholding, employees of LVMH and its affiliates held 0.14% of the share capital, under company savings plans and in registered form in respect of bonus shares identified as having been allocated under plans set up since October 20, 2016.

Kering SA devoted €1.292 million to employee profit sharing in 2020, while its operating income was negative by €27 million and dividends paid out by €1 billion. As regards employee share-holding, the company's policy is to grant bonus and perfor-mance shares to executives and certain group employees. This amounted to €45.719 million in 2020. In total, employees and executive directors held 0.1% of the share capital of Kering SA as of December 31, 2020.

At Hermès International, employee profit sharing, which is linked to the achievement of various corporate objectives, amounted to €113.6 million in 2020, with dividends paid out of €489.6 million. Hermès has set up bonus share plans. In total, as of December 31, 2020, employee shareholding represented 1.09% of the capital, more than €1 billion. This policy undoub-tedly contributes to the company's excellent social climate and the quality of its results.

The group considers that each individual contribution creates value and participates in the collective dynamic that makes it possible to achieve its medium and long-term development strategy.

143

"Winning brands will create a strong sense of belonging among their employees"

Sharon MacBeath, Human Resources Director, Hermès Group

The luxury industry is very demanding, and with the Covid crisis causing further polarization within the sector, as well as further accelerating the impact of pre-existing trends related to the customer experience, digital or sustainable development, to name but a few, candidates considering applying should not minimize demands.

The constant quest for creativity in product design but also in the use of new materials, the quality imperative in everything that's undertaken means that employees in this sector whether in the studio, the atelier or the store must meet the highest standards, always.

When you combine volatility of the world we live in, the intrinsic challenges of the industry, and the ever-increasing expectations of a broad stake holder groups, you need to be a master in the art of managing paradox, very comfortable with ambiguity, agile and resilient.

This is not a business for the faint hearted or those who struggle with complexity.

But can we really list such success criteria for an industry which employs such a diverse range of actors? Indeed, we often underestimate the broad range of professions the sector offers. From design, digital, supply chain, logistics or opportunities for engineers more broadly, candidates in these jobs do not always project themselves in the luxury sector. It's also a business which is resolutely international and as such the career paths on offer are diverse and rich.

While there are business schools and universities increasingly offering specific courses targeting the luxury industry, this is certainly not a prerequisite, since the industry prides itself on a diverse range of backgrounds, values general knowledge, curiosity, and open-minded people above all. It's a highly collaborative business which increasing interdependencies and as such, while there maybe a few stars in the system, most people that succeed are highly collaborative. However, whatever the position you apply for there will always be particular attention attached to personality and *savoir être*.

Cultural fit is so important, and the corporate cultures are very different from one house to the other. For this reason, being successful in one *maison* is not a guarantee you will succeed in another.

I personally think that in a context where retention will be a challenge, the winners will be those houses that manage to create a particularly strong sense of belonging, where the values of the individual align with those of the house and where their work is a source of meaning and fulfilment. Shared humanistic values were important before but I believe there will be a particularly low level of tolerance for working in companies which do not create the conditions for self-accomplishment, well-being, and personal growth.

On top of cultural fit, another element which contributes to a sense of belonging and ownership is the mechanisms that are used to share value creation. While profit-sharing mechanisms exist in many countries, houses that make sure that exceptional performance is shared with those that contributed to it will generate additional good will and build loyalty.

Sharon MacBeath was Managing Director of EMDS Consulting and then Human Resources Director for Redcat, Rexel and Tarkett. She is currently Human Resources Director for the Hermès Group.

6

New Experiences and New Intimacy

Throughout the months of lockdown, luxury brands entered a new dimension – the intimate space of people's homes. Even though the health crisis has brought its share of problems needing to be managed in the immediate future, luxury brands have been able to double down on their creativity and inventiveness to occupy the free space in their customers' homes. They were among the first companies to respond to the health crisis. But beyond the masks and hand gels made and distributed, an essential battle was being played out: being present and bringing comfort to their clients, being by their sides in a time heavy with emotions and worry.

This last year of crisis has also been an opportunity to strengthen essential customer relationships in the luxury sector. Nature abhors a vacuum. "If you can't come to us, we'll come to you," was the motto of the day.

The biggest luxury brands are now going even further. They are aware that they must also render services, enchant our lives, insert themselves into our circle of friends and become our best friends by inviting themselves into our homes. During the lockdowns, many of them increased their communications and sales channels, offering their customers master classes, virtual tours of their stores, while allowing them to purchase their products in just a few clicks on social networks like Instagram. Lululemon, the fashionable fitness clothing brand, is a great example of this with the Mirror, a reflective screen installed at home that lets users follow workouts while watching themselves at the same time.

Imagine what other companies could do: private concerts organized by your favorite brand like Devialet or Bang & Olufsen or a live Instagram session with an iconic rock singer like Bono – all opportunities to build and strengthen relationships with customers. Louis Vuitton customers expected their favorite brand to provide them with travel and discovery experiences to escape the boredom of a world at a standstill and a ban on leaving their homes. It was up to the brand to take us on a journey – its reason for being is the art of travel after all. It had a thousand opportunities to take its homebound customers on journeys by presenting them with multiple formats and online experiences such as visits to museums and cities. Its collection of Louis Vuitton guides has not only given it legitimacy but also substance. The period initiated this change and now the new ideas can be further extended.

With the repeated closures, the obvious challenge was to find a way to get customers who have an even greater expectation of enchantment and wonder back into stores. A growing number of luxury brands are imagining experience centers, creating new spaces for wellness, culture and exhibitions, coworking and recycling, etc. Spaces offering experiences are multiplying. Department stores are boosting their creativity to offer new experiences and services, with themed evenings, the possibility of co-creating as a couple or in a family.

To become our best friends, brands are making the most of their ecosystems with the help of digital technology that gives them detailed knowledge of their customers and their evolution, so they can feed their dreams, come up with solutions to their vintage or avant-garde desires, or offer useful services. They can find these experiences in reinvented and digitalized stores, where the luxury of tomorrow has taken into account the trends that have accelerated during this crisis: digitalization, sustainable development, customer experience, presence on social networks and e-commerce[73]. Luxury brands must have new standards for an increasingly demanding clientele, which is now the new norm.

A whole host of stores are being transformed into museums and hosting exhibitions to provide an artistic and cultural experience. The Prada Epicenters or the Louis Vuitton "Maisons" are excellent examples. The first ones date back to the early 2000s. Contemporary art foundations (belonging to the most famous maisons) have been created such as the Louis Vuitton Foundation, while collaborations between brands and artists are increasing.

The luxury of yesterday, although more lavish and exuberant, was able to establish high-level experiences that many brands are now reclaiming and bringing up to date by drawing inspiration from their heritages. This is a principle that Chanel applied by inviting elite influential women to tea in the apartments of Mademoiselle Coco, in Rue Cambon. The goal was not to sell suits or bottles, but to offer a unique experience.

As opposed to material goods, luxury experiences, essentially composed of shared goods or services, are rapidly growing. According to Bain & Company, the global market for personal luxury goods market in 2019 was $281 billion and luxury experiences $337 billion. Composed of luxury hotels, fine wines and spirits, in-home and out-of-home gastronomy and luxury cruises, it exceeded personal products results by 20%. In 2020, with the

---

73. Yves Hanania, "Le luxe après: les marques, nos intimates?", *CBNews*, December 2020-January 2021.

health crisis, the global market for personal products declined by 23%. Luxury experiences fell by 41%. But the movement towards experiences is well underway.

Being closer to customers

Building and developing brand ecosystems will create greater intimacy with customers. For example, several brands encourage DIY (Do It Yourself), reinforcing their closeness to their customers. The fashion designer Jonathan Anderson, taking note of a knitting fan's initiative, has published tips on how to make one of his creations even though it was originally sold for €1,500. Similarly, Alexander McQueen's design team explained how to recreate a patchwork jacket from the 2020–2021 fall-winter collection. Givenchy tutorials show how to turn a blanket into a cape.

Customers can evolve and consume all of the products and services offered by the brand in a new ecosystem. Soho House, a private English club, now offers a range of places, products, services and experiences around the world. For members, it has become a way of life: you can eat, work, play sports, sleep. The new "houses" have spas, hair salons, projection rooms, swimming pools and gyms. The one in Paris opened in October 2021, the one in Milan at the end of 2021. Soho House now has more than 25 "houses" around the world, some of which are outside of major urban centers. Soho House operates many other brands, including Cowshed spa products and Soho Works shared work spaces. Soho House members have the opportunity to buy Soho Home decoration items, crockery and furniture used in the clubs online; an offering similar to that of the Conran Shop, an iconic trendy English decoration store. Airbnb has invested in luxury by offering high-end properties with specific services and experiences, targeting a wealthy clientele.

Luxury hotels: from storm to recovery

The luxury hotel industry recorded $206 billion in global revenue in 2019. In 2020, the sector lost 65% of its revenue. Forecasts of 5% annual growth by 2023 have, of course, been challenged by the halt or restriction of international tourism. Restructuring is underway in the world's leading luxury hotel chain portfolios, such as St. Regis, The Ritz-Carlton Hotel Company, Four Seasons Hotels Limited, Fairmont Hotels & Resorts, Hyatt Corporation, Shangri-La Hotels & Resorts.

Despite uneven recovery, the major groups have been able to strengthen their positioning, especially in the "ultraluxury" and "lifestyle" segments as evidenced by the Accor group's reorganization.

High-end private rental platforms like Le Collectionist and Onefinestay are taking full advantage of this new situation. *"In the context of the pandemic we, in the luxury industry, were the lucky ones. Even more specifically, private rentals were affected differently as compared to flights and hotels because the product was a perfect fit for the new pandemic context. Originally, in our market we had about 80% foreigners booking with us and very few clientele renting in their home country. But in 2020, everything changed. We had mostly French clients renting properties in France, opening up the market for us with local clients in local destinations. What Le Collectionist has done in the time of the pandemic is make strong growth in the French and European markets, where we previously had a majority of British and American clientele."* explains Collectionist Co-founder Max Aniort[74].

---

74. Interview of Max Aniort by the authors, August 2021.

"Despite the crisis, our customers have continued to go on vacation"

Max Aniort, Co-founder and CEO, Le Collectionist

In the travel market, I'd say you (or at least we at Le Collectionist) have two kinds of clients: those who book in the first quarter in March or April, which are mostly families booking their holidays for the summer in destinations like Corsica, Provence, Cap Ferret. These are mostly French clientele booking in French destinations to be sure to have the best options for the upcoming summer holidays and this has not changed much.

The second group are last-minute bookings, and this is where the attitude has shifted. Whereas previously, booking earlier was preferred pre-pandemic because every destination was an option and booking last-minute limited your options; now it is the opposite. Waiting to be closer to your holiday date means possibly having more options in terms of destinations than you would have if you booked it months in advance due to country restrictions, travel requirements, border closures, and openings.

Of course this is something we've had to adapt to and something that I think everyone in the industry will have to as well.

It's a mad rush, but it's also quite interesting to see how attitudes have changed and will continue to change according to how the global situation pushes forward.

After holding several positions as an analyst and then as a consultant at Chappuis Harper, Max Aniort cofounded the luxury home rental service Le Collectionist, which he is CEO of.

But the luxury hotel industry is no longer the monopoly of large international chains, who are leaders in every sector. Prestigious hotels are increasingly creating concepts which differentiate them. Major brands and luxury groups are developing projects around the world. The Accor group opens over 300 hotels per year, including a significant number in the luxury and lifestyle segment.

LVMH has been making investments for several years. The world's leading luxury goods company has its own brand of small luxury hotels; Cheval Blanc, and it has a project underway in Los Angeles. Olivier Lefebvre, Head of LVMH Hotel Activities, explained to *Les Echos* in September 2021 that Cheval Blanc was *"a collection of Maisons, not an international chain. We could go to London, for example, but not to Munich."* This is because each establishment is custom-designed in exceptional locations. Bulgari (a member of the LVMH galaxy since 2011) has five star hotels around the world.

LVMH's hotel division includes a much larger upscale operator, Belmond, acquired in 2019, which operates 33 hotels, with legendary establishments such as the Copacabana Palace in Rio or the Hotel Splendido Mare in Portofino or seven dream trains like the Orient Express, the Belmond Royal Scotsman or the Cusco-Machu Picchu in Peru. Today, the Orient-Express is "co-managed" by LVMH for the future takeover of the "rail" part of the business and by the Accor group for the hotel part. Accor has also integrated the brand into its "Ultra Luxury" business unit, which also includes Raffles, the famous Singapore brand, which had 15 hotels in 2020. The French leader aspires to build an additional collection of a dozen hotels by 2030.

"Tomorrow's luxury will conquer hearts"

Guillaume de SAINT LAGER, Vice-President, Orient-Express-Accor

Luxury brands have always been seen as something living and breathing, not only because of they are often called after their great creators, but also because they have their own tangible personalities. Energized by the end of the crisis, these living brands will continue to blur the lines, with their complex personalities. Luxury will remain inaccessible, yet it will never have been so accessible to all; it will be both sober and exuberant, both rare and omnipresent. This game of paradoxes has been well thought out, almost meticulously.

Curious, tomorrow's luxury will conquer the hearts of all. Brands are already taking risks, stepping outside their usual fields of expression and emancipating themselves from the boundaries separating the universes of products from services. The goal is to create rich, exhaustive and evolving universes, in which "followers" are invited to immerse themselves in a total experience. For a single brand, luxury can be shape-shifting: a film celebrating the brand (House of Gucci), a café providing a brand experience (Café LV in Tokyo or the Avenue in Paris transformed into a Miss Dior recently), a gym to exercise in with branded accessories (Hermès Fit at Beaux-Arts) or disarmingly simple but incredibly effective collaborations (Balenciaga x Crocs or more recently with the Simpsons).

Guillaume de Saint Lager is Vice-President of Orient Express (Accor), responsible for redeploying the legendary brand in the world of luxury trains and hotels.

Another initiative is designed to "reinvent the mountain". The project involves building a five star hotel, 13 ultra-high-end chalets, each designed as a work of art by 13 renowned designers, 17 apartments, as well as an ice rink, boutiques and an artificial surfing wave, all of which will be built under a single name, WOM, by the end of 2023 in Les Brévières, an Alpine village below Tignes in France. The mammoth, yet eco-responsible project was launched by former freeriding ski champion and ex-rally driver Guerlain Chicherit. And the best part of all is that each chalet owner (expected to sell for several million euros) will be offered a unique car, a specially made electric Lancia Delta collection car[75].

The Barrière group of casinos and hotels will open its first foreign hotel under the Fouquet's label in Manhattan in the summer of 2022, marking the new group strategy headed by Dominique Desseigne. *"Barrière is strengthening its international development, whilst contributing to the promotion of France and French art de vivre throughout the world,"* said the CEO of the Barrière Group in a press release.

After years of unbridled development, the luxury hotel industry offers a double opportunity to brands. The whole product range of a brand, or even a group such as LVMH, can be offered in hotel. Hotels provide unparalleled experiences and brands can vastly increase their offerings. There are a growing number of medium-sized hotels with strong identities. Numerous concepts have emerged, from urban, to country, to ecological, gallery, and literary hotels etc. Authenticity is demanded and expected by a growing number of travelers. The luxury sector is diversifying

75. Claire Rodineau, "WOM Tignes, l'hôtel de luxe qui veut "inventer la montagne de demain," *Le Figaro*, December 9, 2021.

into high-end hotels integrating local aesthetics and cultures, while maintaining international standards of comfort. The pandemic has only reinforced this need to escape, encouraging the development of hotel concepts advocating a return to nature. Covid has led to an unprecedented appetite for outdoor activities in all countries. New offerings are flourishing, enhanced by services related to physical and mental wellbeing.

The eco-chic tourism introduced by Six Senses combines authenticity, emotion and above all experience. A pioneer in this field in 1990, with its first establishment in the Maldives, Soneva Fushi, a chain of 16 barefoot luxury hotels was sold by the American investment fund Pegasus Capital Advisors to InterContinental Hotels Group[76].

A new definition of high-end hotels has been established since 2008 – *"rough luxury"*[77]. The Rough Luxe Hotel, designed by interior designer Rabih Hage and philanthropist Curt Engelhorn, consists of small, rustic rooms with mismatched furniture and peeling paint. By building around the imperfections created by the wear and tear of time, the designers of the Rough Luxe Hotel didn't take the easy way out and chose to preserve the vestiges of the past. Since 2010, Hage and Engelhorn have expanded this concept to a network of hotels, bars, restaurants and stores. Their goal? To offer clients a new, enriched atmosphere, an intellectual and social awakening through unique life experiences. This luxury experience allows people to blossom through encounters, discover art or music, rediscover the taste of natural flavors. Rough luxury doesn't

76. Alexandre Kauffmann, "Six Senses, l'éloge du luxe écolo", *Le Point*, No 2429, March 21, 2019.
77. Yves Hanania, "Un luxe à l'état brut en quête d'authenticité," *INfluencia*, July 9, 2014

intend to please everyone, it is something different – a state of mind which people either like or they don't.

The rough luxury experience network is not about being part of a famous hotel chain. The goal is not to build a standardized chain but to bring together unique establishments that reject luxury as an object of mass consumption. Hotels should have unique and historic architecture, the design should combine the old and the new and include original works of art. For example, Finca Bell-Lloc and Shakespeare & Company, an independent bookstore in Paris, are members of this network. However, rough luxe cannot be reduced to this raw aestheticism and these few rules. Images, objects and ideas from past eras captivate, and the values of yesterday become a refuge. The success of vintage is the best proof of this. An object aged and weathered by time, a bearer of history, where everyone that uses it marks their presence, is opposed to a product without a soul born from recent industry.

In an unprecedented era for the hotel industry, this boom in rough luxe makes sense. It seeks to reconnect with the founding values of luxury: pleasure, tranquility and quality. This desire to embellish the ravages of time symbolizes the rejection of consumption in which only new things have value. Instead of throwing away and buying, destroying and building, things are repaired and rebuilt.

While these difficult economic times have seen the emergence of new luxury concepts, such as lean luxury, accessible luxury and rough luxe, it is important not to misunderstand it. The latter, whose price range remains high, is intended for a minority of customers – those who are prepared to spend very high amounts of money on objects and experiences that look old-fashioned, but which are priceless.

Strong growth in the "lifestyle" hotel business

The luxury hotel industry has not been spared by the health crisis – quite the contrary, and it has responded in many ways. At the same time that it recorded a massive €1.5 billion loss in the first half of 2020, the Accor group undertook its biggest ever reorganization. Rather than trying to defend its position, the French leader chose to go on the offensive by pursuing its strategy of acquiring lifestyle hotel brands, firmly positioned at catering the younger generations. This fast-growing segment corresponds to a hybrid strategy – the convergence of leisure and business travel, while offering a friendly and exclusive spirit in "Soho House style".

Accor has therefore created a new division to bring together all of its brands in this segment. The €300 million invested to buy the remaining 50% of the businesses (22 Delano, Mondrian, SLS and Hyde hotels with restaurants and bars), with no discount despite the other half acquired in 2018, was a surprise in 2020. The merger with Ennismore, the operator of the very popular Hoxton hotels in Amsterdam, Paris, Chicago and London, further confirmed this strategy. Sébastien Bazin, CEO of Accor, said in a press release: *"Lifestyle, entertainment, places with a soul have been at the heart of our development and growth strategy over the last years. Partnering with Ennismore's founder Sharan Pasricha and his great teams will take our Lifestyle ambition to a new and exciting level."* And this will be done *"by creating the largest and fastest growing ecosystem of world class brands"*, with Delano, SLS, SO and Gleneagles for the most "luxurious" part. Other brands in this new division include Jo&Joe, Mama Shelter and Tribe and SO/.

This "platform" brings together nearly 130 hotels consisting of around 2,500 rooms, with another 200 openings planned within three years.

Hoxton, on the other hand, is more of a lifestyle brand, offering a series of open-house hotels inspired by the diversity and originality of the streets and life scenes that surround them. Five new Hoxtons will open in Europe between 2022 and 2023, in Barcelona, Berlin, Brussels, London and Vienna. In the meantime, a tenth hotel has recently opened in Rome. The Hoxton Barcelona will offer a new category of "Homey" rooms, combining a living area with a kitchenette for longer stays. In Brussels, the hotel will also offer a five-story coworking space in partnership with WorkingFrom, similar to the much smaller Chicago space. The company's ambition illustrates the growing importance of this trend and the innovation it brings to the "luxury" hotel segment. The sector is innovating and exploring new models and new formats, while focusing its offering on experience, with meeting and event spaces for the new establishments.

The weight afforded to luxury experiences is a direct consequence of the importance consumers place on discovery, travel and sharing. This form of luxury also expresses the values which are important to the younger generations. The future of luxury for new brand ecosystems is to offer unique experiences beyond just products and services. New players entirely focused on this area will emerge and take their place in the luxury group universe.

Accor's latest initiative has been the launch its twelfth luxury brand in November 2021. With the creation of its Emblems Collection, Accor is consolidating its position in the field of collection brands and seeking to replicate the success it has already achieved with the MGallery Hotel Collection, a portfolio that now includes more than 100 boutique hotels around the world. The Emblems Collection will be divided into three categories: Emblems Collection Heritage will group hotels that contribute to the character of a city or territory, while Emblems Collection Retreat will focus on wellness experiences outside the city (sea, mountains, countryside). The last, Emblems Signature Collection, will offer design hotels. The Emblems Collection network is aimed at existing hotels or buildings undergoing conversion, which will benefit from being part of the Accor brand. It will be the only Accor Group brand deployed as a franchise, with a target of 60 establishments by 2030.

This offering is intended for hoteliers, but also for larger hotel owners who would like to be part of a strong brand and gain access to its extensive know-how. The Guiyang Art Centre Hotel, Emblems Collection in China will be the first flagship hotel of this new luxury brand. This commitment to luxury goods reinforces Accord's strategy of focusing on unique historical properties that are representative of local culture. *"Emblems Collection adds a fresh and exciting new dimension to Accor's luxury offerings. A key focus of our growth strategy is to add aggressively across our strongest lines and leading business accelerators, which includes luxury as well as collection brands, while ensuring all 40+ brands in our global network continue to grow, evolve and flourish,"* said Accor Chairman and CEO Sébastien Bazin in a statement. *"The hotels we will feature in Emblems Collection are those sought out by travelers who appreciate high-end, boutique-style experiences, as well as by hoteliers who cherish the independent brands they've built while desiring the benefits that come with a global partner."*

"A new generation of destination hotels"

Davina Zydower-Cisier, Director Development Luxury & Lifestyle Hotels Europe, Accor

Over the past few years, the meaning of luxury hospitality has shifted from a functional approach to a more experiential and emotional one. Twenty years ago, luxury was embodied through expensive materialistic goods and impeccable service. Today, the focus is on creating memorable and curated experiences in order to spark special emotions in our guests, without losing the attention to detail.

With travel abroad being difficult today, people have been looking to satisfy this hunger for new experiences and emotions through staycations and experiences within their own cities.

This is where lifestyle hotels stand out from classical hotels across every positioning, from luxury to economy. Lifestyle brands are built with an experience-led approach; they aim to evoke emotions through bespoke designs, powered by strong destination restaurants and bars, but more importantly through the hotel staff who are carefully selected according to their unique and sometimes quirky personalities. Lifestyle hotel teams are empowered to treat each guest to a different and creative experience, always with emotions at core of their intention. Because of this, lifestyle hotels are a rocketing trend that are appealing to every generation.

Sustainability is another trend that is here to stay. Today sustainability means more than reducing housekeeping frequency or eliminating single use plastics. Travellers are looking for a more holistic planet-friendly experience; one that is cognisant of preserving the environment and the community in which a hotel operates. It has never been more important for luxury hotels to ensure they are lessening their impact on our planet.

→

→

'Bleisure' travel–a business trip with an element of leisure, will also rebound post-covid as will business trips to foreign cities.

As borders reopen and business travel recommences, people are more and more looking for opportunities to blend their business trips with leisure, preferring hotels offering exceptional experiences across wellness, food & beverage and entertainment.

Overall, the crisis has emphasised the importance of enjoying the moment, which will certainly lead to more spontaneity in travel for all segments.

Davina Zydower-Cisier is Director of Development Luxury & Lifestyle Hotels for Accor. As such, Davina is leading the growth of the Accor Luxury & Lifestyle portfolio in Europe.

Paris, a laboratory for modernity

The luxury hotel industry has been shaken up and rethought over the last ten years, searching for a balance between historic and modern, subtle and bling-bling, authentic and dreamy.

The increase in travelers' purchasing power and their desire to show off their destinations have made the hotel industry a more visible place, and no longer simply a room that welcomes guests for a night. This was a change initiated by the renovations of the Crillon, the Royal Monceau and the Ritz in Paris. When the Royal Monceau reopened its doors in 2010, it was quickly followed by Asian competitors such as the Shangri-La or the Mandarin Oriental. These modern luxury hotels have redefined the standards of the history-filled hotels of the past.

Paris is still a mirror reflecting the hotel world, and each opening reflects strong new trends.

The luxury giants are reinvesting their capital, with the simultaneous openings of the Bourse du Commerce and La Samaritaine, marking a reconquest of Paris' epicenter. With the successive openings of Cheval Blanc Samaritaine by LVMH, Madame Rêve by the Hôtel de La Poste du Louvre or Kimpton Boulevard des Capucines near the Place de l'Opéra, Paris is waking up after Covid to new, unique, unequalled offerings.

These three hotels, in line with the current trends of experience, wellness and design, are moving the goalposts. LVMH uses hotels as laboratories for experimenting with its brands and artists, with a Dior spa, Bulgari showcases and Moët Hennessy also on the list. These initiatives prefigure a fundamental trend: to make a hotel offering the best expression of the essence of a group's brands.

A focus on gastronomy

Like it or not, it's a short distance from the high-end hotel industry to the large-scale restaurant industry. The Cheval Blanc hotels are home to top restaurants, such as the 3 Michelin-starred restaurants in Courchevel by Yannick Alleno or Saint-Tropez and Paris by Arnaud Donckele. The restaurants reinforce the values of these exceptional places, as well as the brands that host them.

Dior has launched its own restaurant with the chef Jean Imbert in its flagship store on Avenue Montaigne. A total of six restaurants and cafés have been created by the brand over the years, with a summer terrace in Saint-Tropez and Dior cafés in Tokyo, Seoul and Miami.

Ralph Lauren, meanwhile, launched restaurants as early as 1999 under the name RL in Chicago, in Paris in 2010 (Ralph's), New York in 2014 (Polo Bar) and London in 2017 (Ralph's). These establishments embody the brand's aesthetic. Their customers become familiar with or even adhere to their world, as a prelude or in continuity to the purchase of their products.

Several high-end gourmet restaurants promote and extend Gucci's collections. The first Gucci Garden opened in 2018 in Florence in the brand's birthplace. The second one in opened in Los Angeles in 2020, the third one in Tokyo in 2021 and the fourth is planned in Seoul. A gastronomic experience is combined with the possibility of discovering and trying on the brand's collections.

Cafés and gourmet stores in outlets are also a way to expand a brand's customer base. Maison Kitsuné's coffees effectively build its reputation. Louis Vuitton created its LV café (restaurant and cocktail bar) and its chocolate boutique in its Ginza Namiki building in Tokyo, after the success of its V café and Sugalabo V restaurant in Osaka. Fendi also runs a café in London, with gourmet products bearing its brand name.

Eco-friendly hotels

Freedom of movement and travel have never seemed more fundamental than during the lockdowns. But consumers also expect different market offerings in terms of sustainable development, responsible tourism and active tourism. *"Tourism has become a powerful and transformative force that is making a genuine difference in the lives of millions of people. The potential of tourism for sustainable development is considerable. As one of the world's leading employment sectors, tourism provides important livelihood opportunities, helping to alleviate poverty and drive inclusive development."* said UN Secretary General Ban Ki-moon, at World Tourism Day 2015.

Accommodation is not usually the most environmentally friendly part of a trip. Valuable resources such as electricity and water are heavily used and have a significant environmental impact. More and more hotels have begun to invest in sustainable, responsible and social practices, whether to conserve resources, reduce their carbon footprint or participate in the economic development of local communities. The ecotourism consulting agency, Inspire Conseil, points out, *"One third of travelers make responsible tourism a choice criterion, and more than one in two travelers state that responsible tourism is a criterion that all travel professionals should incorporate[78]"*.

Six Senses Laamu, in the Maldives, has built its individual villas entirely from environmentally-friendly local materials. A portion of the revenue from the Kalinaw Resort, located above a lagoon in the Philippines, is donated to local communities. Added to this is a search for authentic, original, exclusive experiences above all, such as a stay at Longitude 131, a (luxurious) campsite containing 15 tents in the middle of the Australian red desert, opposite Uluru, the famous rock sacred to the Aborigines, where all construction is strictly forbidden.

The pandemic has further called into question the wisdom of travel. People are calling into question the frivolousness of their motivations for recreational travel when thinking about greenhouse gas emissions caused by transport. With global warming social pressure is expected to put even more pressure on would-be travelers in the next few years. It will be up to them to justify their desires. Themed trips are developing with the search for cultural,

---

78. Inspire Conseil, "Écotourisme: une nouvelle définition du voyage", *Inspireconseil.com*, November 23, 2017.

philanthropic or environmental meaning being the main motivations. The search for places and services that contribute to the wellbeing of travellers – and thus to the prevention of illness – is a current motivation. The demand for a return to nature already makes up a significant market for tailor-made trips. Immersion in nature is a criteria of wellbeing increasingly sought after by city dwellers. Successive lockdowns have exacerbated this desire.

In line with minimizing greenhouse gas emissions due to transport, a new objective has emerged – regenerative tourism. Instead of contributing to climate change and the destruction of early civilizations, it enables people to participate in restoring the planet – its flora and fauna, and even whole communities.

7

Wellness,
a New Planet for Luxury

While baby boomers saw comfort as the ultimate in luxury, Generation Zers have a much higher demand for luxury experiences. More profound and significant, these experiences focus on personal development. Wellness, relaxation and physical and personal development are at the heart of peoples' concerns more than ever, and with the Covid crisis, they have experienced a boom that is only accelerating.

A growing luxury dimension

McKinsey estimates annual growth in the wellness sector at 5–10% depending on the area: 79% of the 7,500 people surveyed in early 2021 in six countries (UK, US, Germany, Japan, China and Brazil) believe it is important. In fact, 42% say it is their top priority.

There are multiple facets to the wellness sector: spas, wellness tourism, fitness, psychological wellbeing, beauty and anti-aging treatments, spaces promoting wellbeing at work, etc. Wellness corresponds to a high-end clientele's need to recharge their batteries and, increasingly, to younger generations in search of new values and new horizons.

"Sports Fashion" and "Luxury Wellness", major trends in post-Covid luxury"

Catherine SPINDLER, Chief Brand Officer, Lacoste

Streetwear is undergoing a revolution. This popular movement, which arose from the emergence of different cultures in the 1970s, is now entering a new era. It is at the heart of fashion inspirations and a prediction of those to come.

Fusing style and comfort, aesthetics and performance, after decades of streetwear following codes where brand and logo were the major standards of the style, the codes have been reinvented to meet the unanimous demand of consumers looking for more comfort, style and practicality in their daily lives. In this new era of streetwear reinvention, Lacoste, now a cross-cultural and cross-generational brand, continues to mix universes, styles and cultural codes to express ever more creativity, free movement and connect cultures.

A rich new vocabulary has emerged to talk about this global trend where most of the growth is concentrated in the fashion industry. We still talk about streetwear, but now we also have "Athleisure", "Activewear", "Active Lifestyle", "Sports Fashion" or "Luxury Wellness".

Luxury and premium brands have seized this opportunity. Creative expression on the catwalks is an ode to this new sportswear that blurs the boundaries between fashion and practicality. New brands have emerged and others have adapted and are embracing this movement and taking their inspiration from athletes.

Their creativity has opened up new territories and new lines which are ever more hybrid and refined.

Catherine Spindler began her career at Guerlain (LVMH) before joining the Yves Rocher group, where she held various positions

→

→

in communications, development and marketing. She then joined Vente-Privée, now Veepee, as Chief Marketing Offier, and more recently Lacoste as Chief Brand Officer. She also sits on the board of directors of the Danish jewelry brand Pandora.

On a global level, the wellness market as a whole was valued at \$4,500 billion by the Global Wellness Institute in 2021. Among the different segments of this huge market, luxury goods represent about one third of the total market. The global market for corresponding luxury services can be estimated at approximately \$1,469 billion, or 32% of the total market[79]. It has been growing rapidly, at about 5% per year since 2010. This assessment does not include the impact of connected health, which will increase preventive healthcare and health promotion activities among consumers and reinforce their need for data analysis and coaching.

Multiple wellness service offerings

The luxury sector has always had the ultimate wellbeing of its customers at heart. Each luxury hotel has wellness areas that very few other establishments, even specialized ones, can match.

Wellness offerings abound in many sectors, including coworking with the Kwerk concept, which we have already mentioned, and in hotels (such as the Waldhotel and the Chenot Palace Weggis in Switzerland or the Sha Wellness Clinic; the hotel complex entirely dedicated to wellness and health on the Spanish Costa Blanca), and even in some stores.

---

79. Luxury wellness includes the following segments: mental wellness, wellness tourism, preventive and personalized medicine, wellness real estate.

The major cosmetics and perfume companies are developing spa offerings: the spa by La Prairie, My Blend by Clarins or the Spa Guerlain. And the services offered have increased. Sisley, in its "Maison Sisley", offers, in addition to its treatments, a reflexologist, a naturopath, a sophrologist, etc. Tomorrow, skincare brands will go one step further and become holistic travel destinations. That's what Susanne Kaufmann, heir to the family hotel Post Bezau in Austria, who created her eponymous organic cosmetics brand 16 years ago, has done. It is a place that she transformed into a location dedicated to wellness and renamed after her brand, which she opened at the same time as a spa in New York.

More and more places dedicated solely to wellness are emerging, bringing together different therapists in one place. The Well in New York City is a members-only wellness club that combines Western medicine with Eastern healing. This health and wellness ecosystem brings together everything under one roof: acupuncture, nutritionists and yoga. In London, the Bhuti Studio offers a range of services: holistic therapies, pilates, hormone experts, yoga, and even a Buddha bowls restaurant. In Paris, the Yuj Yoga Studio has been offering Parisians looking for quietness and a moment of relaxation "an urban refuge" since 2017. On the program are yoga sessions for all levels, an herbal tea bar and a space to discover all of the latest wellness products: eco-friendly mats, organic cotton outfits or accessories to wear in yoga sessions as well as in the city[80].

The wellness offering also extends to travel with dedicated hotel concepts. The Westin brand, part of Starwood Hotels & Resorts Worldwide Inc., has come up with wellness retreats

---

80. Philippe Gaillochet, Yves Hanania and Isabelle Musnik, *Le Luxe demain: les nouvelles règles du jeu*, éditions Dunod, 2019.

called Westin Wellness Escapes, led by experts focusing on meditation, strength training, nutrition, yoga and running. The InterContinental Hotels group has gone one step further and launched a new brand, Even Hotels, with four focuses: eating well, working well, exercising and resting well, with everything based on health and fitness. Guests can work out in their own rooms, which are designed as gyms with different equipment such as an exercise bar, yoga mats, cardio equipment, pull-up bars and videos with 10 to 20-minute classes.

Although they differ from one chain to another, all the fitness or wellness options offered have one thing in common – they provide a response to travelers' growing needs to maintain a healthy lifestyle while on the move. Stores have also understood the goldmine that this sector represents. At Harrods in London, a Wellness Clinic presents itself as "*the ultimate wellness destination*". It welcomes clients in 14 luxurious rooms, where you can find a photo studio with a 3D system to reveal how others see you, or a machine to sculpt your body.

Fitness, a new luxury niche

Peloton, the US brand of connected home fitness bikes, saw its value spike to billions of dollars in the midst of the Covid crisis, far ahead of more established brands like Technogym, known for the excellence and design of its products. The latter, in the meantime, is pursuing its pre-crisis strategy. Established in gyms, luxury hotels and in the homes of affluent individuals, the Italian company invests in content and personalized coaching. It is also a response to a pressing demand from clients who, with Covid, are becoming aware of the fragility of their own existence and are investing in their own wellbeing and health.

"Bringing dreams to life"

Nerio ALESSANDRI, Founder and President, Technogym

We are living an unprecedented historical moment of fast transformation. Over the last years digital technologies and the growing people's sensitivity to sustainability issues have rapidly changed our lifestyle, the way we communicate, the way we choose products and interact with brands. The pandemic has dramatically accelerated these existing dynamics, and health has become a key priority for people across the globe. Bringing a dream to life is one of the luxury industry key goals, and today more than ever people's dreams are linked to a projection of a better, more ethical, more inclusive world.

The ethics of brands and their way to interact with topics like the environment, health and equality of the sexes and races have never been so relevant. The future of luxury will be closely related not only to the ability of creating exclusive, inspiring and attention-to-details driven products, but also to shape a new model of creativity able to combine different layers – functionality, style, purpose, heritage and culture – and create unique and personal experiences for people.

Nerio Alessandri founded Technogym, today's world-leading company offering products and services for wellness and rehabilitation. In the early 90s, Alessandri defined the wellness concept, a lifestyle which aims at improving the quality of life thanks to regular physical activity, a healthy diet and a positive mental attitude.

A whole host of brands has been born with a new relationship to luxury. They respond to new consumer expectations and attitudes, which have increased with the health crisis.

This unprecedented period has provoked the development and success of brands focused on wellness or more precisely a new lifestyle, such as the hotel chains Hoxton or 25Hours, the sports brand Alo Yoga, or the yoga brand Lululemon, already talked about so much for a decade, and that continues to surprise with its agility and creativity. It is not by chance that luxury brands are getting closer to wellness brands. The latest collaboration between Alo Yoga and Saint Laurent in July 2021 attests to this.

Another area less known to the general public is the high-end bicycle sector, with numerous brands offering exceptional products, in terms of cycles, equipment, clothing and services, such as 7Mesh, Specialized, ASSOS of Switzerland or the British company Rapha which has become the champion of chic, expensive bicycles inspired by luxury codes in under 20 years.

Luxury companies' interest in sportswear, especially fitness, can be illustrated by the Hermès Fit. In early December 2021, at the École Nationale Supérieure des Beaux-Arts in Paris, Hermès offered a variety of discovery activities over five days, during which its new scarf yoga, stretch ceinture and haltero'chaussures products were promoted.

The rise of the mental wellness market

According to the Global Wellness Institute (GWI), the global mental wellness market is worth approximately $120 billion, or 15% of the $828 billion global physical wellness market. It is already equal to that of spas and twice that of health cures.

Sleep therapy accounts for almost half of the expenses. Stimulation of cognitive abilities and personal development each account for only about a quarter of the expenditure. Meditation and mindfulness are still in their infancy. Faced with a demand that has increased sharply with the health crisis, the mental wellness service sector suffers from extreme fragmentation and a lack of guaranteed quality from brands.

Mindfulness exercises improve both the body and mind. Their annual market is estimated at \$29 billion[81]. Yoga accounts for nearly 60% of expenditure. Numerous brands are jumping on the bandwagon, such as Beyond Yoga, Yogasmoga and especially Alo Yoga, created in 2007 and which is in eighth place on *Fast Company's* prestigious list of the "10 most innovative companies in the world in 2021". The California-based brand, which now has 10 stores in the US, made its beauty debut with the launch of The Glow System™, a skincare line "made in California" based on Ayurvedic healing. Alo Moves, its digital fitness platform launched in 2018, saw its streaming subscriptions grow sevenfold in 2020, as home fitness became increasingly popular. Alo Moves has expanded its offerings to include more than 2,500 yoga, HIIT, barre and meditation videos, which can be tailored to fit each subscriber's lifestyle.

Hermès offers yoga tutorials on WeChat. Four 13 to 21 minute sessions are devoted to breathing and posture. The companies' products are put in prominent places in the videos.

---

81. Katherine Johnstone and Ophelia Yeung, "What is Mindful Movement? First Global data on a growing, \$29 billion wellness segment," *GWI*, June 28, 2021.

"Returning to oneself and opening up to the world"

Angelic VENDETTE, Vice President of Marketing, Alo Yoga

The traditional definition of luxury has drastically changed for consumers over the last two years, as the world has been grappling with Covid – where an acute focus on health has quickly become our top priority. For GenZ specially, the increased focus on health has been both physical and mental, opening the door for a luxury yoga brand like Alo Yoga to quickly gain mindshare worldwide, with offerings of premium athleisure wear, yoga equipment, clean skincare, as well as the yoga fitness and meditation app, Alo Moves.

In this new world of raised importance for health, true holistic lifestyle brands should be here to inspire, educate, and uplift through innovative activewear, cutting-edge wellness offerings, and powerful fitness content. Wearing Alo is just as prestigious as any other luxury brand, if not more – it's a badge of belonging to a forward-thinking, health-enhancing, consciousness-raising collective.

As consumers, we are writing the story of a different tomorrow, where the pursuit of happiness starts with one intentional breath, where health is wealth, and where winning means joining together to lift each other up in wellness.

… And that, to me, is synonymous with the true definition of luxury in a post-pandemic world.

Angelic Vendette was a Senior Manager at Holt Renfrew, then specialized in digital and social media and influencer marketing. She was responsible for the launch of several brands at Sephora, before becoming Vice President of Marketing for Alo Yoga.

The luxury hotel industry up against the demands of wellness

The wellness offering has become a cornerstone of the hotel offering and is sometimes an important element that differentiates hotels from simple luxury property rentals.

Luxury hotels are transforming themselves into wellness centers to attract and diversify their clientele, increasing their sophistication, as evidenced in Paris, by the construction of new spas and wellness centers constituting a key element of their offering. The Mandarin Hotel's spa was designed as *"a sanctuary entirely dedicated to the pleasure of the senses"*. Covering 900 square meters, it is one of the largest spas in the capital, and nearly one out of every two clients who visit the spa isn't staying in the hotel.

Conversely, wellness specialists are starting to develop hotel offerings. Equinox, a New York-based chain of high-end fitness clubs, has entered the hotel business by opening a chain of hotels in the Netherlands in March 2009 equipped with a sports club. But these establishments do not just aim to provide their clients with a gym. They offer complete wellness experiences, from individual, personalized in-room sports training to restaurants serving nutritionist-approved menus, a juice bar, private fitness classes, a spa and even clothing. The principle is that it is the fitness club hosting the hotel and not the other way around. This is a new offering at the frontier of fitness and tourism. *"Today, we are redefining the luxury experience as a limitless extension of wellbeing,"* explain the directors. Other openings are planned, including in Los Angeles, London and Miami. Among the new generation hotels proliferating is the Sha Wellness in Spain, which claims to be a *"wellness clinic"* offering *"intelligent vacations"* based on wellness, fitness, better sleep, anti-aging, anti-stress and detox, for a minimum of €6,000 a week. InterContinental Hotels Group PLC took this a step further in 2019 with the launch of Even Hotels, now present in many US cities. Guests can enjoy balanced menus with fresh, healthy products in the restaurant. The rooms are both modern and relaxing, and offer equipment (an exercise bar, yoga mat, etc.) so that guests can exercise throughout the day.

After the spas common in luxury establishments, a new niche exists for hotel services, such as multiple individual or collective classes, relaxation, guided meditation, yoga and all other techniques contributing to mental wellbeing. These services can be used by the hotel residents but also by locals. Daycations, or one-day vacations, are a source of additional income. They will push hotels to expand their wellness services ranges.

At the new Cheval Blanc Paris hotel, owned by the LVMH group, wellness is as important as gastronomy and luxury accommodation. They offer Dior Spa Cheval Blanc, Rossano Ferretti hair salon, pool, steam room, sauna, snow shower, fitness and yoga. The Dior Cheval Blanc Spa in Paris, in the new Samaritaine building, takes decor and originality of services to new heights. It is furnished as a Dior-style apartment, with a 30-meter-long pool and several suites furnished with sumptuous decorations. Services include 50 body, face and skin treatments combining ancestral treatments with high-tech advances[82].

The luxury hotel industry is embracing these wellness and health trends, which accelerated during the Covid crisis. Offerings have increased and clients are also choosing locations based on their health and wellness programs.

---

82. Loïse Delacotte, "Dior a ouvert un spa de rêve au cœur de Paris", *Cosmopolitan*, September 8, 2021.

Wellness centers as a luxury travel destination

Several European countries have a long tradition of fitness stays: Austria with the Lanserhof, Switzerland with the Chenot Palaces and the Burgenstock-Waldhotel near Lucerne. More recent European offerings exist in Spain with the Sha Wellness Clinic near Alicante or in Italy with the Palazzo Fiuggi near Rome. The stays offered include a high level of medical supervision for diagnosis and prescriptions on the spot or afterwards. In an exceptional setting and with services fit for royalty, the objectives of such stays are to remedy stress or sleep disturbances, and to offer fitness, wellness, anti-aging, weight loss and detox activities. The European centers are spreading around the world, with the Sha Wellness Clinic present in the United Arab Emirates and Mexico, and Chenot in Azerbaijan.

Asia is setting up equivalent centers in Thailand, Bali and India. The more accessible cost of their services and the integration of oriental methods into their treatments could accelerate their breakthrough into the global market. Major centers include Tri Vanaada in Phuket and RAKxa near Bangkok, Thailand. Their integrated approach to predictive and preventive medicine, as well as wellness methods, is a new way forward. Large luxury groups have the capacity to make the necessary investments to build and operate such centers.

The demand for wellness travel literally exploded during the pandemic. Luxury and classic high-end hotels have clearly been challenged by these new offerings. Similar wellness programs will have to be included in their catalog of offerings, in addition to their exceptional locations and cultural offerings.

Part 2

The Luxury Sector: An Empire Under Pressure

C rises bring out adversity and ambitions, threatening established positions in all sectors. This is no less the case for the luxury sector and Covid-19.

Every luxury brand felt the full force of the consequences of the measures reducing or stopping their activities during the last three quarters of 2020. Using digital communication and e-commerce with varying degrees of success, they have held their ground and their image. The end of 2020 and 2021 saw a resumption of activity, which was very strong in Asia and the United States and much slower in old Europe. Brands have all had to find ways to rebound, even though threats remain, both externally and internally.

Regarding internal threats, some companies have benefited from the luxury craze without thinking about preparing for the future. Others have run out of steam with outdated concepts and will find it hard to emerge unscathed from the crisis. Others, belonging to large groups like LVMH, on the contrary, entered the health crisis with abundant cash, talented human resources and the means to maintain their creativity at high levels. Finally, new types of luxury companies have emerged from the Covid-19 crisis. These meet the new expectations and needs of customers.

But brands are not immortal. With the health crisis, some will die or change hands to find a new lease of life. On the other hand, the better equipped ones will become stronger and the disappearance of some rival brands will offer them new opportunities.

But external threats are also at work. The resistance to the crisis and the exceptional profits of the large luxury groups are inspiring new objectives, mainly on continents other than Europe. These two strategic movements are occurring simultaneously. The fracturing of the world into large geographical zones favors the expression of national cultures that can be embodied in luxury products. The Internet, a major source of supplementary capital, social networks and e-commerce allow people to purchase any luxury product from any point in the globe.

For the moment, France and Italy occupy a dominant position in the world of luxury without question. Their groups have been able to incomparably develop creative and innovative companies and fashions. Their influence is decisive – they are the leaders of global luxury and the creators of tomorrow's luxury.

However, competition remains fierce. Many other groups are also working fiercely and developing strong positions throughout the world.

8

Luxury and the Health Crisis

The year 2020 was the year when the world's economic activity slowed down in a way that had not been seen since the 1929 financial crisis. Despite this, a general rebound, which was very strong in 2021, occurred both globally and in the major economies. The annual evolution of the world GDP was as follows: +2.3% in 2019, -3.6% in 2020 and +5.5% in 2021. For the same years in France it was +1.5%, -8% and +7%; for the European Union, +1.6%, -6.2% and +4.8%; for China, +5.9%, +2.3% and 8.1%; and for the United States +2.2%, -3.5% and +5.7%[1].

The luxury sector did not escape the health crisis, but its rebound began at the end of 2020. In 2021, its performance was brilliant, to the point of exceeding that of 2019 – that is, pre-health crisis[2]. For example, the sales of the world leader LVMH boomed in 2019 with an annual increase of 10%. The annual change in sales was -17% in 2020 and +44% in 2021, to the point of ending 2021 with a +20% overrun of the 2019 figures. Kering has had equally impressive track record: +16.2% in 2019, -17.5% in 2020; +34.7% in 2021 – with a total sales growth of 11% in 2021 over 2019 sales. Hermès recorded the following annual

---

1. Sources: World Bank, Eurostat, Reuters.
2. Sources: universal registration documents and group press releases.

changes in revenue: +12.4% in 2019, -6% in 2020 and +33.4% in 2021, with an outperformance of +30.4% in 2021 compared to 2019. The other major groups have followed similar trends. In this way, the luxury sector is amplifying the growth or decline rates of the global economy.

VISION & PERSPECTIVE

"Every crisis is an opportunity"

Nicolas SANTI-WEIL, CEO, AMI Paris

The health crisis has been a real catalyst for fashion brands. It has forced brands to accelerate transformations that sometimes had been dragging on for years.

The difficulty for managers was to define the short and long term. In the short term, they needed to navigate the storm nobody was prepared for by sight. But the real issue was the ability to keep their long-term vision in mind. This vision was essential because it enabled them to stay the course and thus reassure their teams, but also all of their partners (suppliers, shareholders, agencies, etc.), because many more structural changes were taking place under the surface.

They had to be agile enough not to take in too much water in the middle of a storm by adapting their course if necessary. But at the same time, it was necessary to avoid making sharp turns and look far ahead.

Sudden changes in direction can cause brands to lose their souls and break the bond built with their customers. Brands that were not yet present in China and which suddenly invested their entire budgets there, sacrificing their original markets will inevitably suffer the consequences in the medium to long term.

Conversely, those that stayed the course and which continued to move forward through the storm, solidly anchored in

→

→
their values despite the lack of visibility, have emerged from this crisis stronger.

It was certainly easier for small structures where decision-making chains are shorter than for larger companies which were structurally much more complex.

However, size is not everything, agility is a state of mind that consists in constantly questioning oneself so as to better advance. Customer, employee and partner expectations have somehow aligned to demand more transparency and, above all, more coherence. This search for meaning and a tiredness of opportunistic dialog have created an extraordinary call for authentic brands that did not need to recreate or disguise themselves too much to get through the crisis.

The post-pandemic years will be a unique opportunity to get back to basics and will allow some houses to achieve in a few seasons what they would have had difficulty doing in 10 or 20 years before the crisis.

Every crisis is an opportunity if we know how to open the doors it presents us with!

Nicolas Santi-Weil cofounded The Kooples in 2008 and managed it until 2012.

He is now the CEO of AMI Paris, the designer brand founded by Alexandre Mattiussi, which he joined in 2013 as CEO and investor, taking the lead in strategy and development.

The shock of 2020

Globally, sales of luxury goods and services in 2020 were down 21% compared to the previous year, according to Bain[3]. The causes were due to the pandemic: population lockdowns, closure of sales outlets, prohibition or strong limitation of international travel. However, not all sectors of the economy experienced the same degree of crisis.

The hardest shocks were for luxury cruises (-65%), high-end hotels (-55%), art objects (-35%) and personal luxury goods (-23%). Less affected were sales of luxury cars (-8%), wines and spirits (-10%), private jets and yachts (-10%), furniture and decoration (-10%), and gourmet products and restaurants (-15%).

The main collapse in personal luxury goods sales was in those related to tourism, in "travel and retail" (-70%). Personal goods sales reached €217 billion in 2020, down 23% compared to €281 billion in 2019.

Among luxury products, it was, of course, the products that did not need to be tried and tested and which were easily deliverable that did the best. Footwear, jewelry and leather goods held up best, with declines ranging from 12% to 18%. Beauty products and cosmetics lost 20% of their sales. The decline was more marked for clothing and watches (-30%).

Not all brands performed equally well. The most accessible, such as Furla in leather goods, suffered more vertiginous drops. Many historical brands have held up better, because they are "safe havens" for their customers. But their roots and heritage did not

---

3. Claudia d'Arpizio, Federica Levato, Filippo Prete, Constance Gault and Joëlle de Montgolfier, "The Future of Luxury: Bouncing Back from Covid-19," *Bain*, January 2021.

always guarantee their resilience: Delvaux changed hands in the middle of the storm, while its sales were in free fall.

According to McKinsey, declines in 2020 were 10 to 15% for jewelry and 25 to 30% for watches. Online sales represented only 13% for the first sector and 5% for the second. Asia-Pacific, led by China, accounted for nearly half of all revenues. For the consultancy firm, the major luxury brands in this sector could significantly increase their market share in the future, provided that they respect their depth, roots, transparency and traceability to meet the widespread demand for sustainability. The development of retailers with high quality and high ambitions has replaced multi-brand retailers.

The year 2020 also saw a profound reshaping of distribution channels. Department stores and multi-brand boutiques lost 40% of their sales. Physical stores that limited the damage are single-brand stores (-22%) and sales outlets (-15%). The only channel to do well was online shopping, which doubled its share of total revenue to 23%. The world leader LVMH, and the star of artisanal luxury Hermès, outperformed their competitors in the sector.

All the luxury groups, which are diversified to varying degrees, were therefore impacted by the progressive closure of global markets.

Full speed adaptation

An immediate counter-attack

The cloud-free growth of the late 2010s had partly obscured the need for companies to adapt. However, even before the pandemic, profound changes were already taking place in the luxury economy, both in terms of supply and demand.

VISION & PERSPECTIVE

"Luxury is a tennis game."

Alexandre FAUVET, CEO, Fusalp

Luxury is no longer a monolithic block with standard shapes for familiar clients. It is complex, multiform, technological, and increasingly dominated by services that will inevitably change its business model. Its will to significantly extend its social influence amplifies its political dimension. From influencing culture, luxury companies are now becoming influential in social issues. This is the price of making luxury available to all.

Luxury is a tennis game. It can be played on any surface, producing constantly changing effects. Its equipment is evolving fast, which makes the game faster and faster. Speed and mobility take precedence over power as the game progresses.

Oppositions of style create its interest and richness. They develop its innovative spirit.

Players must constantly adapt without forgetting their game plan. They interact with a wide variety of people who will try to take them out of their comfort zone. They have to accept this and feed off it to constantly improve their game. Their secret is constant questioning. Their driving force is doubt, even if they will never admit it. They must be obsessed with the details that make them progress. They hate losing.

Alexandre Fauvet began his career in the fashion industry in 1999 as Executive Vice-President of Lacoste. At the same time he was also President of Club V.I.E. He became CEO of Fusalp in 2014.

The different national markets differed in their growth rates and in the evolution of consumer expectations. Asia-Pacific, with China taking over from Japan, was growth fast based in the traditional product range, with these products penetrating ever wider geographical areas. In Europe and the United States, growth was slower. Changes in behavior were beginning to emerge, with a rise in societal and environmental concerns among consumers. Digital technology was gradually taking over the entire operation of luxury brands – from the supply chain to Internet communication and customer relations. Online shopping began its breakthrough as a new distribution channel. The closure of stores, department stores, duty free stores and the halt to international tourism during the pandemic represented a mortal danger for the sector, with its economic model being violently challenged.

As their revenues plummeted in 2020, luxury companies rushed to respond and demonstrated their unique responsiveness by launching numerous initiatives to survive. Digitalization, virtual fashion shows, widespread online shopping and sustainability have all gone wild. The health crisis was a tremendous accelerator for this.

A gradual return to normality from the end of 2020

The year 2020 ended better than it started. Thanks to the economic recovery in Asia and the United States in the fourth quarter, the luxury sector limited its damage in 2020, contrary to many so-called "non-essential" consumption sectors.

In the first nine months of 2020, LVMH's sales were down 21%. The sharpest drop was in selective distribution, watches and jewelry. The freezing of airport activity was the main cause. At LVMH, the strongest resistance to the decline came from fashion and leather goods as well as wines and spirits. In the fourth quarter of 2020, fashion and leather goods saw sales increase, so the final decline for the year was limited to 17%.

E-commerce and Asia-Pacific activity picked up in the summer of 2020, and at the end of the year for the United States. On the other hand, selective retailing continued to plunge, feeling the full brunt of the airline shutdowns and the closure of nonessential stores. Dual diversification in sectors and geographically has proven to be an extraordinarily successful strategy.

The Kering group recorded a 16.4% drop in revenues in 2020[4]. The slowdown was more marked for Gucci (-21.5% if we take comparable data). In the midst of the pandemic, the Florentine label was able to count on a 70% increase in online sales in 2020, boosted by the acceleration of digital use in the Covid-19 period, as well as by the company's digital transformation policy. In addition to revamping its mobile app in spring 2020, Gucci also strengthened its presence in Chinese online shopping in December with the installation of its Fashion Division on Alibaba's Luxury Pavilion. On the other hand, thanks to its efforts to relaunch during Covid, Bottega Veneta grew by 4.8%.

Chanel saw its sales fall by 18% to €10.1 billion[5]. This slowdown was slightly more severe than that of its competitors due to the closure of its own stores and multi-brand distributors for perfumes and cosmetics, as well as less advanced digitalization and online shopping. Despite the explosion of online sales, the brand on rue Cambon continues to refuse online sales for its fashion department.

---

4. On a like-for-like basis, i.e. at a constant scope of consolidation and exchange rates. The same is true for Kering's other results.
5. On a like-for-like basis and at constant exchange rates.

Hermès posted sales of €6.1 billion, with a limited decline of 4.8%[6]. Leather goods, which account for nearly half of its sales, is a segment that has held up well, as it has for its competitors too. Another stability factor is the development of its online offering in an increased number of geographical areas: China since 2018 and Hong Kong, Macao and the Middle East in 2020. Asia-Pacific accounted for almost half of its revenues. Hermès' 2020 results show the importance of Asia in the recovery of luxury goods. The growth of the Chinese luxury market had reached 48% in 2020. Representing 51% of Hermès sales in 2019, Asia-Pacific increased to 59% in 2020, with an increase in absolute value of 8.6%.

Other growth drivers include the growing appetite of Generation Z for luxury goods and the strong expansion of e-commerce, which initially compensated for the closure of boutiques, but has since become a channel in its own right, inflating demand. Globally, e-commerce is a fundamental evolution for the sector. If its turnover had not almost doubled, from €33 to 49 billion, the closures of boutiques and stores would have had much more serious consequences. E-commerce in 2020 accounted for an estimated 23% of total luxury sector sales, compared to 12% in 2019.

In fact, despite its strong impact on tourism, the impact of the pandemic shock on luxury goods was much less than that of most other sectors such as air transport, tourism, hotels and restaurants, culture and events, automobiles, and non-food retailing in particular.

The good results of late 2020 were amplified in early 2021, with the same drivers. But by early 2020, luxury companies had strongly accelerated the transitions begun in previous years.

© Dunod – Toute reproduction non autorisée est un délit.

---

6. At constant exchange rates. The decline was 6% at current exchange rates.

A return to growth: segment situation

The 2021 V-shaped economic recovery did not involve all sectors of the economy, and health constraints did not disappear all at once. What is more, demand has undergone major changes.

Uneven recovery across segments

The same disparities exist in the luxury sector. During the deep decline of the global luxury market in 2020, not all segments declined as much and not all countries reacted in the same way. Recovery is also uneven.

Due to lockdown rules and the ban on international tourism, the cruise and luxury hotel markets lost almost half of their revenue. The return to normality is being further delayed by Covid-19 variants and new lockdowns in some countries or regions.

For personal products, there are still gaps in recovery. Sales of leather goods, accessories and beauty products have rapidly grown. The different fashion segments have had a different pace of recovery. Streetwear, casual and athleisure are benefiting from the self-reflection encouraged by teleworking, fitness and home-based activities. Other fashion segments are facing new market demands, including the rise of second-hand and rental.

Geographically, China's economy expanded dramatically in early 2021. Chinese consumers show a continued strong attraction to luxury goods, even if their purchases are made on domestic soil. But since then, political directions aimed at towards reducing inequalities could contain the expansion of Western luxury. The question is whether these policies will affect luxury in the long-term.

Rapid vaccination campaigns and successive stimulus packages in 2020 and 2021 led to strong economic recovery in the United States. This market has become an important growth pole for the luxury sector.

As for Europe, despite a rebound driven by "local" consumption, the absence of international customers still weighs heavily on luxury brands' results. Above all, those of department stores, which experienced an unprecedented shock. The almost total disappearance of foreign tourists caused Galeries Lafayette to lose half of its revenue in 2020, representing €1.7 billion, and is leading to the sale of more than ten stores across the whole of France in 2022. The French group obtained state aid of €300 million in January 2021 to help make it through this troubled time.

The reaction of luxury groups

The first half of 2021 confirmed the extraordinary ability of luxury groups to rebound. LVMH's revenue for this period – €28.6 billion – exceeded that of 2020 by 56% and even 2019 by 14%. The strongest recovery came from the fashion and leather goods division, followed by the wine and spirits division. Faced with continued restrictions on stores and international tourism, the selective retailing[7] division was down 25% on 2019.

In 2021, LVMH saw its global sales increase by +44% compared to 2020, with a stronger recovery in the United States and Asia. 2019 levels have been exceeded, except for in the perfume and cosmetics and selective distribution divisions, the latter suffering from the continued restrictions on international travel.

---

7. That is Sephora and DFS (duty free).

Kering's earnings growth was along the same lines. In 2021, its revenue was 11.1% higher than in 2019. Gucci surpassed its 2019 level with a +1.1% rise, after a -22.7% decline in 2020, the highest of all the Hering brands. Yves Saint Laurent largely outperformed with 23% growth over 2019. The most spectacular growth has been Bottega Veneta, which was up +28.7% in 2021 compared to 2019.

L'Oréal also got back to normal in the first half of 2021. Its overall revenue amounted to €15.19 billion, up 20.7% compared to the first half of 2020 and 6.6% compared to the same period in 2019. A key player in French luxury goods, L'Oréal's luxury division (36% of revenue) outperformed the market, particularly after the acquisition of the Mugler and Azzaro brands.

In Italy, recovery was similar. Armani saw a 34% increase in revenue in the first half of 2021 compared to the first half of 2020 to €1.6 billion. Prada's revenue jumped 60% to €1.5 billion. The recent results of the main luxury groups show that beyond simply catching up, they have rebounded amazingly.

From the Asian El Dorado to Chinese dependency?

Dependence on the Asian market is a key factor in the development of the luxury goods sector in France and Italy. While Japan was a tremendous springboard for brands like Louis Vuitton in the last decades of the 20th century, China now accounts for at least a quarter of major luxury group revenues. Sales there collapsed in early 2020, and then recovered before all other zones. Chinese customers, both locally and internationally, are expected to account for almost half of global luxury goods sales by 2025[8]. China is an El Dorado for companies more than ever, but this success must not become a mirage in the desert.

China and its tourists – markets without limits?

China played a key role in the rebound of the luxury market in 2021. Although the halt in international tourism led to a drop in Chinese purchases abroad, almost all of their consumption was transferred to the domestic market, which recovered before all others. China's share of the global market in fact doubled to 21% in 2021 from 11% in 2019[9]. The limited slowdown in August and September 2021 was only temporary. By 2025, the mainland China market is expected to continue to grow, reaching 25–27% of the global market, ahead of Europe and the United States (23–25%).

After the revival of intercontinental tourism, Chinese purchases, both locally and abroad, are expected to rise to 42% of the global market. Being present in China is, more than ever, a key objective for luxury brands. Reuters announced in November 2021 that Louis Vuitton, which has always favored a very strict distribution policy and never offering discounts, would consider, *"opening its first duty-free store in China, in the highly touristy island province of Hainan."* It is a strategic choice for the luxury brand since tax-free purchases on the island of Hainan, which has become the preferred destination for Chinese people deprived of international travel and trips in 2020, have seen a sharp increase: total duty-free sales there had already reached €2.9 billion as of October 31, 2020, with an online purchase rate of nearly 55%. Other luxury brands are also expected to set up shop there in 2022.

---

8. Claudia d'Arpizio and Federica Levato, "Luxury is back to the future", *Bain & Company*, November 2021.
9. *Ibid.*

The CEO of Balmain, Jean-Jacques Guével, announced the opening of a store on the island of Hainan, as well as in Chengdu and Chongqing.

Geopolitical risks?

China's assertion of its desire to become the world's leading power is accompanied by a series of internal developments that may give rise to concern about the reality of its openness to the world.

In the field of technology, China is implementing a classic policy of protecting its domestic market and providing massive subsidies to domestic companies. In fact, the Great Firewall has enabled the development of BATX, whose goal today is to fight the American giants: the search engine Baidu against Google, the marketplace Alibaba against Amazon, Tencent with WeChat against the Facebook universe, Xiaomi against Apple. Another characteristic of China's technology leaders is their strategy of cooperation and hunting in packs to better develop internationally. The clampdown on technology giants like Alibaba and Didi and restrictions on the use of video games would seem like key sectors of the Chinese economy are being taken over.

The promotion of national culture is now a major political focus in China. The aim is both to reconquer the domestic market and to project Chinese soft power abroad. Luxury goods are not yet explicitly included in China's domestic market reclamation program, but luxury brands are an integral part of Western soft power. It is feared that they will be subject to new restrictions, such as increased customs duties or the creation of new entry or operating barriers, not to mention the creation of national champions with public aid. For the moment, the luxury sector is not receiving any.

Sustainable market fundamentals

However, essential political and geostrategic constraints should guarantee the opening of the Chinese market to foreign luxury products. China's rapid economic growth has resulted in considerable inequalities between urban and rural areas, and between the eastern urban provinces and the western rural provinces. The Chinese president's call for "common prosperity" is directed primarily at the wealthier sections of the population.

As the predominant market for European luxury brands, the Chinese upper middle class shows a strong attraction for international luxury products, which represent a territory of individual freedom. The hardening of the regime does not seem to be able to restrict it, without encountering serious political inconveniences.

China is not only one of the largest markets for consumer products, it is also the world's factory and as such has a vital need to export. While it has the world's largest trade surplus – $366 billion in 2020[10], ahead of Germany ($220 billion)[11], its position in terms of exports and imports is far from being the same. In 2020, China's exports accounted for only 13.1% of the world total. The European Union's weight in world trade is almost three times greater. Its imports represent 33.3% of the world total and its exports 35.2%. With its dominant global position, the European Union therefore has considerable leverage in terms of retaliatory measures to counter any new barriers to entry into the Chinese market.

The fundamental question for the European luxury sector is therefore how to take into account its economic importance and

---

10. WTO, 2021.
11. The deficits of other countries are huge: United States – $651 billion: France – $53.1 billion: Japan – $1.6 billion.

its interests in any commercial tug-of-war with China. Hence the urgent need for strong action to represent its interests to the European Commission and the governments of the European Union.

In any case, the rest of Asia offers expansion opportunities that can complement those of China. Southeast Asia represents a new opportunity. 80% of consumers in Singapore, Malaysia, Indonesia, the Philippines, Thailand and Vietnam are familiar with e-commerce.

The threat of platform dependency

To effectively and thoroughly reach Chinese consumers who are extraordinarily present on the Internet, luxury brands have greatly increased their presence on multi-brand platforms such as Lyst, Farfetch, Mytheresa, Net-a-Porter and, in China, JD.com and Tmall Luxury Pavilion.

The dependence on large e-commerce platforms may eventually threaten a significant part of the European luxury sector's turnover. Online shopping on these platforms could reach up to 25% of the sector's revenue, according to projections.

There are several kinds of threats. The most serious is the outright interruption of service that strong tensions between China and Europe could cause. Another threat which is also very dangerous, has already been clearly made by Tmall Luxury of the Alibaba Group. Playing a key role in the sale of European brands online, the platform wants to invest in physical stores. With its lead in digital, maximizing customer experience in its stores could be one of its distinctive assets. Retail chains such as Sephora could face serious competition.

The use of large Chinese platforms has helped overcome the crisis caused by the pandemic. But a growing number of groups such as Hermès and Louis Vuitton are already planning to bring their Internet presence back in-house to control their costs, communication, and customer data.

Europe, international luxury model and leader[12]

The pandemic has widened the gap between heritage brands and more commercial brands or those not having the same resources, particularly financially, to invest so they can rebound. The risk remains that there will be a two-tiered recovery and that small groups will struggle longer than the leaders. Previously strong brands such as Salvatore Ferragamo, Tod's and Hugo Boss are not expected to return to their 2019 sales levels until 2023, or even later[13], despite Hugo Boss' stated ambition to reach sales of €4 billion by 2025 and then €5 billion, according to its new president Daniel Grieder. The major rebranding effort launched in early 2022 should accelerate its recovery.

According to analysts, this polarization has become a feature of the sector over the past decade, and the pandemic risks

© Dunod – Toute reproduction non autorisée est un délit.

---

12. For the following developments relating to the various regions of the world, the analysis is based on the 2019 ranking of the top 100 global luxury companies in terms of revenue, compiled by the audit and consulting firm Deloitte and published in May 2021. This ranking also includes the compound annual growth rate of each group for the period 2016 to 2019. Its particular interest is that it presents the 2019 results, the best year in the history of luxury, on the eve of the Covid-19 crisis. This information is supplemented by the groups' official publications – press releases, financial documents, universal registration documents. The group's performance for 2020 and the first few months of 2021 is based on these official documents.
13. Industry Leading Data, Refinitive Eikon.

accentuating this divide. Over the past year, customers have turned to more classic, timeless clothing and brands that convey a sense of heritage, favoring Hèrmes and Chanel. Even Gucci, which usually opts for boldness and excess, has toned down some of its designs. One of its new handbags, Diana, comes in brown leather with a bamboo handle that evokes the 1950s.

In the current situation, brands have an exceptional asset if they are able to anchor themselves in centuries-old traditions. Most European brands, whether they be French, Italian, Swiss, British or German, have this incomparable asset. In fact, most of the international luxury brands are European. They occupy a predominant place in the world, in the imagination of globalized consumers and in sales figures.

In 2019, the most recent year in which the global economy ran smoothly, European luxury brands held more than two thirds of the world market[14]. So European luxury is a strong market, yet one which has numerous challenges and opportunities today, which all of the other countries and players in the luxury sector are reacting to by taking "strong positions". In 2019, based on the sales figures of the top 100 international companies offering personal luxury goods, Europe achieved 67.4% of the global total.

The top European countries for luxury are France followed by Italy. French groups accounted for 35.7% of the world total and Italian groups for 13.6%. The next largest European luxury goods producers are Switzerland with 12.4%, the United Kingdom with 2.1%, Germany with 1.5% and Scandinavia (Denmark and Sweden) with 1.1%.

---

14. "Global Powers of Luxury Goods 2020," Deloitte.

Associations and organizations promoting the luxury industry in Europe

In each of the major European countries, organizations exist which represent and promote the luxury sectors. In France, the Comité Colbert, an association founded in 1954 and governed by the French law of 1901, campaigns for its members, which include 90 luxury companies, 17 cultural institutions and six European members. What they have in common is that they embody the culture of beauty and share the same passion for know-how. The Committee is chaired by Laurent Boillot, CEO of Hennessy. Elected from among its members by the Committee's General Assembly, the President heads the board which is composed of 25 members, six of whom are directors of major companies[15]. The board approves the Comité Colbert's strategy decided on by the General Delegate in collaboration with the presidents of the working commissions.

In 2020, the Comité Colbert adopted a new raison d'être: "To passionately promote, patiently transmit and sustainably develop French savoir-faire and creation in order to inject a new sense of wonder." *"Every word was carefully thought out,"* explains its CEO Bénédicte Épinay. The Committee's strategy is developed within eight working commissions offering a place of exchange and forward thinking for the French luxury players. The "Ethics and New Members" commission, chaired by Jean-Michel Delisle, President of Delisle, works to bring the world of intangible luxury into the Committee and to get closer to the world of culture. The "Forward-Thinking" commission, chaired by Christophe Caillaud, President of Liaigre, aims to lead collective reflection on

---

15. Margaret Henriquez (Krug), Françoise Montenay (Chanel), Hélène Poulit Duquesne (Boucheron), Florence Ollivier (Bréguet), Saskia de Rothschild (Lafite Roithschild), Nathalie Tribouillard (Léonard).

future issues and collaborate with experts, particularly in the field of economic forecasting. The role of the "Advocacy and Public Policy" commission, chaired by Bruno Pavlovsky (Chanel), is to *"suggest legislative or regulatory measures capable of creating a favorable context for the development of this industry and to monitor the evolution of regulations in France and in Europe in order to alert the authorities to their possible impacts"*. The mission of the "International" commission, chaired by Jean-Marc Gallot (Champagne Veuve Clicquot Ponsardin), is *"to fly the flag of French luxury by organizing events that highlight the sector's cultural dimension and promote the French art of living around the world."* The "Sustainable Development" commission, chaired by Cédric Charbit (Balenciaga), leads discussions between the Maisons *"on best practices, and monitors issues that arise in the luxury industry and elsewhere so as to share them"*. And the "Craft & Creation" commission, chaired by Nicolas Bos (Van Cleef & Arpels), is responsible for *"coordinating transmission through actions that promote know-how and creation but also through collaborations with training institutions*[16]*"*.

In the UK, the Walpole, founded in 1992, includes 250 brands across many luxury sectors, with a wide international reach. A special feature is that the major British orchestras and opera houses are full members of Walpole. The big car brands which the UK is privileged to have are also part of it. The major universities and fashion and design colleges are absent, the only notable link with the academic world being with the London Business School. Its stated mission is to promote, protect and develop British luxury goods, a sector that is worth £48 billion to the country's economy.

---

16. See the Comité Colbert website.

In Italy, Altagamma has assigned itself a very broad mission, namely the promotion of Italian production, provided that it is high-end. Its motto sums up its mission: *"Creativita e cultura italiana"*. Its members all participate in the Italian way of life. So mass consumption brands like Illy or San Pellegrino are there, along with Ferrari or Prada. Another characteristic of Altagamma is its links with the Bocconi University of Milan and the studies commissioned by Bain, BCG, Deloitte or Accenture, which are worldwide references.

In Spain, Circulo Fortuny is particularly interested in developing links between the national cultural scene and the luxury economic sector, which have suffered from the long-standing priority given to sacred art.

The Meisterkreis, or "master circle" the German sector association is a name that has a significant meaning for the association's ambitions. One of the major focuses of its mission is the training of "masters", "foremen" and artisans of the highest level. The areas covered by its members are relatively narrow. In particular, prestige car manufacturers, such as Porsche or Daimler, are not included. On the other hand, various industrial companies are part of it. The Meisterkreis is, like the industrial Mittelstand, the basis for the German economy's success.

Finally, the EECIA – European Cultural and Creative Industry Alliance – brings together the continent's national associations. Its goals are to promote their common interests, in particular through promoting savoir-faire and skills in Europe, protecting and promoting creativity through intellectual property, through the war against counterfeiting, advocating for a fair access to European and world markets, and promoting the attractiveness of Europe through tourism.

201

All in all, while each of the European countries has brands that are emblematic of luxury anchored in its national culture, the size, structure and performance of their groups are extremely diverse. For most of them, their ambition is to become a leader in the protection of the planet.

9

France, a Leading Role in World Luxury

I n their first book of March 2019, the authors of this book pointed out with Renaud Dutreil, who wrote the preface, that the French luxury groups – the KHOLCs (Kering, Hermès, L'Oréal, LVMH and now Chanel) are France's GAFAMs (Google, Amazon, Facebook, Apple, Microsoft). Three years and a pandemic and economic crisis later, they have increased their strength in the world and their essential role in the French economy.

The financial markets weren't mistaken. As of November 2, 2021, the top ten market capitalizations on the Paris stock exchange included three luxury groups, including LVMH in first place with €345.7 billion, Hermès International in third place with €147.6 billion and Kering in eighth place with €80.3 billion. L'Oréal, whose division groups its luxury brands, is in second place with a capitalization of €223.1 billion[17]. While these capitalizations are subject to stock price volatility, they do reflect the power of the French luxury groups which are major flag bearers for the national economy.

---

17. Laurance Boisseau, "CAC 40: en vingt et un ans, le luxe a supplanté les télécoms comme moteur de l'indice," *Les Echos*, November 2, 2021.

LVMH, an unparalleled success

The LVMH group is the world luxury goods leader. It is also the world champion in external growth and export. The group began with the merger of Louis Vuitton and Moët Hennessy in 1987 by Alain Chevalier and Henry Racamier. The idea was to combine the strengths of leather goods (Louis Vuitton) with those of wines and spirits (Moët champagnes and Hennessy cognacs) to cushion any market downturns in these two segments. The takeover of LVMH by Bernard Arnault, who already owned Dior and Céline, ushered in an extraordinary wave of acquisitions of previously independent luxury brands. Today, LVMH is made up of 76 luxury brands.

The financial strength thus acquired has enabled the group to accelerate its growth, in particular by drawing on the creative reserves of Italian brands. It has also enabled the various brands to project themselves internationally with the major resources of an integrated group. The main takeovers or acquisitions made by LVMH have been in fashion and leather goods: Kenzo, Givenchy, Loewe, Céline, Emilio Pucci, Fendi, Loro Piana and Virgil Abloh; in perfumes: Guerlain, Acqua di Parma, Patou; in watches and jewelry: Tag Heuer, Zenith, Hublot, Chaumet, Bulgari, Tiffany; in wines and spirits: Krug, Château d'Yquem, Glenmorangie, Belvedere, Château Cheval Blanc; in selective distribution: DFS, Sephora, Le Bon Marché and La Samaritaine.

Over the 2016–2019 period, LVMH's sales increased by 16.5% per year[18]. The group's 2019 revenue was €53.67 billion, with the French market only accounting for 9% of its sales. Its main market was Asia, excluding Japan, i.e. mainly China, with

---

18. In compound annual growth rate.

30%, followed by the United States with 24%, Europe, excluding France, with 19% and Japan with 7%.

The pandemic caused its 2020 revenues to fall to €44.65 billion; a 16.8% drop. Fashion and leather goods played a remarkably effective role as a shock absorber, with a decline limited to 3%[19], as did wines and spirits with a decline reduced to only 14%. On the other hand, store and duty free closures led to a 23% decline in watches and jewelry and a 30% decline in the distribution division.

As soon as business picked up at the end of 2020 in China and in 2021 in the United States, then in Europe, LVMH resumed its forward momentum. In the first nine months of 2021, its activity recovered and even exceeded its 2019 level, with revenues 11%[20] higher than in the same period in 2019[21]. After playing a crisis shock absorber role, the fashion and leather goods division played an accelerator role with 38% growth compared to the first nine months of 2019, followed by wine and spirits with 10%, while the distribution division still suffered with -23% compared to the same period in 2019. The watches and jewelry division rebounded by 4%, with the consolidation of Tiffany & Co, estimated at 10% for the first three quarters of 2021 compared with 2020. Tiffany's revenue was $4.4 billion in 2019 and it was able to stay at over $4 billion in 2020.

Hennessy, a benchmark brand since 1817

Founded in 1765 by Richard Hennessy, an Irishman who had served in the armies of Louis XV, the Hennessy cognac house began by specializing in high quality eaux de vie and immediately began to expand internationally. This strategy continues

---

19 to 21. On a like-for-like basis, i.e. at comparable structure and exchange rates.

today with a new dimension – protection of the environment. Hennessy weathered the crisis well and quickly recovered as of 2021.

Hennessy launched its special quality VSOP (Very Superior Old Pale) cognac in 1817. 1870 saw the introduction of its X.O cognac, which was presented in a special decanter from 1947. Hennessy Paradis was created in 1979 and the Richard Hennessy brand in 1996. These new brands aim for higher quality each time. Limited editions of its products also aim to innovate in terms of bottle or decanter presentation, such as those developed with Julien Colombier, Frank Gehry or V.S. and Faith XLVII.

The company works with a community of 1,600 wine growers, on 32,000 hectares of vineyards. The house has entrusted the blending to the same family line of master blenders for 200 years and tests its products within a tasting committee made up of in-house experts who meet every day.

The brand has been present internationally since its creation. It has delivered to America since 1794, to Russia since 1818 and to China since 1869. Today, the brand is present in over 160 countries through its worldwide distribution network.

Hennessy is a pioneer in environmental issues. It is ISO 14001, 22000 and 45001 certified for 11 sites and 12 facilities are classified for environmental protection (ICPE). Its vineyards are doubly certified "High Environmental Value" and "Cognac Environmental Certification", and favor the use of biocontrol products and the protection of biodiversity. *"My goal is to firmly establish Hennessy as the most prestigious and responsible spirits brand in the world,"* says its CEO Laurent Boillot.

Hennessy's organic sales growth was 7% in 2019, with volumes up 6%. In addition to cognac sales, which it has long been the leader of (with 100 million bottles exported each year),

Hennessy has become the leading international premium spirits brand in terms of value[22]. At the height of the health crisis in 2020, the company maintained its value strategy focusing on the highest quality products. It benefited from a strong recovery in the second half of the year in the United States and an improvement in China. It had a limited decline in volumes. The rebound in sales was in the premium X.O segment and through retail and e-commerce, as the brand's customers shifted a significant portion of their consumption from restaurants, bars and clubs to the home. The brand is also developing rare editions for "High Net Worth Individuals" (20 million people in the world who have a direct income of at least €1 million) for whom it has developed a dedicated entity. For the Chinese New Year, for example, in collaboration with the Bernardaud factory, it produced 550 copies of a decanter decorated by the Chinese artist Zhang Enli, sold for €8,000 each.

In the first three quarters of 2021, Hennessy cognacs recorded a 4% increase in sales compared to 2019. *"The crisis and the dynamics of 2021 have shown us that the big brands are doing better than the others because consumers need quality references."* Says Laurent Boillot[23]. Hennessy's strategy has once again proven its relevance.

LVMH-Tiffany: a perfect marriage?

With the purchase of Tiffany & Co at the end of 2019 for an estimated €13 billion, LVMH is enriching its portfolio of American brands (it already owned Marc Jacobs, Benefit Cosmetics and

---

22. LVMH, financial documents, December 31, 2019.
23. Stéphane Reynaud, interview with Laurent Boillot, "Chez Hennessy, nous allons aussi travailler à l'unité avec des artisans d'arts ?" *Le Figaro*, July 2, 2021.

Kat Von D Beauty), which until now were underrepresented amidst the group's mainly French or Italian brands. In the jewelry industry, 80% of products sold are not associated with a particular brand. There is therefore an enormous development potential for brands able to impose themselves and become essential references. The acquisition of Tiffany by LVMH is far from trivial, and could change the entire luxury sector, creating new dynamics in a fast-growing segment[24].

For LVMH, this acquisition is of major importance. As an industry expert points out, *"not only has the LVMH group done very well by buying Tiffany & Co, but its competitors have made a very bad deal by leaving the field open to Bernard Arnault, who now has an unrivaled strike force in the jewelry market."* LVMH will have a global brand that can move upmarket in a fast-growing luxury segment, and Tiffany will have unprecedented investment capacity, particularly for its supplies and boutiques, as well as greater operational efficiency.

LVMH's new territories

In its financial communication, LVMH presents itself as the *"world leader in high-quality products"*. This choice of wording has been carefully thought through. LVMH's forays outside of luxury goods are increasing. Collaboration with consumer brands can bring significant, rapid profits. For example as seen by Stella McCartney with Adidas, Dior with Nike or Louis Vuitton with the NBA. LVMH's partnership with Rihanna for its Fenty Beauty line has proven to be a huge success. A new maison, named Fenty, was launched in 2019 within the group with its ready-to-wear, footwear and accessory designs. Its multicultural approach

---

24. Yves Hanania, "LVMH-Tiffany: un mariage parfait ?" *Harvard Business Review*, December 4, 2019.

broadens the group's spectrum. The singer previously collaborated with Kering and Puma on sneakers and jersey dresses in 2015 and then in 2017 with TechStyle Fahion Group on her lingerie line. On September 8, 2018, she launched a line of Fenty Beauty by Rihanna cosmetics[25] with Kendo Holdings, LVMH's Californian start-up, available in 1,600 Sephora stores and 17 countries. *"We have had incredible success with our Rihanna and Fenty Beauty launch, reaching about 500 million euros in sales, starting from zero,"* Bernard Arnault announced on January 29, 2019, at the presentation of the group's results. This global launch, perhaps one of the first in the history of cosmetics, means the world leader can reach generations Z and Y on every continent.

This line of cosmetics for all skin types and complexions was so successful that LVMH and Rihanna joined forces in May 2019 to create the house of Fenty. The last time LVMH had launched a similar operation was in 1987 with Christian Lacroix. Bernard Arnault explains the reason behind the decision: *"Everybody knows Rihanna as a wonderful singer, but through our partnership at Fenty Beauty, I discovered a true entrepreneur, a real CEO and a terrific leader. She naturally finds her full place within LVMH. To support Rihanna to start up the Fenty Maison, we have built a talented and multicultural team supported by the Group resources. I am proud that LVMH is leading this venture and wish it will be a great success.[26]"*. The brand describes itself in this way, *"Inspired by a worldwide community beyond traditional boundaries, FENTY embraces a fundamental freedom: a freedom from convention and rules."*

Given the scale of the investment needed to develop a "billionaire" fashion brand, LVMH and the singer decided to

---

25. Juliette Garnier, *Le Monde*, January 18, 2019.
26. LVMH, news, May 10, 2019.

stop this activity in February 2021 and focus their efforts on the Savage X Fenty brands and on Fenty Beauty and Fenty Skin cosmetics. Although Fenty Beauty's sales have not been made public since 2018 (that year it made around $550 million in sales), LVMH has said that they continue to grow. *Forbes* estimates that the company made over $600 million in sales in 2019 and Rihanna's stake was $375 million, making it its most valuable asset.

Despite the closure of Fenty, LVMH continues to invest in small brands. In July 2021, it announced its support for the launch of Phoebe Philo, by Céline's former creative director, taking a minority stake in it.

One of LVMH's shareholders, the L. Catterton fund, has also acquired the German sandal manufacturer Birkenstock. Rimowa, a manufacturer of high-end luggage, is also part of the LVMH universe. In early 2021, LVMH also increased its stake in Tod's, which was struggling due to Covid-19. Similarly, Tiffany represents an opportunity for the French group to explore new territories. The recent announcement of its collaboration with Supreme heralds a new era. Tiffany's involvement with the American streetwear leader is the latest indication of the 184-year-old brand's new direction under its LVMH ownership and the leadership of its new CEO, Alexandre Arnault. The redesign of the label included a controversial campaign, *"Not your mother's Tiffany"* as well as a high-profile communication campaign featuring Jay-Z and Beyoncé. This expansion and diversification strategy is also played out in high-end hotel services.

With its 76 maisons, LVLH had widely overcome the consequences of the pandemic by 2021 and resumed its growth. A giant, diversified, highly export-oriented company with the largest stock market capitalization in Europe, LVMH is one of the leading lights of the French and European economy.

Kering, creativity at the heart of the group's vision

In less than 20 years, the Kering group has built up a portfolio of brands that have distinguished themselves through their creativity and daring. Today, along with a few other big names, they are the world's leading fashion brands. Kering benefits from an image of daring and agility that gives it a special status as the world's second largest luxury group. The group has chosen to concentrate its resources on a small number of very strong brands, which has made it one of the world champions.

The Pinault family group entered the luxury sector in 1999 under the name Pinault-Printemps-Redoute, with the acquisition of 40% of Gucci Group NV. In the same year, the Gucci Group acquired Yves Saint Laurent, YSL Beauté and Sergio Rossi, followed by jeweler Boucheron, Balenciaga and Italian Bottega Veneta, Swiss watchmaker Girard-Perregaux and Italian men's tailor Brioni. After taking full control of Gucci, followed by a number of changes through the sale of the retail division, the group renamed itself Kering in 2013 and continued to grow externally by making smaller acquisitions. Over 2016–2019, Kering's sales grew rapidly at 23.3% per year[27], almost one and a half times higher than LVMH. In 2019, Gucci, which provided 63% of the group's revenue, was the main driver of its expansion.

Gucci is known for its blazing successes followed by periods of inactivity. Between 2015 and 2019, its revenue multiplied by 2.7. Between 2015 and 2019, its operational result almost quadrupled. The brand has experienced moments of pause, then rebound and acceleration, for example with the iconic duo of

---

27. Compound annual growth rate.

Domenico De Sole and Tom Ford. Today, Marco Bizzarri and Alessandro Michele have revolutionized the brand in synergy with marketing, merchandizing and communication.

The pandemic affected Kering, as it did the entire luxury sector, but in the first nine months of 2021, the group not only forgot about the crisis, but outperformed the first nine months of 2019 by +9.0%, with total revenues of €12.235 billion. After a brilliant first half of 2021, Kering continued to accelerate in the third quarter. For the first nine months of 2021, Gucci did see a 4.7% decrease in sales compared to 2019, but Bottega Veneta outperformed itself by 28.5%, the other companies by 26.2% and Yves Saint Laurent by 14.8%. The group is currently rebalancing its various brands.

VISION & PERSPECTIVE

"Creativity is the essence of luxury"

François-Henri PINAULT, Chairman and CEO, Kering

The mission of the luxury industry is to show the way. And it's to take creative risks. I think luxury up to a certain point in the period between 2008 and 2010 forgot that; it became something very much immobile, with a great marketing skill on some points, but things weren't moving a lot, [we were] forgetting that creativity is the essence of luxury. It's part of the definition of luxury and this industry has to take creative risks to be relevant. If you stop taking those risks, what's your purpose in this industry? Nothing, nothing.

And of course everyone talks about creativity, but when I mean creativity, everything has to come from it. So everything has to be encompassed in that creative vision. Not only one category or one sort of product, all the product categories and all the image and all the touchpoints of the company. That's the vision that we develop inside the group as we [talk
→

→
about] modern luxury. If there's no risk, I don't see how you can sustain the reward.[28]

François-Henri Pinault has been Chairman and CEO of the Kering Group since 2005. He has also been President of the family holding company Artémis since 2003.

Balenciaga, a pioneer for the group

For its 100th anniversary, Gucci surprised the fashion world by collaborating with another group brand, Balenciaga. This is a first for the two brands, but also the first of this type of collaboration.

The two brands, known for their boldness and creativity, are innovating together by creating a unique new kind of collection that is not a normal collaboration, but a tribute paid by Gucci's creative director since 2015, Alessandro Michele, to Demna Gvasalia, Balenciaga's creative director since 2015. To build this collection, Michele was inspired by the mythology that surrounds the brand. At the same time, the Florentine house continued its diversification with the launch of a line of fine jewelry.

Bottega Veneta takes flight

Bottega Veneta's rebound is due to a new interpretation of the brand. Noting the growing influence of young Millennials and Generation Z and their new expectations, Bottega Veneta reinvented itself in 2018 by making 32-year-old Daniel Lee its creative director.

---

28. For the Kering Group, this statement made to *Business of Fashion* in 2018 is still relevant. Imran Amed, interview with François-Henri Pinault, "How François-Henri Pinault unites profits and purpose," *The Business of Fashion*, September 11, 2018.

Lee immediately took significant risks by injecting his vision, while remaining true to the extraordinary savoir-faire of the brand. His collections are bolder, more colorful and more flamboyant. In particular, he has given more importance to ready-to-wear items, which had never been the priority under the previous creative director Tomas Maier.

Bottega Veneta is now one of the few leading brands that are setting trends and enjoying incredible commercial success at the same time. The brand has established itself as an innovative creative force, while capitalizing on its core strengths: timeless design, extraordinary craftsmanship and materials, and a contemporary dimension that both reflects and influences the times. The spring-summer 2022 collection, presented in Detroit and inspired by America, illustrates this. Bottega Veneta's sales reached €1.2 billion in 2019. Sales jumped in Q3 2021, with +18.4% growth over Q3 2019. Daniel Lee offered an *"ultra-inventive collection with a focus on distinctive textures, playing between casual style and playful glamour"*,[29] while innovating in its marketing, with a pop-up store in a disused fire station, and offering a series of products created with local artists and partners. Daniel Lee stepped down as Bottega Veneta's creative director in November 2021 and was replaced by his right-hand man, Matthieu Blazy.

Saint Laurent, priority to creation

During the 2020 health crisis, the Saint Laurent brand helped to slow the decline in Kering's revenues. Its sales had fallen by only 13.8% compared to 2019 to €1.744 billion compared to

---

29. Dominique Muret, "Bottega veneta explore de nouveaux territoires avec un show insolite à Détroit," *Fashion Network*, October 26, 2021.

16.4% for the group overall. Its share of total sales rose to 13.3% compared to 12.9%. Over the first three quarters of 2021, Yves Saint Laurent's growth was +45.1% compared to 2020, with €1.698 billion in total.

A strong acceleration occurred in 2021, as its Q3 sales exceeded those of Q1 of the same year by 26.4%. Its share of Kering's revenue in the last quarter was 15.5%, compared with 8.7% for Bottega Veneta.

Saint Laurent confirmed its role as one of Kering's historical, stylistic and commercial pillars. The brand's history is one of the most brilliant in the world of fashion. From the creation of his first collection in 1962, Yves Saint Laurent gave free rein to all of his talent. This was the beginning of a life of original creation entirely centered on movement and fluidity – from haute couture to high-end ready-to-wear, from typically feminine clothes to clothes inspired by menswear, from abstract art to fashion, etc.

Today, as Francesca Bellettini, the brand's CEO, puts it, it's all about giving priority to creativity[30]. Stylistic heritage is one thing. The spirit behind the creation of the house's aesthetic is even more fundamental. In any case, for the director, it is not a matter of responding to consumer demand, but of creating the dream and emotion that will naturally lead them to the brand. In terms of organization, to reflect this creation priority, designers need to be supported and have a direct relationship with management.

---

30. Francesca Bellettini, talk at Kellogg School of Management, in Gregory Carpenter and Yves Hanania's luxury marketing course, May 2021.

The increased role played by the group's other brands

Other brands in the group include Balenciaga, Alexander McQueen, Brioni, Boucheron, Pomellato, Girard-Perregaux, Ulysse Nardin and Qeelin. Kering gives each of them a great deal of autonomy. This ensemble is becoming increasingly important for the group.

In the third quarter of 2021, their total revenues reached €843 million, or 20.2% of the total (26%[31]). They have been expanding steadily since 2019, especially thanks to Balenciaga and Alexander McQueen. Balenciaga passed the €1 billion revenue mark in 2019 and continues to grow at a steady pace after the Covid crisis. Also noteworthy are the successes of prestige jeweler Boucheron in China and Korea.

Finally, Kering Eyewear, founded in 2014 and including Richemont as a shareholder since 2017, provides high-end eyewear manufacturing for a series of 16 prestige brands, including Danish brand Lindberg and luxury and lifestyle brands Gucci, Cartier, Saint Laurent, Bottega Veneta, Balenciaga, Chloé, Alexander McQueen, Montblanc, Brioni, Dunhill, Boucheron, Pomellato, Alaïa, McQ and Puma.

L'Oréal Luxe, 26 brands including 17 international brands

L'Oréal is the world leader in cosmetics and perfumes. Founded in 1909, its activity today is structured into four divisions: professional products and the company's first productions account for

---

31. Using comparable data.

12% of its revenue[32]; consumer products, which account for more than a third of its revenue (39%); L'Oréal Luxe, which has an equivalent weighting (37%); and the Active Cosmetics division, which is growing rapidly, and which is of equivalent importance to its professional products (13%). The L'Oréal group as a whole has experienced strong growth for several decades. Its 2019 sales exceeded its 2018 sales by 10.9%. The group held up well over the pandemic, with revenues down only 6.3% in 2020 compared to 2019.

The establishment of a luxury division within the group began in 1964 with the purchase of Lancôme, and then continued with Kiehl's, Shu Uemura, YSL Beauté, Urban Decay, and IT Cosmetics. L'Oréal Luxe's strategy is to produce cosmetics and perfumes under license which are acquired or negotiated with fashion or cosmetics brands, some of which may be sold, like Roger & Gallet in 2020. Its main brands at the end of October 2021 were Lancôme, Yves Saint Laurent, Giorgio Armani, Kiehl's, Helena Rubinstein, Urban Decay, Biotherm, Ralph Lauren, Shu Uemura, Victor & Rolf, Diesel, HR, It Cosmetics, Atelier Cologne, Valentino, Mugler, Azzaro, Prada, Maison Margiela, Cacharel and Yuesai.

L'Oréal Luxe's growth reached 12.9% per year[33] over 2016–2019. The division even accelerated its growth at the end of the period, with a growth rate of 17.6% in 2019. L'Oréal Luxe, ranked fifth in Deloitte's global ranking of luxury groups, had a turnover of €11 billion in 2019. With a turnover of €10.2 billion in 2020, 7.6% less than the previous year, L'Oréal Luxe's slowdown was slightly more marked than for the group as a whole (-6.3%). But overall recovery was very fast in 2021. For the first nine months

---

32. Over the first nine months of 2021.
33. Compound annual growth rate.

of 2021, the entire group's growth reached 5.5% compared to the same period in 2019, and 8.7% for L'Oréal Luxe.

The group's success is the result of a combination of several key directions. From the outset, research and development have been at the heart of its product development. It is segmented into different niches to which brands are attached which are heavily promoted by traditional or digital advertising. The group operates worldwide, with Europe accounting for only one third of sales. E-commerce, where technological innovations are multiplying, accounted for 26.6% of sales in the first nine months of 2021. Finally, L'Oréal is at the forefront when taking into account its social and environmental responsibility. As Jean-Claude Le Grand, the group's chief human relations officer, points out, *"The group has been committed to professional equality for almost 20 years, and it has also taken up issues related to disability or socio-economic and cultural origins. In today's world of major social and societal challenges, L'Oréal has also set up a Global Diversity, Equity and Inclusion Advisory Council, a forum for discussion among internal stakeholders"*[34].

Chanel, a jewel in the crown

Gabrielle Chanel opened her first boutique in 1910. Originally a milliner, her presence in fashion expanded in 1913 with clothing, in 1921 with her N°5 perfume and in 1932 with a collection of high jewelry. The house's development accelerated after the Second World War, when, in competition with Dior, it asserted a style whose motto was women's emancipation. Adopting certain codes from men's fashion, Chanel used soft, light fabrics

---

34. Interview of Jean-Claude Le Grand by the authors.

and invented loose-fitting clothes. At the same time, her evening fashion was both sophisticated and refined. Her color palette favored black, white and neutral tones.

There was complete symbiosis between Coco Chanel's style and Karl Lagerfeld's, who was at the helm of the house from 1983 to 2019. Karl Lagerfeld set Chanel at the forefront of fashion, perfume, cosmetics and watchmaking. The creative director's style and media genius was essential to his success, as the house was in great difficulty when he arrived.

In 2019, Chanel was ranked 6th among the world's top 100 luxury groups, with revenues of €11 billion. Deloitte's top 100 shows one of its limitations here. Indeed, more than simply being a group, Chanel is a brand present in several luxury segments, but always – or almost always – under its own name. As a brand, Chanel should be compared to Louis Vuitton or Gucci and not to LVMH or Kering. In this respect, Chanel undoubtedly has a place on the podium with the top global brands. The group, which is totally independent, not listed on the stock exchange and owned by the Wertheimer family since the early 1950s, managed to grow by 12.5% per year over 2016–2019[35].

Chanel is unique in that it gives its name to all of its products, whether fashion, ready-to-wear, perfumes and cosmetics, jewelry or watches. The company has subsidiaries in the arts, such as feather-work, millinery, embroidery and goldsmithing. External growth is small and limited. It focuses on its excellent crafts-manship internal to its parent company to ensure its continuity. Chanel's only fashion subsidiary is Eres, for high-end swimwear and lingerie, which it acquired in 1996.

---

35. Compound annual growth rate.

The pandemic didn't spare Chanel. Its 2020 revenue was $10.1 billion, down 17.6% from 2019. The fact that sales in Asia-Pacific fell by only 3.1%, compared with 36.4% in Europe, attests to the company's outstanding performance in that region. The brand, which invested a whopping $1.36 billion to bolster its business in 2020, rebounded strongly in 2021. *"We're beyond what some have called revenge buying, we believe it's a deep and lasting momentum, which may not be true for all the players in the luxury industry but it's true for the big brands which continued to invest, as we did"*[36], the group's CFO Philippe Blondiaux explained to Reuters in June 2021. In an interview with the *Financial Times*, he even said,

"We expect sales this year will be 35% over 2020, and we are confident we can rebuild margins very close to 2019 levels."[37]

"Our growth will be in the double digits," confirmed Chanel president Bruno Pavlovsky at the presentation of its cruise collection in Dubai in November. Demand is so high that to avoid speculation on the most popular handbag models, such as the Coco Handle or the 11.12 – through online sales of used goods – the brand limits the number of items sold to one per person.

Chanel, which today has some 360 points of sale worldwide, is continuing to open new stores (with eight to ten in 2021) but is still refusing to hear of a web presence for its fashion, watch and jewelry items, unlike its competitors. By maintaining this position, the brand gives reason to the theory defended by some,

---

36. Reuters Dispatch, "Chanel expects strong business recovery in 2021," June 15, 2021.
37. Leila Abboud, "Chanel finance chief "happy to be wrong" as luxury group shrugs off pandemic," *Financial Times*, June 15, 2021.

according to which, in the long term, the online sales of luxury houses will be only carried out by themselves.

Hermès, quintessential French luxury

Hermès International is the generalist group that has best withstood the consequences of the pandemic, and above all the one that rebounded most strongly in 2021. The success of Hermès has always been, and still is, based on organic growth.

Organic growth as a constant strategy

The group has gradually expanded its activities from its original business of saddlery and leather goods by developing new internal skills.

Remaining true to its values of savoir-faire of excellence and extreme quality, Hermès has invested in clothing since 1925, watchmaking since 1927, silk scarves since 1932, perfumes since 1951, women's shoes since 1972, tableware since 1984, fine jewelry since 2010, upholstery fabrics since 2011, lighting and bath lines in 2014, and then a makeup line with its first lipstick in 2020. "*A new métier is the continuation of what we know how to do. We have been artisans since the beginning, and beauty has been at the heart of our concerns for 183 years*," explained Pierre-Alexis Dumas, CEO of Hermès, at a presentation of the new products in February 2020.

Only three other brands in the group are active in related fields, but they don't compete with Hermès products: John Lobb shoes, Saint Louis crystal and Puiforcat goldsmiths. In upholstery fabrics, the company completes its offering with Métaphores, Verel de Belval, Bucol and Le Crin.

The health crisis: what crisis?

Hermès' turnover of €6.9 billion in 2019, only fell by 7.2% in 2020 to €6.4 billion. This small decline concluded a stellar four-year period from 2016 to 2019, when its compound annual growth rate reached 9.8%.

Hermès more than overcame the crisis in 2021 and far surpassed its previous records for 2019. For the first nine months of 2021, its sales exceeded those of the same period in 2019 by 35.3%. Thus, the global quintessential luxury champion overcame the health crisis in 2021 with an astounding three times faster growth than its rivals. Moreover, its exceptional performance in the most dynamic international markets – Asia-Pacific and the Americas – exceeded that of all its competitors.

Hermès is a national manufacturer that is 90% oriented towards international markets. France only accounted for 8.9% of its sales in the first nine months of 2021, down 5.8% from the same period in 2019.

Asia-Pacific, including Japan, accounted for 59.7% of 2021 revenues, up 56.7%. The Americas absorbed 16.1%, up 30.4%.

Successful diversification

Today, Hermès offers a myriad of products resulting from its savoir-faire: clothing, accessories, silk and textiles, perfumes, watches, jewelry and tableware. Hermès' activities outside its core business are grouped together in an entity called "Other métiers", jewelry, art of living and tableware. In 2020, it generated €643 million, or 10% of its total revenue, up 23.9% from 2019, while maintaining its strong identity and developing one of the richest universes in the luxury sector.

In the first nine months of 2021, Hermès' original segment – saddlery and leather goods – recorded sales of €3.076 billion, up 27.2% compared to the same period in 2019. Despite its historical importance and the status conferred on its customers, leather goods and saddlery accounted for only 46.6% of total sales for the period. Over the course of several decades, Hermès has developed an ecosystem that today includes multiple products, services and experiences, strengthening brand attachment while developing its desirability among the younger generations.

The second largest métier is "clothing and accessories"[38]. Over the same period, it accounted for 24.8% of total sales, with growth of 43.1%. The third largest is "other métiers"[39]. It accounts for 11.1% of the total, with extraordinary growth of 98.3%. Silk and textiles accounted for 6.6% of total sales, up 10.1%. The other areas of activity are "perfume and beauty" (4.4%), "watches" (3.7%) and "other products" (2.9%)[40]. Among these, the "watchmaking" sector is experiencing the strongest growth (77.3%), followed by "perfume and beauty" (17.8%) and "other products" (11%).

Without undermining its image as an ultra-luxury specialist, Hermès has succeeded in offering a wide range of products for under €1,000. Regardless of the segment in which Hermès operates, it remains the benchmark of French luxury.

---

38. The "clothing and accessories" métier includes men's and women's clothing, belts, jewelry accessories, gloves, hats and Hermès shoes.
39. The "other Hermès métiers" segment includes jewelry and Hermès Maison products (Hermès Art of Living and Tableware).
40. "Other products" correspond to production for non-group brands (textile printing, tanning) as well as John Lobb, Saint-Louis and Puiforcat products.

Pernod Ricard, world leader in premium spirits

"The upheaval created by the crisis has been terrible, but at the same time it has brought new opportunities for those who are able to see and create them. […] I am convinced this crisis has strengthened your Group, and we are even better placed now to face the future," said Alexandre Ricard, Pernod Ricard's Group CEO, at the presentation of the 2020–2021 annual report to its shareholders. The world's number two in the wine and spirits sector has taken up the challenge[41] and brilliantly weathered the pandemic, with sales of €8.8 billion in the July 1, 2020 to June 30, 2021 fiscal year, up 4.4% compared to the previous fiscal year. The level reached in 2021 even exceeded that of 2019. In July through September 2021, sales continued to rise.

FY2021 sales were 29% in Europe, 30.1% in North and South America, and 41% in Asia and the rest of the world. Growth was strongest in the Americas (14%), Asia and the rest of the world (11%), particularly in China, South Korea and Turkey, but remained modest in Europe (4%). The group has its own sales forces in 73 countries.

Pernod Ricard's business is based on a dozen international brands[42], which account for 63% of its sales, with annual growth of 11%. Its so-called prestige brands[43] represent 13% of its sales,

---

41. Impact Databank, 2021 figures, using 2020 data.
42. Ricard, Mumm, Perrier-Jouët, Martell, Malibu, Ballantine's, Chivas, Royal Salute, The Glenlivet Absolut.
43. In addition to Mumm, Perrier-Jouët, Martell, Ballatine's, Chivas and Glenlivet, the following brands have been added: Jameson, Midleton Very Rare, Rabbit Hole, Havana Club, Secret Speyside, Avion, Absolut Elyx and L'Orbe.

with annual organic growth of 15%. Pernod Ricard claims to be the world's number one in premium spirits[44]. Another group of brands, known as specialty brands, accounted for 5% of sales, with organic growth of 28%. Strategic wines account for 5% of sales and local brands for 18%.

To ramp up its development, Pernod Ricard has identified four major accelerators: portfolio management, continued premiumization and a move towards luxury spirits, innovation and digital acceleration. The group is committed to a policy of sustainable development, with its Road Map 2030. All of its subsidiaries are committed to the protection of biodiversity. Its own vineyards will be required to adopt regenerative practices by 2025 in eight wine regions. The census of risks related to agricultural inputs should be completed in 2022 and the certification of inputs in 2030.

The "Transform and Accelerate" strategic plan, committed to by Pernod Ricard in 2018 has been translated into action. Knowledge of consumers and demands is at the heart of the activity of its 18,306 employees. Their objective and the group's signature is *"Créateurs de convivialité"* (*creators of conviviality*). *"Our mission is to transform Pernod Ricard into the world's leading Conviviality Platform Company,"* promises Alexandre Ricard.

44. Statement by Alexandre Ricard at the *Show Me* event at the Champs-Elysées Theater, October 19, 2021.

"Luxury is about sharing a unique sensory experience"

Alexandre RICARD, Chairman and CEO, Pernod Ricard

The definition of luxury is very subjective and subject to debate. For many of us, luxury remains synonymous with rarity, beauty, unique skills and history. We make this luxury concept our own by producing exceptional wines and spirits from ancestral terroirs. But these bottles also have a characteristic feature. With them we can share the intimate, sensory experience of a moment of pleasure that cements memories and that, in its own way, constitutes a pure moment of luxury.

Today, consumers are more than ever attached to brand authenticity and to the values they convey through their social and environmental commitments.

These expectations are fully legitimate and luxury products are no exception to this requirement. They even have a duty to set an example. This is why, for example, our vineyards are actively developing regenerative farming methods and our distilleries are using the latest technologies to gradually eliminate all emissions.

To seize the tremendous opportunities of a very buoyant market, it is not enough to simply develop excellent products. We also need to offer consumers experiences. Tasting a 50 year old scotch, acquiring a bottle engraved with one's name, or having an extraordinary gastronomic experience in a champagne house are priceless experiences.

With the Covid-19 pandemic, consumers have expanded their choices, made new experiences via digital technology and, at times, increasingly emphasized their preferences. As they are now spending more of their budgets on certain purchases, they have moved towards more upscale products.

→

→

After difficult times, consumers feel the need to indulge themselves even more, and their choices veer more and more towards products rooted in their local areas.

Alexandre Ricard has been Chairman and CEO of Pernod Ricard since 2015. He joined the group in 2003. Since then, he served as CFO of Irish Distillers and then as CEO of Pernod Ricard Asia Duty Free and Chairmand and CEO of Irish Distillers. In 2012, he was appointed Director of Pernod Ricard, then Deputy CEO and COO before being appointed to his current position as Chairman and CEO.

Rémy Cointreau, world leader in exceptional spirits

Rémy Cointreau was created in 1991 from the merger of the two family-owned companies; Rémy Martin and Cointreau. It specializes in high-quality spirits. Founded respectively in 1724 and 1849, the two companies retained their individual identities after their merger, with the two original families controlling more than half of the capital and two thirds of the voting rights.

Cognac, with Rémy Martin and Louis XIII accounted for almost three quarters of the group's revenue of €1 billion over the period 1 April 2020 - 31 March 2021. Its other prestigious brands include Cointreau liqueur, Metaxa Greek spirit, Mount Gay rum, St-Rémy brandy, The Botanist gin, Bruichladdich, Port Charlotte, Octomore, Westland and Domaine des Hautes Glaces single malt whiskies, Brillet cognacs and liqueurs and Telmont champagnes.

Rémy Cointreau's products have a strong international presence through marketing subsidiaries in its strategic markets. In 2020–2021, the Americas accounted for 52% of its sales, Asia-Pacific 29% and Europe, Middle East and Africa 19%. The group has weathered the health crisis remarkably well. The beginning of 2020 saw a sharp drop in sales, but recovery was spectacular in the second half of the year – thanks to the upturn in China in the summer and in the United States at the end of the year. The structure of Rémy Cointreau's sales changed significantly during the crisis. After the collapse of sales linked to reduced air travel and out-of-home consumption, new practices have taken over, according to its president Marc Hériard-Dubreuil, which include the rise of mixology, in-home consumption, e-commerce and an increased priority given to high quality products by customers.

Rémy Cointreau is also a leader in sustainability. Nearly two thirds of its suppliers' land is made up of responsible and sustainable practices, more than 90% of its waste is recycled, and the group has received CDP leadership status for reducing its greenhouse gas emissions.

Listed on the stock exchange but controlled by the original families, the Rémy Cointreau group has set itself a medium-term roadmap: to affirm the unique positioning of each of its brands, to fast-track growth-driver brands, to develop a special emotional bond with its customers, to optimize the distribution network in line with the development of the brand portfolio, to boost the group's agility and responsiveness, and to make CSR a cornerstone of the group's strategy. The objective, in the words of Marc Hériard-Dubreuil, is to give themselves "the ambition to become the leader in exceptional spirits".

"Staying true to your roots and to the special relationship to time required for unique savoir-faire."

Éric VALLAT, CEO, Rémy Cointreau Group

Tomorrow's luxury is yesterday's luxury. That is to say that they are not opposites. A true luxury brand is timeless because it has all the attributes to be able to respond to its customers' aspirations, which are evolving: the logo for customers looking for status, craftsmanship for those seeking quality, selectivity for those seeking exception, ceremony and service for those seeking experiences, values for those seeking meaning.

The challenge for luxury brands is not to deny their past, but to adapt their models and build on their strengths to best meet their customers' new expectations.

We have been looking after our vineyards for almost 300 years so that we can pass them on to the next generations in the best possible condition. In addition to quality, which is still essential, the notion of respect for our planet has been added, which was not an issue just a few decades ago.

The pandemic has strongly accelerated underlying trends such as the rise of digital technology and e-commerce, and social and environmental awareness. This will force the luxury industry to adapt even more rapidly, while remaining true to its roots and to the special relationship with time that unique savoir-faire requires.

Éric Vallat has held management positions within several luxury groups including LVMH, Richemont, EPI and Rémy Cointreau. He was Head of the Fashion and Accessories Maisons of the Richemont group, where he was a member of the executive committee.

French luxury, a major asset for the national economy

The fashion and luxury goods industry in France contributes to the economy in an equivalent way that the automobile or aeronautics industries do[45], with a value added of 1.7% of GDP and 3.1% if its indirect effects are taken into account.

In 2019, before the crisis, exports of luxury goods amounted to €55.9 billion and those of aeronautics and space to €64.2 billion. Their trade balances (exports minus imports) were comparable, €27 billion for luxury goods and €31 billion for aerospace. The pandemic caused both sectors to plunge in activity, but the luxury sector held up much better in terms of foreign trade in 2020. Compared to 2019, exports from the luxury goods industry fell by only 14% in 2020. Aerospace exports collapsed by 45%. In fact, in 2020, the contribution of luxury goods to the trade balance amounted to €48.1 billion of exports and a positive balance of €24 billion. Aerospace exports only reached €35 billion and its positive balance reached €16.5 billion.

As a major employer in the French economy, the luxury industry represents more than 600,000 direct jobs, to which nearly 400,000 indirect jobs can be added[46]. According to the survey conducted by the Comité Colbert in 2020, the sector has created 3,500 production jobs with in-house training. 20 new production sites have been opened in France. The sector's activity is evenly

---

45. Industrial and distribution activities of haute couture, ready-to-wear, jewelry, watchmaking, textiles, leather, leather goods, footwear, cosmetics and perfumes. Strategic industry contract–Fashion and Luxury–2019–2022. National Industry Council.
46. Institut Français de la Mode/Quadrat, strategic contract for the fashion and luxury sector, 2019–2022.

distributed across all territories. Each year, there are still 10,000 jobs to be filled in the sector. At the end of December 2020, LVMH had 150,479 employees. France accounted for 21.8% of the total, the other European countries 25%. Asia and Japan accounted for nearly 30%, the United States for half that. At the same date, Hermès had 16,600 employees, 63% of whom were in France, where 80% of its production is carried out[47].

The luxury sector is also very active in training its employees. The 90 luxury brands in the Comité Colbert run 14 training schools for luxury businesses. Continuing education is another area of responsibility for the sector. On average, more than 10% of its employees are in training each year. However, there is a shortfall of 10,000 production positions.

The Institute of Métiers d'Excellence, founded in 2014 by LVMH, provides vocational training in the creative, craft and sales professions. Since its creation, this institute has trained over 1,400 young people in France, Switzerland, Italy, Spain, Germany and Japan. Training is provided by the group's companies as well as by partner schools. To accommodate its growth, LVMH offered 400 apprenticeship contracts in 2021. *"Nothing could be more essential to LVMH than the Métiers d'Excellence [...] It is vitally important that we encourage a shift in perceptions among younger generations concerning these exceptional professions, because they are truly meaningful and because they are perfect avenues to build excellent careers. More than 30,000 recruitments are planned as part of the Group's vision for the future between now and the end of 2024, including about 8,000 in 2022,"* says Chantal Gaemperle, the group's EVP Human Resources and Synergies. In July 2021, the group, emphasizing that nearly 200 excellent professions are at the heart

---

47. 14% in Asia-Pacific, 12% in Europe excluding France and 6% in America.

of its business, announced the strengthening of its actions at the global level in favor of information on these professions and internal promotion in this area.

Hermès trains its own artisans. It takes 18 months to master the expert skills needed to make high-end leather goods. Its employees may initially be completely new to the trade. Each high-end item has the name of the artisan who made it, like a work of art. To ensure the best possible cooperation and transmission of skills, the Hermès factories don't exceed 250 to 300 artisans.

VISION & PERSPECTIVE

"The future of luxury will be local."

Bénédicte Épinay, President and CEO, Comité Colbert

On 21 September 1972 French President Georges Pompidou held a press conference during which, in a questionable shortcut, he described the luxury industry as being a sector of the past.

50 years later, the French luxury industry is a heavyweight in the country's economy, contributes positively to its balance of trade and is a major employer thanks to the existence of a long-standing industrial network which spreads to all regions. Better still, its extreme resilience since the pandemic means it is still able to consider new locations.

Unlike other sectors, the French luxury industry has been able to maintain and develop local activity. Numerous workshops and production sites continue to be built in France, contributing to the development of local employment in this industry, which today employs 1 million people, directly and indirectly.

This local anchoring marvellously shows the persistence of French genius born with the Age of Enlightenment and the

→

→ perpetuation of unique savoir-faire that appeared in the Royal Manufacturing era. It is this anchoring in our regions that allows French luxury brands to embrace the values of local and sustainable development so dear to the younger generations. Finally, it is this same French identity that has made the iconic products of our major brands so successful abroad, and whose history is the stuff of dreams. It is also, without doubt, a non-negotiable part of their future.

Bénédicte Épinay started at Les Échos where, after having directed the luxury section, she created its two weekend magazines, for whose editorial staff she was responsible. In 2016, at Les Échos she took over as the general manager of Pelham Media where she developed a division dedicated to the luxury industry. Today Bénédicte Épinay is CEO of the Comité Colbert.

Luxury, a paradoxical promoter of social ties

The luxury groups contribute to the rebirth of manual labor and give birth to artistic and creative vocations among young people. In this context, Hermès has been organizing "Hermès hors les murs", a traveling festival of savoir-faire since 2011.

The annual success of the opening of certain LVMH workshops during the "Journées Particulières" shows the fascination of the French people for their high quality artisanal creations. These days attracted more than 180,000 people in October 2018, passionate about high-level craftsmanship and, for some, interested in its business lines. Antonio Belloni, Group Managing Director of LVMH, indicates that "*several major initiatives have been taken in the social field, such as partnerships with sensitive suburban cities to promote the inclusion of young people*"[48]. Under agreements with Clichy-sous-Bois and Montfermeil, the Group offers tours of its facilities and internships to young people from disadvantaged neighborhoods. The "Cultures and Creation Fashion Show" in Montfermeil, designed to highlight young local creative talent, has been sponsored by LVMH since 2005. Schools such as La Fabrique and the Simplon school, which help people retrain to return to work, also benefit from the group's partnerships.

The growing commitment of public authorities

The current strategic industry contract for fashion and luxury for 2019–2022 was signed in January 2019 by Guillaume de Seynes, then chairman of the Strategic Industry Committee, with Bruno Le Maire, French Minister of Economy and Finance, as well as with Franck Riester, the French Minister of Culture. This contract followed on from a similar contract signed by Isabelle Guichot in April 2013 with Arnaud Montebourg, French Minister for Productive Recovery. The financial amount at stake from the government and the private sector over 2019–2022 is however only €10 million.

As part of the €100 billion France Relance plan for 2020–2022, three companies in the luxury goods sector have been granted state aid: Bronzes de France, Ateliers Pinton specialized in luxury carpets and rugs and Pivaudon in perfume bottles.

As one of the 54 competitive clusters in existence in 2020, Cosmetic Valley, the cosmetics and perfume competitive cluster in the Centre-Val-de-Loire, Île-de-France and Normandy regions, is an exceptional success story that has contributed significantly to the development of French production in this field. In 2021,

---

48. Interview with the Group Managing Director, LVMH 2017 business report.

the Cosmetic Valley, created in 1994, represented 246,000 jobs. In 2019, its 3,200 companies exported €15.7 billion. The creation of other competitiveness clusters in fashion, perfume, leather goods, and especially footwear, for example in Limousin, would be able to produce positive results in terms of productivity and employment. For example, a competitiveness cluster could be created straddling the Drôme, the Alpes de Haute-Provence and the Alpes Maritimes. The Biovallée association, which promotes organic crops, could be the promoter.

Based on the model of the advances on earnings which the film industry benefits from, a procedure of reimbursable advances was set up in 2018 for young fashion designers. With the support of Balenciaga, Chanel, Louis Vuitton, and the Ministries of Economy and Culture, the Institute for the Financing of Cinema and Cultural Industries (IFCIC) is aimed at fashion start-ups which are between 1 and 15 years old and with a turnover of less than €5 million. Various aid schemes are also planned to help the sector develop a traceability system and create new textile recycling systems.

10

Italy, the Envy of All

T he Italian luxury sector is renowned throughout the world. It is deeply rooted in Italy's history, culture, art of living, incomparable landscapes, and architecture. The same is true for its prestigious brands in many areas, such as gastronomy, automotive, leather goods, textiles, and clothing. Italy, and especially its most coveted brands, have always been lusted after by large luxury groups, whether they are European (especially French) or international. Italy has often historically been a supplier for French brands. The two largest luxury countries in the world have always enjoyed a special relationship.

A rank to be decided on

Twenty-two Italian luxury companies were included in the Deloitte 2019 global top 100, and the cumulative sales of these houses reached $43.6 billion in 2019. Their share in the turnover of these top 100 companies is 13.6%, which makes these Italian groups the second largest luxury goods power in the world after France.

Apart from EssilorLuxottica, the result of the merger of Essilor and Luxottica, the most notable independent Italian companies are Prada, with its brands Prada, Miu Miu, Church's, Car Shoe;

Giorgio Armani with its Emporio Armani, Armani Privé, Armani Jeans, Armani Casa and Armani Ristorante universe; Max Mara, Moncler, Dolce & Gabbana, Ferragamo, Emenegildo Zegna, Valentino, Brunello Cucinelli, Furla and Liu Jo. The OTB Group, which was built on the success of its iconic brand Diesel created by Renzo Rosso, counts among its brands contemporary Italian fashion gems such as Maison Martin Margiela, Viktor & Rolf, Marni and Jil Sander.

In the face of global competition, the Italian groups have two important assets: creativity and exclusivity. Several dynamic Italian brands have literally exploded since 2016 thanks to these assets. For example, Moncler, with sales growth of 16.1% per year, Brunello Cucinelli with 10% growth, Euroitalia (perfumes) with 16.6% growth and Liu Jo with 8% growth[49]. Despite their conventional diversification into many adjacent niches, Italian brands retain their rare, "ultra chic" image, stemming from centuries-old culture and their deep roots in the fashion industry. Beyond its incredible creativity, the Italian luxury sector preserves its high manufacturing quality, inherited over several centuries.

However, many Italian gems have gone over to foreign groups. Kering is the French group that owns the most Italian brands – Gucci, Brioni, Bottega Veneta, Sergio Rossi and the jeweler Pomellato. LVMH counts Bulgari, Loro Piana, Fendi and Emilio Pucci among its brands. This has enabled these prestigious brands to both successfully develop and improve their financial situations at the same time. Other countries have invested in Italian brands. Qatar has taken over Valentino, China has Krizia, while La Perla has become Dutch. In 2018 the Italian fashion house Versace was sold to the American group

---

49. Compound annual growth rate.

Michael Kors, best known for its handbags. Of the 327 acquisitions in the luxury industry between January 2017 and March 2018 globally, 21% involved Italian companies.

France and Italy: friendly competition

Based on Deloitte's figures[50], the share of French and Italian groups in the top 100 global personal luxury goods companies is 49.3% of the total, for a combined turnover of €157 billion. The two countries combined are therefore two undisputed leaders in the world's luxury industry. However, the French groups in the top 100 have a turnover 2.6 times higher than their Italian counterparts. This balance of power needs further explanation. A significant part of French group sales are of products from previously independent Italian brands. But it is only under the French groups' wings that these brands have achieved the success they know today. There is also a fundamental structural difference in French and Italian groups. There are 10 French groups in the top 100 as opposed to 22 Italian groups.

Many Italian companies have a family structure and independence that they wish to maintain, at the risk of limiting their growth prospects and incurring difficulties in passing their businesses on from one generation to the next. To compensate for the handicaps of being small, Confindustria, the Italian employers' federation, stressed the urgency of increased cooperation between Italian companies in 2021. With a surge in global luxury goods consumption over the four years from 2016 to 2019, the ten French groups in the top 100 registered 11.3% growth per year[51]. The 22 Italian groups only grew by 3.1%.

---

50. "Global Powers of Luxury Goods," Deloitte, 2020.
51. Compound annual growth rate.

The impact of the pandemic on Italian luxury

In the midst of the Covid crisis, Italy saw the capitalization of its companies fall by 40% in the first quarter of 2020; *"one of the worst performances in the financial markets"* (figures provided by the study "The State of Fashion 2020"[52]). Prada, Tod's and Zegna demonstrate the range of possible responses.

Prada's rebound

Prada, the Italian luxury leader, was not spared by the crisis. The group, which has 637 brand outlets in 70 countries and controls other brands such as Miu Miu, Car Shoe and Church's, saw its revenue fall by 24% in 2020 to €2.4 billion in turnover. Over the four-year period of 2016–2019, its sales had already been declining by 3.1% per year. In 2019, Prada accounted for 83% of sales, Miu Miu for 14.2% and Church's for 2.2%. Prada made 32% of its 2019 sales in Asia-Pacific – including China – and 12% in Japan. The group recovered at the end of 2020 and in the first three quarters of 2021. Retail sales in the third quarter of 2021 were up 18% compared to the same period in 2019, and the luxury group is aiming at an increase in revenue to €4.5 billion per year in the medium term, representing 40% growth (compared to its record revenue of €3.6 billion in 2013). At its November 2021 results presentation, the company also announced that it would double its online penetration rate to 15% of its retail revenue. It is a project that comes as the brand's online sales are already booming (+400% in the third quarter compared to the same period in 2019). Its CEO, Patrizio Bertelli, also clarified that he

---

52. McKinsey in partnership with Pitti Immagine and Camera Nazionale della Moda Italiana.

had no intention of partnering with a global luxury conglomerate, nor was he looking for a financial investor, as he did not need additional capital: *"The Prada Group has a thoughtful and pioneering vision of fashion. At a time of significant cultural and societal change, luxury needs to continue evolving coherently with the market [...]. Our dialogues and fluid perspectives continually reinterpret luxury. By being relevant, sustainable, and impactful, we will drive long-term growth[53]."*

In the meantime, Lorenzo Bertelli, the eldest son of Miuccia Prada and Patrizio Bertelli, is making the green shift a priority, even though he is still in charge of marketing and will only take over the group's reins in 2024.

Tod's rebounds

Several brands have emerged shattered by the pandemic, with the ever-present threat of another wave. The Italian luxury sector is once again facing another phase of restructuring. Today, brands such as Dolce & Gabbana, Ferragamo, Furla, Cerruti and Trussardi are all new targets.

Tod's, one of the most prestigious Italian leather goods manufacturers, had its first international success in the 1980s with its iconic lightweight Gominno moccasin with its spiked sole. It was brought to the top of Italian fashion by famous clients such as Gianni Agnelli and Hollywood stars. In footwear, Tod's has expanded its collections, created a new brand (Hogan) and acquired Roger Vivier. Its territory has expanded to include leather goods and fashion, under its own name or that of Fay. The group was hit hard by the pandemic, with a -30.4% drop in sales in

---

53. Huw Hughes, "Prada reveals CEO succession plans as sales surpass 2019 levels," *Fashion United*, November 22, 2021.

2020, after five years of erosion[54]. Its 2021 results showed a clear turnaround with fourth quarter sales +9.6% higher than the same quarter in 2019. In April 2021, LVMH increased its stake in the group to 10%[55].

The financial markets to Zegna's rescue?

Zegna went public in the U.S. on December 20, 2021, becoming the first Italian fashion label to be listed in New York, the aim being to strengthen its presence in this key market to boost its future development. Before Covid, 90% of the brand's sales were generated internationally, with half in China. Originally specializing in men's clothing, Zegna turned 111 years old in 2021. Having retained its independence, it is one of the most successful businesses in the sector, present in 80 countries and with a network of directly managed boutiques in more than 300 stores by 2022. It has the undeniable assets to be able to continue its progress and compete with the biggest companies in the future.

Strengthened national cohesion around Italian luxury

A major role in the Italian economy

The Italian textile and clothing sector employs 40,000 people in nearly 50,000 companies[56]. Its revenue was €56 billion in 2019.

---

54. Dominique Muret, "Tod's: les ventes chutent de 30% en 2020," *Fashion Network*, February 3, 2021.
55. Reuters, "LVMH porte sa participation dans Tod's à 10%", *Les Echos*, April 26, 2021.
56. Source: Sistema Moda Italia.

Adding accessories, jewelry and beauty, the fashion industry represented nearly €95 billion in the same year. The health crisis resulted in an approximately 23% decline in industry sales. But recovery was rapid in 2021, with a catch-up of more than €90 billion expected[57]. Many small and medium-sized companies with unique savoir-faire are scattered throughout northern Italy. Significant investments have been made to modernize and increase their production. In April 2019, Gucci unveiled Gucci Artlab, its first leather goods and footwear industrial complex over 37,000 square meters, located in Caselli, south of Bologna. The Brunello Cucinelli house, specialized in cashmere, is located in Solomeo, a small village in Umbria, where it employs 1,600 people in its ultramodern facilities. The brand considers its roots in the Perugia region to be part of its Italian identity, its mission to renew local heritage and its social responsibility.

Altagamma, promoter of national luxury since 1992

The Altagamma Foundation, the Italian equivalent of the Comité Colbert (association to promote luxury), has 102 members. It brings together the best high-end Italian cultural and creative companies[58]. The foundation promotes Italian excellence and art of living, with a cross-sectoral approach.

Generally speaking, the various brands bolster each other within the Foundation, through their exchanges of experience, skills and contacts, in a cross-fertilization approach that pulls all members upwards. This cooperation enables the brands to be even stronger on an international level. During the Covid crisis,

---

57. Dominique Muret, *Fashion Network*, 2020, 2021 and 2022.
58. *"Altagamma gathers the best High-End Italian Cultural and Creative Companies and promotes the Italian Excellence and Lifestyle with a cross-sectional approach,"* Altagamma, 2019.

the association was particularly active in helping its members cope with this unprecedented period. Its strategy for 2020–2022 focuses on internationalization, sustainability, contemporary outlook and high-end tourism.

11

Switzerland, a Third Luxury Land

Originally specializing in watches and high-end hotels, Switzerland is now a major competitor in the international luxury market. In the personal luxury goods sector alone, ten Swiss firms are among the world's top 100 luxury companies. The country ranks third in Europe, after France and Italy.

Richemont, the flagship of Swiss luxury

The group's origins are closely linked to the Geneva watchmaking industry. Its oldest brand is Vacheron Constantin, created in 1755. Ranked fourth in the 2019 top 100 with revenues of $16.2 billion, the Geneva-based group owns some 20 world-class brands. Its jewelry houses are among the most prestigious in the world: Cartier, Van Cleef & Arpels and Buccellati. Its watchmaking companies are also internationally renowned: A. Lange & Söhne, Baume & Mercier, IWC, Jaeger-LeCoultre, Panerai, Piaget, Roger Dubuis and Vacheron-Constantin. Richemont is also present in online distribution with Yoox Net-A-Porter and Watchfinder & Co. Richemont's fourth division is made up of the fashion brands Alaïa, Chloé, AZ Factory and Peter Millar; the writing instrument, leather goods and watch specialist

Montblanc; the English ready-to-wear and accessories brand Dunhill; and the arms manufacturer Purdey.

More recently, in July 2021, the group strengthened its leather goods division. After buying Lancel in 1998 and then selling it in 2018, Richemont acquired the Belgian company Delvaux. A pioneer in modern leather handbags, the iconic brand, which has around 50 stores, has suffered from the pandemic, particularly from the restrictions on travel for Chinese tourists who are big consumers of its products, and lost 40% of its sales, which before the crisis exceeded €120 million. With Dunhill, the Richemont group has two stars in high-end leather goods and luggage.

Richemont, steadfast during the health crisis

The group didn't escape the pandemic's impact, with a 26% drop in revenues in the first half of the April 1, 2020–March 31, 2021 fiscal year, due to the closure of sales outlets, logistics centers and manufacturing sites, as well as the halt in international tourism. But sales picked up in the second half of the year, growing 12% at real exchange rates since September 2020 (+17% at constant exchange rates). They then increased in the last quarter of the year, from January to March 2021, with a 36% jump at constant exchange rates. Overall, Richemont has weathered the health crisis well with a limited 8% decline in revenues to €13.1 billion for the period April 1, 2020–March 31, 2021, compared with €14.2 billion for the previous period.

In his letter accompanying the results, Richemont chairman Johann Rupert explained the drivers of its recovered dynamism to be the *"jewelry houses, online retail and Asia-Pacific[…]Jewelry houses grew their business beyond their pre-health crisis level, delivering a 31% operating margin, underscoring the enduring appeal of Cartier, Van Cleef & Arpels and Buccellati."*

Jewelry is indeed Richemont's most important division (and, according to Morgan Stanley's estimates, Cartier accounts for about 75% of this division). For the April 2020–March 2021 period, it accounted for 57% of the group's revenues, with an operating margin of 31%. Its sales even increased by 3% over the period. The watch division accounted for 17% of total sales, but its operating margin was only 5.9% and its sales plunged 21% year on year. Online distribution contributed to 16% of total activity, with a negative margin of 10.2% and sales down 9%. The other brands – fashion, leather goods, office products, watches and shotguns – accounted for 10% of total activity, with a negative margin of 25% and sales down 25%.

Like most groups that have weathered the pandemic well, Richemont benefited from its presence in China, where it performed well, contributing to the 19% growth in revenue in Asia-Pacific, with triple-digit growth in the fourth quarter of the year, at the beginning of 2021. Over the same annual period, Europe plunged by 31%, Japan by 22% and the Americas by 15%. Since April 2021, Richemont has been buoyed up by the strong economic recovery in Asia-Pacific and North America, where 2019 results for the three months from April to June were exceeded by nearly 40% in 2021. Europe is lagging behind, and it is the jewelry houses that are once again keeping the group going.

Listed in Zurich, Richemont is of particular interest to investors and other luxury groups. Nevertheless, the group seems to have all the necessary assets to maintain its brands' independence. Recently, the group announced that its executive committee would now focus on *"strategic direction, capital allocation and governance"*, while brand managers would focus on brand development. Cartier and Van Cleef & Arpels *"have reached a size and scope that requires the full attention of their managers and the group's support"* to continue their growth, said Johann Rupert.

Cartier, the jewel in the crown

Founded in 1847 and now present in more than 60 countries with 270 stores, Cartier, which was acquired by Richemont in 1964, generated sales of €10.29 billion in 2020. The *"jeweler of kings and the king of jewelers"*, which is one of the world's top 7 most valuable luxury brands, continued to successfully launch all of its products and maintain solid revenue growth. This success can be explained in particular by a premium on sustainability and by a refocusing on its iconic products.

"Jewelry shows more resilience than other sectors and plays a very important role in providing reassurance in this context. Cartier is considered one of the luxury goods companies on the market with the strongest image and the most incredible desirability. Our items are recognized as having strong symbolic value – like the Love bracelet and its concept of attachment – and this resonates even more today. People want to please themselves and others. In the watch industry, which is a very complicated market, we were very dynamic and worked very hard on products and communication. We have seen the results of this in recent months, and now in April 2020 with the relaunch of the Pasha watch, first in France, then in China and Korea in July and in the rest of the world in September. And we were 100% right to do so. The overall results are very good everywhere, it is the launch of the year in watchmaking", explained Arnaud Carrez, its marketing director, to *INfluencia* in January 2021[59].

---

59. Isabelle Musnik, "Je crois profondément au "new retail" par toutes les générations", *INfluencia*, January 5, 2021.

The brand has begun to transform of all its stores. The new flagship store at 13 rue de la Paix in Paris opens in August 2022 and the 5th Avenue store is also on the list for future renovations. "*It's a total reinvention,*" says Cyrille Vigneron, Cartier CEO. The brand has also greatly accelerated in terms of digital technology – which saw triple-digit growth in 2021 – including the opening of a virtual store on Tmall's Luxury Pavilion.

Its digital innovations are important, especially for the Chinese market. In its Pudong store, interactive screens capture the heart beats of the future bride and groom and engrave them on their wedding rings. Thanks to augmented reality, the customer can visualize the appearance of the jewel on their hand and follow how it changes according to the type of gold or the light. 3D scans of clients' heads are being researched, which would let them visualize the appearance of special orders. Cartier has also worked on its new digital platforms[60]. So when the Watches and Wonders show was canceled in April 2020, it found "*alternatives to this physical meeting by creating an international website dedicated to new watches, Cartier Watchmaking Encounters*", says Arnaud Carrez. Finally, Cartier is pursuing an active policy of diversification into accessories, leather goods, eye wear, perfumes and, recently, toys and gifts for babies.

The other gems: Van Cleef & Arpels, Montblanc, etc.

Another star is Van Cleef & Arpels, founded in 1906 and acquired in 1999. Since then, the brand has developed a very strong identity in the jewelry and watch segments, where it

---

60. *Ibid.*

has always worked and focused its development, thanks to its uncompromising creative management. According to some sources, its revenue exceeded €2 billion, compared to a revenue of 600 million francs (less than €100 million) at the time of its acquisition.

Another jewel in the group's crown is Montblanc, which built its reputation around luxury pens when it invented the first fountain pen with an integrated inkwell in 1910. In 2009, the brand still held 60% of the global market for premium pens. It has realigned itself to focus on the "luxury business lifestyle" with a new mission: *"at Montblanc, we encourage people to impose their brand: in design, product manufacturing, stories and experiences – all by making life easier every day."*

It has agreed to collaborations with Kitsuné in high-end headphones, leather goods, connected objects and writing accessories. *"We have a long history of collaborations, particularly in writing instruments, where we have worked on our product lines with several artists. Our customers recognize us for our savoir-faire as a century-old luxury brand, but also for our watches and leather goods. Our logo is a fantastic tool. But we hope that our customers will enjoy the entire Montblanc universe. We need to evolve from a business luxury brand to a business lifestyle luxury brand,"* said brand president Nicolas Baretzki in June 2021.

Montblanc has continued its development, kept consumer confidence, improved its desirability and, above all, developed customer experience and emotion. Its objective is not to diversify in any old direction, but to offer products in line with the brand's DNA. Despite the crisis, its turnover should quickly reach €1 billion.

The Swatch Group, much more than just the Swatch watch

Swatch Group is ranked 10th worldwide in Deloitte's 2019 Luxury Goods Group Rankings[61], with revenues of $8.29 billion. Its growth over the four years 2016–2019 was 2.9% per year. The group owns 18 watch brands, which it classifies into four categories. The prestige and luxury range includes Breguet, Harry Winston, Blancpain, Glashütte Original, Jaquet Droz, Léon Hatot and Omega. The high range is composed of Longines, Rado and Union Glashütte. The middle range includes Tissot, Balmain, Certina, Mido, Hamilton and Calvin Klein. The basic range consists of Swatch and Flik Flak. The group diversified in 2013 with the acquisition of jeweler Harry Winston, whose production was later supplemented by high-priced watches. The watch and jewelry business, which includes sales of branded products and components as well as jewelry, accounts for 96% of revenue. The remaining 4% is provided by its electronic systems business, under the Renata, EM Microelectronic-Marin and Micro Crystal brands, with strong positions in low energy microchips.

The year 2020 saw Swatch Group sales plunge by 32.1%. As with other luxury groups, its recovery began at the end of the year. In the first half of 2021, sales growth reached 54.4% compared to the same period of 2020, while remaining 12.3% lower than in 2019. China and the United States initiated its recovery as early as the second half of 2021. In its financial communications, the group notes a very strong demand for Harry Winston jewelry, as well as for its Blancpain, Omega, Longines and Tissot brands, whose production has been slowed down by production bottlenecks. Swatch's outlook for the second half of the year was encouraging, with sales expected to be higher than in 2019.

---

61. "Global Powers of Luxury Goods 2020," Deloitte.

Independent Swiss watchmakers at the forefront of global luxury

Watchmaking and jewelry are the essence of Swiss luxury, but the large groups listed on the financial markets don't actually possess the top Swiss luxury watch brands. It is in fact quite the contrary. Although they own 37 watch brands, the groups' share of 2020 sales represents only 55% of the total. 41.8% of sales are made by five large independent houses: Rolex, Patek Philippe, Audemars Piguet, Richard Mille and Breitling[62].

The big independent brands have, for the most part, unmatched levels of prestige. Their prices can be very high. In 2020, average prices were €32,878 for a Patek Philippe, €32,159 for an Audemars Piguet and €171,195 for a Richard Mille[63]. From the brands belonging to the large groups, only Lange & Sohne (€33,188), Van Cleef & Arpels (€32,544), Breguet (€20,228) or Piaget (€19,177) can compete. Rolex and Breitling have lower selling prices -€9,176 for the former and €4,908 for the latter–but they have a very special status.

A deep, but well overcome crisis

At the peak of the health crisis, the Swiss watch industry saw its sales fall by almost 33% in volume and 21% in value, and its exports by 21.8%. Because of their high-end positioning, the independent brands cushioned the blow much better. Rolex sales fell 19% in volume, but the brand partially offset this decline with a 5% price increase, according to Theresa Di Martini[64]. On the other hand, Audemars Piguet sales fell by only 9%[65].

---

62. "Spot the watch," *The Everest Journal*, April 2021.
63. "LuxConsult," Morgan Stanley Research, estimates.
64. "Spot the Watch," *op. cit.*
65. J.X. Su, interview with François-Henry Bennahmias, CEO Audemars Piguet, *Watches by sjx*.

However, Rolex continues to fascinate its customers, as do Patek Philippe and Audemars Piguet. During the pandemic, the demand for certain models exploded on the second-hand market, especially on marketplaces such as Chrono24. On a global level, premiumization further increased in 2020. Exports of watches valued at €6,539 or more accounted for 70% of the total in terms of value, with a volume of only 10%.

The Swiss luxury groups have several assets that allow them to maintain their leadership in this segment. The first is that Swiss watchmaking is recognized as a world leader for its product quality. The second is that these groups accounted for a total of 12.4% of sales in the 2019 top 100, covering all market segments, including components. The third is that almost all of these brands are positioned at the very high end of the market, which is more resistant to crises. Very high-end or ultra-luxury watches have even become investments in their own right, with their value rising steadily as their clientele expands. This is evidenced by the inflation and speculation on certain models of some brands, especially Rolex, Patek Philippe and Audemars Piguet. The fourth reason is that the Swiss groups have a several centuries-long technological history and a technical savoir-faire that is very difficult to copy or match. The entry barriers are very high. This is evidenced by the difficulties French brands have in finding a place for themselves in the luxury segment of the watch industry.

"King" Rolex

Rolex, founded in 1905, occupies an unrivaled position in the Swiss luxury watch industry thanks to the image of its time-pieces, its innovations, its sales volume, and its numerous sponsorship and patronage programs. Hence the nickname given to the brand by Morgan Stanley: King Rolex[66]. Through its watch

---

66. "King Rolex," Morgan Stanley–LuxeConsult, March 2021.

production alone and that of its subsidiary Tudor, Rolex occupied 12th place in the top 100 luxury groups in 2019, with a turnover of $6.74 billion and a growth rate of 8.1% per year. In 2020, Rolex accounted for 26.8% of Swiss watch sales.

Patek Philippe

Patek Philippe achieved an estimated $1.5 billion in sales in 2019. With its very high-end watches, Patek Philippe is ranked 40th in the world's top 100, with growth of nearly 5% per year from 2016 to 2019. The exceptional quality of its watches justifies its famous signature, *"You never actually own a Patek Philippe, you merely look after it for the next generation."*

Audemars Piguet

Audemars Piguet ranks 48th in Deloitte's top 100 with an estimated revenue of $1.187 billion in 2019 and growth of 10.5% per year over 2016–2019. Founded in 1875, it specializes in the most extraordinary watch complications. Its signature, *"to break the rules, you must first master them"* demonstrates its philosophy of permanently overcoming technical barriers. The brand's focuses on a limited production of 40,000 watches per year and extremely rigorous management of its stocks[67].

According to François-Henri Bennahamias, CEO of Audemars Piguet, the importance of the Chinese market should not lead to uncontrolled expansion of production or to underestimation of the American market. High-end watches fascinate the younger generations who, like their elders, are attached to tradition, high-level craftsmanship and sustainability. The Audemars Piguet

---

67. François-Henri Bennahamias, CEO, Audemars Piguet, "The State of Fashion: Watches and Jewellery Report", *The Business of Fashion* and McKinsey & Company, 2021.

Houses offer a club-like experience to current and prospective clients. By opening its first private apartment in Asia, Audemars Piguet has redefined the notion of hospitality. At the end of 2020, seven Houses had already been opened throughout the world with increasingly large surface areas, from 600m² for the Houses in Madrid and Bangkok, to more than 800m² for the one in New York. New ones are expected to be set up in Tokyo. The brand is part of a movement running counter to the old model of selling through resellers which has run out of steam, especially so during the pandemic. Direct sales to customers currently account for 70% of Audemars Piguet sales.

Richard Mille, a billionaire brand for billionaires

Richard Mille, in its "ultra-luxury" segment, has not been spared by the crisis. If Covid hadn't hit, Richard Mille would have joined the very closed club of watch brands that have passed the billion Swiss franc mark for its twentieth anniversary[68]. Richard Mille had 2019 sales of $9.06 million – up 200% from the previous year. Over the 2016–2019 period, its average annual growth rate was 58.7%.

Breitling, a responsible brand

As for Breitling, ranked 67th in the 2019 Deloitte Top 100, its revenue amounted to $0.584 billion that same year. The brand has developed models adapted to the specific needs of aviation, space and diving professionals. Its culture and communication are rooted in aeronautics, as well as in Bentley luxury automobiles. CVC Capital Partners took control of Breitling in 2017, with an 80% stake in the watchmaker, and then 100% in 2018.

---

68. Christophe Roulet, "Richard Mille set to join the billionaires club", *Watches and Culture*, January 13, 2021.

The development focus for the new shareholder is its presence on the Chinese market. Recently, Breitling has made a commitment to the planet, notably by designing the Superocean Heritage 57 Outerknown watch with the sustainable clothing brand dreamed up by Kelly Slater, a living surfing legend and company ambassador.

Chopard and Franck Muller, two other exceptional manufacturers

Chopard is another independent luxury watch and jewelry group. In 2019, the company had revenues of $936 million, ranking it 53rd in the top 100. Its growth was 4.3% per year from 2016 to 2019. Its positioning for watches is at the top end of the market, with average prices of €6,383 in 2020 and a market share estimated at around 1%. Chopard invented the concept of Happy Diamonds, a watch with a dial containing several mobile diamonds. Diversifying into perfumes and accessories, the company stands out because of prestigious ambassadors such as Julia Roberts and the sponsorship of extraordinary events, such as the Cannes Film Festival or vintage car rallies.

12

Other European Players

British chic, a real luxury brand

Eight UK luxury companies are in the top 100 worldwide. In total, their share of the global market amounted to 2.1% in 2019. Remarkably, their cumulative growth reached 9% per year over 2016–2019. Burberry (20th), Ted Baker (55th), Graff Diamonds International Limited (66th), TFG (72nd), J. Barbour & Sons Ltd (90th), Paul Smith Group Holdings Limited (91st) and Charles Tyrwhitt Shirts Limited (97th) all have their roots in British culture, with a blend of tradition and unbridled imagination.

Despite its limited number of brands, British aesthetics are well represented in several luxury concepts and products – decoration, high-end automobiles, formal wear and outdoor wear.

Burberry's rebound

Burberry's revenue declined by 4% over April 2019 to April 2020 and 11.5% over April 2020 to April 2021[69]. These relatively limited drops, due to the accounting method used, reflect

---

69. Fiscal year 2019 (April 2018 to April 2019), fiscal year 2020 (April 2019 – April 2020), fiscal year 2021 (April 2020-April 2021).

the strong performance of markets through the end of 2019 and their recovery in early 2021. Burberry has a strong presence in Asia-Pacific, where the company generated 52% of its revenue from April 2020 to April 2021, compared to 27% in Europe, the Middle East, India and Africa and 21% in the Americas. Results were expected to improve in the 2022 fiscal year. Thus, the three months of April through June 2021 exceed the same three months in 2020 by 86%. Compared to the same period in 2019, sales were slightly higher at 1%.

Burberry's turnaround is primarily due to the markets. But there are other internal factors that strongly contribute to this. *"In the last three years, we have transformed our business and built a new Burberry, anchored firmly in luxury,"* CEO Marco Gobbetti said in a press release, who believes the group has reported *"strong results"* thanks to the upmarket strategy implemented since he took over in 2017. After a few years of creative stagnation, the brand has resumed its forward march by adapting and revolutionizing its great classics. Burberry has also put an end to its image-dangering policy of price cuts and the destruction of unsold clothing, while at the same time placing great emphasis on its sustainability.

As part of this major strategic transformation, the brand has also worked in depth on distribution and digital. Burberry opened a model concept store in Shenzen at the end of July 2020. It invites its Chinese customers to discover a new immersive experience mixing the physical and social worlds. It is an innovation that is part of its desire to *"redefine the expectations of the luxury industry"*, especially for generation Z. This *"social retail store"* is built around ten rooms, all generating personalized experiences (interactive windows, QR codes, etc.). Burberry has finally also actively embraced the world of video games.

The image of British chic is also helping other companies prosper. Of note is the very strong growth of Ted Baker (accessible fashion) at 10.8% per year and Barbour (traditional outdoor clothing) at 13.3% per year, between 2016 and 2019.

Ignored in the world rankings, other rarer brands[70] delight numerous connoisseurs, both British and Anglophile around the world.

Spain, at the forefront of the perfume world

Three Spanish groups appear in the top 100: Puig, S. All SL and Sociedad Textil Lonia, with a total share of 1% of global sales 2019.

The Puig Group achieved a turnover of €1.537 billion in 2020, down 24% from 2019. After having based great hopes on fashion with the Nina Ricci brand acquired in 1998 and Paco Rabanne, the pandemic led the company to give priority to its Beauty and Fashion division. Its iconic brands include Paco Rabanne, Carolina Herrera, Jean Paul Gaultier, Nina Ricci, Dries Van Noten, Penhaligon's and L'Artisan Parfumeur. The company also has licensing deals with Christian Louboutin and Comme des Garçons Parfums, as well as Lifestyle brands such as Adolfo Dominguez, Antonio Banderas, Shakira and Benetton. Puig is now the fifth largest selective perfume company in the world, with a market share of close to 10% and three brands in the top 20 worldwide. Its Charlotte Tilbury brand of "digital native" cosmetics, acquired in 2020, and its Derma dermocosmetics division (Uriage, Apivita and Isdin brands) constitute its two other major areas of development for the coming years. *"The company aims to exceed revenues of €3,000 million in 2023 and reach €4,500 million in 2025. This would mean doubling*

---

70. For example, Mulberry and Ettinger: leather goods, Jo Malone: perfume, Henry Poole: tailoring, Emma Willis: sportswear, Turnbull & Asser: shirts.

current turnover in 2023 and tripling it in 2025. The plan is based on forecasts of significant growth through promotion of the digital channel and an increase in revenues in Asia, which will represent 30% and 25% respectively in 2025." explain its managers in a press release. Puig is also the third-largest player in the dermocosmetic sector sold in pharmacies in Europe.

VISION & PERSPECTIVE

"Getting back to brand fundamentals"

Javier BACH, CEO, Puig

The concept of luxury has evolved over time and is experiencing an even faster pace of change nowadays. How to develop your brand in such waters becomes an even more amazing endeavour. Think of the connections with the consumer in what relates to how and where the brand actively communicates and engages with its community, which products and experiences it offers, and how this may evolve over time. Think of the endless opportunities ahead fostered by technological innovations both in the physical and in the virtual world, where the possibilities seem limitless. Let's also consider the sustainability agenda that is and will be even more relevant going forward. Think also about the future of consumption in terms of consumer trends or geographical expansion and how the brand will have to adapt to that.

All these realities, in my opinion, make it even more relevant to go back to the fundamentals of purpose, values and commitments. What do I stand for? This should be the North Start in our future journeys.

Javier Bach has more than 25 years of experience in running beauty brands worldwide. As Puig's CEO, in charge of international markets, operations and technology, he has driven the company's global growth and its digital and ESR transformation.

Sociedad Textil Lonia is a company that designs, produces and sells clothing and accessories for women, men and children. Founded in 1997, the group recorded sales of €0.41 billion in 2019, with its main brands Purificación García and Carolina Herrera. In fast fashion, Spain also has, of course, world champions like Zara or Desigual. For the moment, these groups do not seem to want to develop luxury brands.

The other luxury players in Northern Europe

In Germany, whose share of the global market in 2019 was 1.5 percent, the leader is Hugo Boss, with sales of $3.2 billion. The group is 23rd in the 2019 Deloitte Top 100. Wempe, a retailer and producer of jewelry and watches, is the second largest company, with sales of €0.6 billion, but with growth of 6.5% per year.

Three accessible luxury brands are rapidly developing – Marc O'Polo and Flake in sportswear and Marc Cain in casual fashion.

Philipp Plein, king of ultramodern, hit but not sunk

German designer Philipp Plein has had one of the most dazzling success stories in modern fashion. His brand, founded in 1999, reached an estimated €250 million in sales in 2018[71]. Its positioning is extravagant luxury. Philipp Plein shows off his jet set life and uses social networks with ease. His eccentric shows are very popular, thanks to the presence of celebrities chosen for their media impact such as footballers, young

---

71. Dominique Muret, "Philipp Plein forced to downsize," *Fashion Network*, September 9, 2020.

singers and rising stars. These shows are programmed as a counterpoint to the fashion weeks which he is kept away from by the fashion establishment. Philipp Plein's products, as well as those of its subsidiary, Billionaire, are priced without any relation to their intrinsic or aesthetic quality. Above all, they are a testament to the success and purchasing power of their customers. With the health crisis reducing its sales by almost a third, Philipp Plein has reduced its workforce and the number of stores in the world's capitals and has recruited seasoned industry professionals.

The rise of Scandinavian design in fashion

Sweden and Denmark still don't have a large place in personal luxury goods, with 1.1% of the total top 100 and only two groups listed: Pandora and Acne Studios.

In 2019, Pandora recorded sizable sales of €3.3 billion with its accessible jewelry sold around the world. Acne, with 13% annual growth over 2016–2019, demonstrates the potential of a bold brand incorporating requirements like exclusivity and modernity. Founded in 2000, Ganni is a Danish brand which is very popular with influencers, positioning itself as accessible luxury with its cool Scandinavian casual-chic style[72]. Its range extensively features dresses (19% of total sales), accessories (38%) and shoes (moccasins and boots). Its items range in price from €55 to €1,300, more affordable than its direct competitors Acne Studios, Isabel Marant or The Kooples, and it also offers a lower number of items. The brand currently relies on 25 of its own stores in Scandinavia, the United States and the UK and

---

72. Mathilde Lemaire, "Style, product range, price positioning the secrets to Ganni's success", *Fashion Network*, 23 novembre 2021.

some 600 partner distributors around the world. Sustainable development is a major concern for the brand, which offers a collection made with upcycled fabrics and clothing rentals. Ganni's originality led L. Catterton, a French-American investment fund involved in LVMH to acquire a majority stake in 2017.

VISION & PERSPECTIVE

"Sharing instead of hiding"

Andrea BALDO, CEO, Ganni

From an industry point of view, the level of carbon emission generated by the current production and distribution practices in fashion and luxury fashion are simply not sustainable while our planet is experiencing major climate change that could become irreversible.

From a consumption point of view, the level of carbon emission generated is unequally distributed, with the top 10% richer households contributing for more than half of total CO_2 emissions. Luxury customers are pressured to change their consumption behaviour, and the young generations admit that sustainability is already affecting their luxury purchasing decisions.

This trend towards sustainability is not a fad. It is an acceleration of a secular trend towards a more responsible form of doing business. This is confirmed by the recent growth of the B-Corp movement and the use of benefit corporate legal status, where for-profit companies aim at having a positive impact on the society (employee, customers, suppliers) and the environment as well as making money. All this is creating the "perfect" storm for the luxury industry.

If luxury brands and maisons are willing to keep their relevance in the future, they will have to embrace more inclusive
→

→

and diverse practices, share more than hide, act more than talk and finally align their core values with an ever-evolving luxury consumer.

Andrea Baldo has over 20 years of experience in the fashion and luxury goods industry. He held top General Management positions at brands including Diesel, Marni, Maison Margiela and more recently as CEO of Coccinelle and currently of Ganni. He is also Lecturer of Strategic Management at IESE Business School in Barcelona.

In this context, young fashion brands, born with an authentic responsible mission, with the ambition to be transparent and the desire to contribute to changing the fashion sector from within, have an advantage over their older rivals. Their young histories make a strong case for them with younger generations of consumers.

13

North America, the Great Powerhouse of Accessible Luxury

North America has 16 luxury groups in the Deloitte top 100, representing 18.1% of global revenue. The United States and Canada together were in silver place on the podium in 2019, ahead of Italy. Their very ambitious luxury groups are divided into two main areas. The first is firms specializing in perfumes and cosmetics, and the second is companies in accessible luxury products–fashion and leather goods. In the field of perfumes and cosmetics, three world champions are American.

The strength of American cosmetics and perfume groups

Estée Lauder comes in in third place in the top 100 global luxury groups. Its 2019 revenue was $16.2 billion. Its brands have excellent reputations in skincare and makeup: Clinique, Estée Lauder (including its Advanced Night Repair product), Darphin,

Bobbi Brown, LaMer, JoMalone, MAC: DKNY, Tom Ford, Michael Kors, Tommy Hilfiger.

There are two other international luxury cosmetics groups. Coty Luxury had 2019 sales of $3.3 billion, growing 21.5% annually over 2016–2019. To further accelerate its growth, the group sold its professional products division and decided not to prioritize its so-called "mass beauty" fragrances, but to focus its investments on its prestige division, which includes licensed fragrances; the most high-end of which carry the Gucci, Burberry, Bottega Veneta, Tiffany, MiuMiu, Boss and Calvin Klein brands. The turnover of Revlon, which bought Elisabeth Arden in 2016, reached $1 billion in 2019. The group also develops a line of perfumes, some of which are named after celebrities: Elizabeth Taylor, Christine Aguilera, Britney Spears, Jennifer Aniston, in particular.

Accessible luxury in fashion and leather goods is the other area of excellence for American firms.

PVH, the iconic American brand group of Calvin Klein and Tommy Hilfiger

PVH is the American champion of medium-high-end products with very high distribution. Its investments are focused on the two major global brands, Calvin Klein (37% of sales in 2020) and Tommy Hilfiger (51%). Three lingerie brands – Warners', Olga and True & Co – complete its offer. PVH ranked 9th among luxury groups worldwide in 2019, according to Deloitte, with revenues of $9.7 billion in 2019 and growth of 8.7% per year over 2016–2019.

2019 saw good growth for both major PVH brands in Europe (+8.8%) and Asia-Pacific (+16.3%). However, in 2019, the

North American continent accounted for 48.2% of its revenues and Europe for 36.9%. Asia-Pacific only accounted for 13.7%. Its sales in 2020 fell to $7.13 billion, down 28% from 2019. Its international expansion has slowed, but the declines in 2020 (-13.8% in Europe and -12.1% in the Asia-Pacific region), were less pronounced than in the United States (-42.5%) and Canada (-48.1%). In 2021, the February to April quarter saw sales pick up and accelerate in the following May to July period. Based on the cumulative results for the six months from February to July 2019 levels have already been achieved and were expected to be confirmed for the year.

PVH's strategy is to refocus and concentrate its resources on Calvin Klein and Tommy Hilfiger to move them upmarket.

Ralph Lauren, archetypal American lifestyle

The Ralph Lauren Group, founded in 1967, has become known worldwide for its men's and women's American and British-style accessible luxury collections. Limiting its designs to a few signature pieces, Ralph Lauren offers products that are strongly rooted in traditional American style, with a strong focus on quality across all product lines.

Its many brands are organized into three divisions. The Ralph Lauren Luxury division includes the premium brands Ralph Lauren Collection for women's fashion and Ralph Lauren Purple Label for men's fashion. The Double RL brand updates western American outdoor clothing. The Ralph Lauren Home brand offers decorating and furnishing accessories that are representative of beautiful traditional American homes. The luxury division includes watches and jewelry inspired by North American upper-class style. The products are sold in the brand's most prestigious boutiques, as well as in its online shop.

The Polo Ralph Lauren range is the second division, which includes more accessible products with a wider distribution; the Polo Ralph Lauren Children's brand, as well as the RLX Ralph Lauren brand of casual clothing. The Pink Pony brand of gender-neutral casual clothing donates a portion of its sales to cancer charities. The third division is called Lauren Ralph Lauren, and offers a more affordable range of men's and women's clothing than the first two.

The brand also has its own restaurants in New York, Chicago and Paris, located in its local flagship stores, whose role is to give its prospective customers a luxury experience from across the Atlantic, naturally leading to a combination of spending, both on food and clothing. The role of the brand's founder, Ralph Lauren, is absolutely key in the group. Financial reports put his presence at the helm of creation at the forefront of the conditions for its success.

Ralph Lauren Group's 2019 revenue was $6.3 billion, bringing it to 13th place on the Deloitte list. However, over 2016–2019, the average decline was 5.2% per year, which led Ralph Lauren to cut the number of brands and distributors. The group also focused on its high-end products, while scheduling the sale of its Chaps and Club Monaco brands, which took place in May 2021. This policy initiated the brand's recovery, as the last year of the reporting period saw its sales increase by 2.1%. But the pandemic hit the group hard. Over March 2019–March 2020, revenues decreased by 2.4% and then by 28.6% from March 2020–March 2021. Representing almost half of its sales; Ralph Lauren's American market collapsed by 36.6%, while its European market; the second largest, lost 28.6%. The brand has benefited little from the rapid recovery of the Chinese market, where its sales have only stabilized. The 2020 difficulties, however, appear to simply be a brief interlude. From March to September 2021, thanks to the recovery of the U.S. and European economies, revenues increased by 71% compared to the previous year.

With its strong North American style and after the streamlining of its brands in favor of its top-of-the-range, the Ralph Lauren group seems to be in a position to resume regular growth in the coming years.

Tapestry, the first accessible luxury group

Tapestry, ranked 14th in the 2019 rankings, with $6 billion in revenue and 10.3% annual growth over 2016–2019, is the holding company for three brands. Coach is progressively developing, with its bestsellers in bags and leather goods and other product lines (accessories, shoes, ready-to-wear) and its revisited and modernized classic style. Kate Spade, acquired in 2018, implements a similar strategy with marked originality. Stuart Weitzman, who joined the group in 2015, is a specialist in women's shoes.

Tapestry has two major features. On the one hand, the group's main market is North America, which accounts for 61% of its sales year upon year. On the other hand, it specializes in women's bags and accessories, which accounts for 70% of this market. In the 2020 fiscal year, which ran from the end of June 2019 to the end of June 2020, Tapestry's revenue was $4.961 billion; down 17.7% from 2019. Coach accounted for 71% of group sales, Kate Spade for 23.2% and Stuart Weitzman for 5.7%. From June 2020 to June 2021, sales recovered by 15.8%. Recovery in the U.S. and China began in late 2020 and early 2021. Although sales of the group's products in China from 2019 to 2021 increased by 20%, their volume is still insufficient (19%) to take advantage of development of this huge market. As a result, the June 2020–June 2021 revenue of $5.746 billion remains 4.7% below 2019.

Capri, another luxury player in the United States

Capri Holdings Limited, 17th in Deloitte's top 100 with 2019 revenue of $5.2 billion, is considered British by the consulting firm due to its registration in the British Virgin Islands and the presence of its headquarters in London. While Jimmy Choo is a British brand of Malaysian origin and Versace is a large Italian brand, Michael Kors, which accounts for three quarters of its sales, is of American origin, hence its placement in the United States chapter of this book. In fact, Capri Holdings Limited was formerly known as Michael Kors Holdings Limited.

Capri Holdings Limited had revenues of $5.551 billion for fiscal year 2020, which actually runs from April 2019 to March 2020. During this period, its Michael Kors brand accounted for 75% of the group's sales, Versace for 15% and Jimmy Choo for 10%. In fiscal year 2021, from April 2020 to March 2021, corresponding to the peak of the Covid pandemic, Capri's revenue decline was 29.6%. The Michael Kors brand saw its sales fall by 29.6% and Jimmy Choo by 24.7%. Versace, acquired in December 2018, experienced a limited decline of 14.8% over the entire period. But in the first calendar quarter of 2021, when the Capri Group saw its sales rise by 0.4%, recovery was much stronger for Jimmy Choo (+15.9%) and Versace (+10.3%). Capri's internal evolution through the health crisis demonstrates once again that the high-end luxury segment has been better able

270

to withstand the economic downturn than other market segments and has recovered more quickly.

Tory Burch, on the way to being premium

Growing rapidly at 7.4% annually from 2016 to 2019 – privately held, unlisted Tory Burch offers a range of products – clothing, accessories, shoes – in the niche market of modern, chic, yet quirky and trendy New York fashion. The brand is positioned as a new, typically American segment, with products of equal quality to the major European brands. Pierre-Yves Roussel, at the helm of Tory Burch since 2019, makes this clear, *"We sit between the European luxury brands and the accessible luxury brands in the United States[73]."*

A new strategy is being implemented accordingly. Improved product quality goes hand in hand with higher prices. A new logo, a monogrammed T, is used for a new collection of bags, shoes and other accessories. Production, inventory and supply chain management are now managed with the utmost rigor. Direct sales to consumers represent 80 to 85% of total sales. The brand's boutiques are designed to be not only showrooms, but also places for socializing and selling decorative products or antiques. The brand, which has a strong presence on the Internet and social networks through influencers, has its own e-commerce platform. *"Customers who get information on the web and also go to the stores buy three or four times more than those who use only one channel,"* says Pierre-Yves Roussel[74].

---

73. Christina Binkley, "Tory Burch CEO on building the new-age American luxury brand," *Vogue Business*, November 12, 2021.
74. *Op. cit.*

With sales of $1.3 billion in 2019 and a goal of $1.5 billion in 2021, Tory Burch could well establish itself as a future challenger to Ralph Lauren, even if it is four times smaller at the moment.

14

Asia-Pacific, a Vital Market

Asia is well represented in the Deloitte global ranking of luxury groups. In 2019, 17 of its luxury groups were in the top 100, representing 12% of the total revenue of the world's top 100 companies. The average annual growth of these groups was 7%. The prospects for China, Japan and India cannot be underestimated, both in their domestic and international markets.

China, an empire in the making?

Chinese firms dominate the Asian luxury brand rankings. Their image is still not very well-formed, and often confused in the West. The largest groups have their origins in jewelry, which they have begun to diversify from, though this remains limited for the moment.

The large number of large local jewelry groups

Chinese jeweler and watchmaker Chow Tai Fook had sales of $8.5 billion in 2019, placing the group 8th in the world (compared to Swatch Group's place in 10th position). Its goal is to make the notion of branded jewelry popular. From products with Chinese aesthetics, it is also developing new brands with a Western feel and aesthetic: T Mark for diamonds and the Disney Classics collection. It has been growing at 5.2% per year. Chow has taken many initiatives in the field of jewelery technology. Blockchain guarantees the origin of T Mark diamonds. Artificial intelligence is integrated into the brand's web applications to guide consumers to products that meet their questions and profiles.

Lao Feng Xiang has a dual business of selling precious raw materials and producing and marketing finished products – jewelry and items made from gold, silver or platinum. For this second activity, the group occupied 16th position in the top 100 in 2019.

Chow Sang Sang, ranked 30th in the top 100, with 2019 sales of $2.2 billion, specializes in jewelry. Its jewelry collections embrace all specialties. For its diamond pieces in the "Infini Love Diamond" range, the firm has developed new cutting and polishing technologies. Chow Sang Sang's main market is local, but it aims to strengthen its export presence.

With revenue of $2 billion in 2019, comparable to Chow Sang Sang's, Luk Fook completes its jewelry offering by selling western watch brands such as Omega, Longines, Rado and Tissot.

Among the four other Chinese groups in the top 100, two deserve special attention. Chow Tai Seng, which is approaching $1 billion in sales, is experiencing strong growth, at 22.5% per year on average over 2016–2019. This group has the particular feature of conducting its own jewelry product marketing activities and selling its skills to other companies wishing to accelerate their development in the same area. This original model may pave the way for the gradual reconquest of the national market by local brands.

Trinity, China's last top 100 group, is a specialist in men's apparel and has acquired the Cerruti 1881, Kent & Curwen and Gieves & Hawkes brands. These brands could ensure real growth in the local market. With a strong boost in financial results,

Trinity could revitalize the international presence of these three prestigious European brands.

VISION & PERSPECTIVE

"China, from follower to leader of tomorrow's luxury"

Isabelle CAPRON, International Vice President and General Manager Paris, Icicle Shanghai Fashion Group

Even if studies say so, we underestimate the capacity of China to be the real luxury industry "game changer" in the decades to come because we don't know much about this continent from the inside and we don't yet see all the new brands that, too busy benefiting from the domestic reservoir, will gradually consider an international destiny, proposing new approaches, and, against all odds, Western ones, marked by quality, modernity, style and creativity.

I have been a privileged witness since my arrival at Icicle of the rise in power, vision and quality of China in sectors as varied as tech, digital technology, e-commerce, cashless transactions, clean cities and mobility, AI, etc., and of course, luxury goods.

And this is happening at breakneck speed as a result of deep confidence in the future (China's century), the motivation of the younger generations aware of this historical "momentum", and the hard work of a positive nation aspiring to a "Happy Life".

Since 2012 (the year of the creation of WeChat, which is now used by more than 1.3 billion people), China has been able to increase its influence on the luxury sector, for several lasting reasons:

– mindset: "the Chinese dream", as a contender for the rank of first economy in the world China is showing its desire for quality, security and consumption;   →

→
- ambition: to spread new offerings brimming with culture and meaning, stemming from its thousand-year-old history, which are today a source of creation;

- size: the growth of the middle classes underway and still to come, a solid demographic pool of 600 to 800 million people, with potential travelers who will leave China to discover the world, with Europe as their first cultural and shopping destination;

- purchasing power: of young people (the average age of luxury consumers is 28, 10 years younger than in the West), products of the one-child policy, combined with that of women, who are now very active and independent, educated and looking for enjoyment;

- industrial capacity and the mastery of a now very high-quality production process, giving significant strike force to possible luxury brands on the international scene.

Thus, the luxury sector's center of mass is unavoidably moving towards Asia, with China at the heart of economic growth inside and outside China, apart from a few viruses to contend with, of course!

Isabelle Capron was notably involved, as Executive Vice President, in the relaunch and international expansion of Fauchon. She is currently Vice President of ICCF Group, in charge of global marketing and brand strategy.

Products that are "made in China" are gradually taking root in the luxury sector thanks to high-end Chinese brands that have set up shop in Paris, the fashion capital, to reach a more international clientele such as Icicle, Shiatzy Chen and Stella Luna shoes. Not to mention the fact that new designers, who proudly assert their Chinese identity, are seducing an increasingly patriotic youth, and launching new brands such as Bosideng (luxury down jackets present at London Fashion Week in 2020[75], Li-Ning, Peacebird, or Labelhood. *"We show fashion that comes from China but that is addressed to the whole world, creating new references for this country. We are promoting a new "Made in China" of quality and refinement"*, explains Isabelle Capron[76].

The new presence of French brands in China

French luxury goods relations with China have been, until now, essentially unilateral. For a large number of groups, China is first and foremost an export market – certainly a vital one – but first and foremost a market. The establishment of French factories in China is a trend that has been followed by other brands. LVMH, Kering and Hermès are leading the way.

In 2008, LVMH decided to repeat its success in the production of wine in California in China, with the production of a high-end red wine. From vineyards in Yunnan province in the foothills of the Himalayas, not far from the city of Shangri La, its Ao Yun brand delivered the first bottles of its 2013 vintage in 2018. Chandon completed the same process in 2013 in the Ningxia province of northern China. Semi-dry sparkling red wines are produced from vineyards located at an altitude of 1,100 meters, under the brand Chandon Xi.

Kering is committed to developing its Qeelin jewelry brand, which is produced in China and sold mainly on the Chinese market. Its oriental aesthetic is in line with its distribution, which includes 28 stores in Greater China.

---

75. Julie Zaugg, "Mode : quand le Made in China devient cool", *Les Echos*, August 26, 2021.
76. AFP, "Le "Made in China" de luxe prend ses quartiers parisiens," *Fashion United*, December 2019.

Hermès is collaborating with artists or artisans representative of Chinese culture to spread the brand in China and offer it an opening to the French market. To this end, the Shang Xia brand was created in 2010 by Hermès and the designer Jiang Qiong Er. Its stores in Paris, Beijing, Chengdu, Hangzhou and Shenzhen offer both high-priced clothing and art objects designed and produced in China based on its own aesthetic. At the end of 2020, Hermès reserved an €80,000 million capital increase in Shang Xia for the Agnelli family's Exor Group. The aim is to revitalize Shang Xia and make it *"the world's leading luxury brand focusing on authentic Chinese tradition[77]"*, as the group explained in a press release, and perhaps one day to extend the scope of collaboration between the two French and Italian groups.

Japan, the potential of a luxury giant

The world's third-largest economy behind the United States and China, Japan, is a country of contrasts. Its major groups–Sony, Hitachi, Toshiba and Canon in high-tech; Toyota, Honda, Nissan in the automotive industry; Keyence (industrial automation) or Toray (chemicals) in industry–operate worldwide, although its production mainly comes from small and medium-sized enterprises. The Japanese standard of living is equivalent to that of the French standard, but they hold financial assets six times greater than their GDP. Japan has the world's second largest trade surplus, but is virtually absent from the luxury goods sector, despite traditional high quality craftsmanship and local demand for high-end products.

---

77. Dominique Chapuis, "Hermès cède les commandes du chinois Shang Xia aux Agnelli," *Les Echos*, December 10, 2020.

From 1989 to 2004, Japan was the world's largest luxury market with a share that peaked from 1997 to 2002 at an average of 30.5%, according to the "Luxury Business in Japan" study by professor Pierre-Yves Donzé[78]. But since 2005, this share has decreased. Japan doesn't have any luxury groups in the world's top 10 and only four in the top 100. Their share of global sales in 2019 didn't exceed 3.4%.

Japan's largest luxury goods group and the 15th largest in the world, Shiseido, had sales of $5.8 billion at that date, with an annual growth rate of 16% over 2016–2019. This skin care and cosmetics firm has world-renowned expertise, combining oriental values and high technology. The group markets its formulations under its own brands, such as BareMinerals or Benefique. It also owns foreign brands such as Issey Miyake, Serge Lutens and Dolce & Gabbana for its perfume range.

The Kao Group owns other very high luxury cosmetic brands such as Sensai, Kanebo, Ascience or John Frieda. There are few other Japanese luxury groups and most are small. The Onward conglomerate, which generated $1.8 billion in revenue in 2019, was a top 100 global luxury group in 2019, with brands including Joseph and Jil Sander, as well as a collection of Italian footwear and knitwear factories. Polar Orbis, with $2.1 billion revenue in 2019, specializes in beauty care for the domestic market. There is also Mikimoto, a jeweler specializing in cultured pearls.

Despite their smaller distribution compared to the heavyweights of the fashion industry, several Japanese brands are well known: Kenzo (a LVMH company since 1993), Issey Miyake (an independent Japanese firm), Yohji Yamamoto and Comme des Garçons by designer Rei Kawakubo.

---

78. Published in Pierre-Yves Donzé, Véronique Pouillard and Joanne Roberts, *The Oxford Handbook of Luxury Business*, Oxford University Press, 2020.

The Japanese have a high appetite for luxury. Western groups—especially French ones—are favored. Japan used to be the primary growth driver in this sector, far ahead of China.

South Korea, a young luxury market

The luxury sector in South Korea is booming, driven by the strength of its industry and exports. Cosmetics and beauty products are the leading segment, followed recently by fashion and leather goods.

One of the least impacted by the Covid-19 pandemic, the Korean economy was expected to drop from 11th in the world in 2019 to 9th in 2021. Thanks to the strength of its industry (33% of GDP, compared to 27% for Germany) especially in electronics and semiconductors, South Korea was the 7th largest exporter in the world in 2019. The luxury sector is supported by the public authorities, who promote domestic growth and support exports. South Korea's GDP per capita rose above $30,000 as of 2017.

The first luxury sector to emerge, cosmetics or "K-Beauty" took off in the early 2000s. Like Japanese women, Korean women pay great attention to their skin care. The increase in the standard of living has increased the number of large firms and brands in the national market, which are beginning to expand internationally.

The Amorepacific beauty care and cosmetics group reached sales of $6.2 billion in 2019. Founded in 1945, it owns some 30 brands, the best known of which are Sulwhasoo, Laneige, Mamonde, Étude and Innisfree. Other groups are taking off, such as Korea Ginseng Corp, whose "ultimate cream" brand Donginbi, is sold at stratospheric prices.

All Korean beauty and cosmetic brands rely on the use of local natural ingredients, biotechnology or traditional Korean medicine. Brands like Innisfree are already distributed by Sephora.

In addition to this segment's performance, the fashion segment is also taking off. Brands show very modern creativity: eye wear company Gentle Monster (whose LVMH and Arnault Group investment fund, L. Catterton, became the second largest shareholder behind its two founders in 2017) is calling on daring artists and designers for its 23 stores worldwide. The brand We11Done has made a good place for itself in streetwear.

The expansion of Korean luxury goods has benefited from the breakthrough of K-pop, a fundamental element of new national soft power. The Korean appetite for famous western brands makes it an important market. Despite their rapid emergence, local brands do not seem to be able to oust them, in fact, quite the contrary. The move upmarket in Korean consumption will benefit all brands, both domestic and international.

India, a long way to go

India had a population of 1.38 billion in 2020. Its population, which is growing at 1% per year, is expected to surpass that of China (1.41 billion in the same year)[79] in the next few years. It is the sixth largest economy in the world, with a GDP close to that of Italy[80], but its level of income inequality – one of the highest, if not the highest, in the emerging economies – is only slowly diminishing.

---

79. World Bank, 2018 forecast.
80. OECD, 2019.

Based primarily on a growing upper middle class, the luxury market was estimated to be worth around $20 billion[81] in 2017, with a consumer base of around 9 million[82]. In recent years, its growth has been based on jewelry, cosmetics, gourmet products and luxury cars. The most promising additional niches for the future are perfumery and watches. Given the growth of certain sectors, such as high-tech, some forecasts predict local luxury spending of $200 billion in 2030[83].

A protected market

The establishment of luxury brands has long been hampered by high customs duties, a lack of commercial infrastructure (specialized stores, insufficient number of luxury shopping malls), as well as slow and complex administrative procedures. The domestic luxury market remains highly protected in India, with taxes ranging from 5% to 28%, resulting in prices that are on average 20% higher than their European counterparts.

Luxury goods are mainly distributed in malls located in the main urban areas – Delhi, Mumbai, Bangalore, Chennai, Kolkata. E-commerce platforms are developing rapidly. These include Ajio, Tata Cliq Luxury and Luxepolis. Second-hand sales are also increasing.

Foreign brands have difficulty accessing the Indian market. Many brands try to establish themselves there, then give up, replaced by others with the same results. French and Italian luxury brands are most often established through licenses

---

81. Lighthouse, May 2020.
82. Forrester Research, *Vogue Business*, March 2020.
83. McKinsey, *Morning Brew*, 2021

granted to distributors and retail chains. Moreover, the Internet is a formidable accelerator for the establishment of luxury brands in India, as in all the new economic powers. However, a gradual opening of the market is underway, with the recent possibility for a foreign company to own up to 51% of an Indian company and up to 100% of a subsidiary if 30% of its sales are from products manufactured in India. In addition, the Internet has remarkably improved information about French and Italian luxury brands, increasing their desirability.

"India will be the next India"

India is not the next China; the culture and history of the two countries are very different. China has the particular feature of living under the communist regime for over 70 years. It is as much a political as a cultural model. The economic relaxation of the regime has brought about major changes in society. The Chinese are finally able to choose their clothes, the color of their walls or their lipstick. As a result, Chinese consumers have literally rushed to luxury.

India does not have the same history. It still has its traditions and culture. While in China you can see whole families wearing Balenciaga or Gucci, this is not the case in India. Indians adopt, and will adopt fashion according to their culture, habits and customs. So India will probably not have the same growth as China because of cultural and historical differences. However, the Indian economy is growing and major luxury players like Reliance Brands Limited expect the luxury industry to develop sector by sector, in several waves.

"Offering our potential customers Indian brands that are free from their local origins"

Darshan MEHTA, President and CEO, Reliance Brands Limited

The Indian fashion and lifestyle consumption landscape is not pyramidal in shape; more a kind to a flat disc with a "blip on the top". Luxury consumption is still thin air. Having said that as wealth creation trickles from top to bottom and aspirational consumers rise from below to the surface above, the pyramid formation will start taking shape. We currently have the largest number of newly minted billionaires in the country as also the second largest number of Unicorns, next only to China.

Luxury sales have truly had a sharp V shaped recovery, soaring past 2019 numbers. A combination of factors - large number of full vaccinations in urban cities, creating a heightened health confidence in a post pandemic period, an unparalleled appreciation across asset classes, a continued boom across most business and industry verticals leading to significant employment opportunities and the ensuing rise of the "gold collared professionals and finally the well-heeled and habitual international traveler and shopper, being "trapped" inside the country! These customers, who, in the past, took pride in always shopping for luxury internationally, have now discovered the convenience, the freshness and width of merchandise assortment and most importantly the personalized and warm service (not available in the western shopping world) in India. These customers have now tasted blood and have thus become big converts and ambassadors of the joys of luxury shopping in India!

The pandemic, a first real-life experience for most consumers, have also made them acutely aware of their mortality, leading to a clear trading up to shopping for timeless luxury products; very often a symbol of expression of their feeling for their loved ones.

The big fat Indian wedding is back with a bang, after a hiatus in 2020. "Let's grab this window, before the next wave of health care and related restrictions" is the emotional theme.

The over indexation of everything digital has also fueled this consumption rally, creating an outreach to consumers who were hitherto beyond physical reach and who were thus sporadic consumers, limited only to their travels. These and related factors have underpinned the new narrative on luxury consumption In India.

The top $10 million in terms of income and thus disposable spends is the ready size of "luxury audience" in India. There is another cache of $25 million, who are fast up and coming, given their increasing exposures through digital media and international travel.

In an increasing "flat world", the circle of influence for any brand is determined less and less by geography. The ability to create "unboxing delight" with consumers sitting across different continents is both fast and economically affordable. Newer trends such as pop-up stores, interesting cross category collaborations, social commerce, livestream commerce and increasingly nomadic customers who are cosmopolitan in their outlook, has reshaped our approach to looking at current and potential customers for India originated/inspired brands, in a geography agnostic way.

Having said that, every true brand has its own beating heart, its own cache of consumer following and its own re-imagination of itself. It's this journey that we have undertaken alongside our partners Manish Malhotra, Ritu Kumar and Raghavendra Rathore.

Darshan Mehta, after having headed a communication agency and a financial agency, founded Reliance Brands Limited (RBL) in 2007, today the reference retailer in India for fashion and luxury goods with 1,500 outlets and a presence in 17 countries. He is considered to be one of the architects of luxury retail in India.

The same type of luxury consumer doesn't exist in India

Consumers from several generations live together and make up a diverse group. We are witnessing the emergence of a wealthy upper-middle class, as well as the expansion of traditional wealthy circles to Indian tycoons. However, growth is now being driven by new consumers, particularly the younger generations, including the famous HENRYs. This segment is all the more interesting because it corresponds to the many students that India, like China, sends abroad. A majority of them return from their studies with new consumer habits similar to those of the major luxury markets. They are, or become, trend-setters, influencing the entire market. Across all generations, luxury goods customers have gained confidence in their identity and are assimilating western trends into their own culture. Product acquisition and ownership have always been important in India.

A long way from production to creation

Why is it so difficult for an Indian brand to go global? India started developing its economy from scratch. As a newly independent nation, it began with manufacturing.

For many, "*Made in India*" means produced in India, rather than being created in India, an essential nuance in luxury. However, if we refer to Japan, with time, a growing number of Japanese brands have gained their place in the very closed club of world luxury brands. Examples are Yoshi Yamamoto or Rei Kawakubo's Comme des Garçons, who even had the luxury of creating one of the most innovative concept stores in the world, Dover Street Market.

Although the domestic market is still relatively undeveloped, India is a producer and exporter of materials and luxury goods.

In textile exports, India is a major subcontractor for certain products – high quality textiles, woven fabrics, embroidery – used by major brands, notably French and Italian. For the sector as a whole, however, India's share of global textile exports in 2020 was ten times smaller than China's.[84]

In jewelry, India is one of the world's leading manufacturers and exporters. Jewelry and precious stones are a very important economic sector, representing 7% of GDP and 15% of its exports. This labor-intensive industry employs nearly 5 million people. India is the world's second largest market for gold, 70% of which is used by the jewelry industry. The local jewelry industry is expected to reach a turnover of $89 billion within five years[85].

However, there are only four Indian luxury groups in Deloitte's 2019 top 100. Their share of global revenue is only 2%. The Titan watch, jewelry and accessories group dominates the industry with sales of $2.7 billion in 2019 and an annual growth rate of 19.8% from 2016 to 2019. The next largest are the jewelers Kalyan Jewellers, PC Jeweller and Joyalukkas, with sales of around $1.2 billion.

India is committed to the development and growth of its luxury sector. The government also supports companies' export efforts. Several fundamental movements are at work, heralding the creation of an Indian luxury industry. First of all, economic growth and the development of sectors connected to the world, such as IT and telecoms. Second, the emergence of an upper – middle class and millennials with rapidly increasing purchasing power. Finally, the affirmation of Indian identity in luxury products.

---

84. Statista, 2021.
85. "2020 Annual Report," *Kalyan Jewellers.*

Several Indian brands are modernizing and westernizing traditional fashion: Ritu Kumar for urban youth, Sabyasachi Mukherjee for wedding dresses, Manish Malhotra which is well established in Bollywood, Anita Dongre for an Indian touch which is accessible for global markets. Manish Malhotra and Raghavendra Rathore have the means to expand rapidly, with the recent acquisition of the giant retail group Reliance Brands Limited[86]. Manish Malhotra is present in the huge local market for wedding dresses, which represents $50 billion a year. The brand is developing its haute couture, jewelry and cosmetics lines on these foundations. Raghavendra Rathore offers a men's wardrobe consisting mainly of a line of dressy clothes and sportswear with a modern Indian aesthetic.

The central issue is the up-marketing of local Indian brands. Only strong local economic growth will make this possible. After a sharp 7.3% recession in 2020, the IMF expected India to return to an annual growth rate of 9.5% in 2021 and 8.5% in 2022. So its conditions for development seem to have been met.

Australia and "natural, casual and typical" luxury

Australian fashion and design are going through a remarkable development. The sector reached a turnover of $27.2 billion with exports of $7.2 billion in 2019. Australia's image as a continent of preserved open spaces contributes to these good results. The casual style of various local brands met market expectations during the Covid crisis and lockdowns. E-commerce enabled expansion to continue and even accelerate in the country itself and in exports.

---

86. Jeena Sharma, "Indian conglomerate Reliance gets big on luxury," *Morning Brew*, October 18, 2021.

Brands such as UGG, Double Rainbouu, Holiday the Label and Bassike are taking advantage of new trends in comfortable fashion and have a global presence through online sales. The emergence of Australian luxury is far from being something negligible for the major groups. Australian perfumes offer natural and original fragrances that are becoming increasingly successful in the export market. LVMH, Guerlain and Estée Lauder are beginning to show interest in this new niche.

15

The New Generation
of Brands

T he beginning of the decade has seen a proliferation of new
brands. Their limited initial size is not an obstacle to their
survival. These brands, in line with the demands of the
younger generations, have taken the lead in all sectors. They are
part of the zeitgeist and luxury is no exception. On the contrary,
given the large groups' resources, it is likely that other brands
will emerge, filling a gap between established brands and the
new generations. The Covid crisis has only strengthened their
presence and development.

DNVBs – Digital Native Vertical Brands

Digital Native Vertical Brands (DNVBs) focus on direct customer relationships. They are based on digital marketing and focus
on customer experience. These brands have other decisive assets,
with traceability of supplies and revitalization of their intrinsic
ecosystems.

Maximizing the benefits of digital technology

Pure play companies, based on "direct to consumer" business models, are not necessarily luxury brands, but with their new development models, they have been able to inject new dynamics and market standards.

All over the world, independent brands – such as Glossier, created by the beauty blogger Emily Weis –, brands by influential stars halfway between the luxury and premium markets (Kat Von D, Huda Beauty, Fenty Beauty), or Rent the Runway, Girl Meets Dress, Chic by Choice, specializing in the rental or sale of luxury items, are flooding into the markets with the aim of overturning the established order.

Amazon's creation of a store dedicated to independent brands on its marketplace has only reinforced this trend. All luxury segments are concerned; from personal products such as beauty, fashion, leather goods, watches and jewelry, to luxury experiences, hotels, gastronomy, travel, furniture, etc.

These new brands have integrated customer aspirations and respect for the planet. Founded in 2018, the Courbet jewelry brand, a specialist in synthetic diamonds, follows the same line. *"Our mission is to offer the next generation of modern and ethical, sustainable and creative jewelry that respects the traditions of the art of luxury jewelry"*, announces the jeweler. Its founder, Manuel Mallen, formerly of Poiray and Richemont, explains, *"We have built our brand around two pillars, ecology and technology. Gold and diamonds are ubiquitous, and it is precisely technology, through the recycling of gold from electronic device circuit boards and the creation of diamonds in our laboratory, that enables us to be ecological"*[87] Courbet has

---

87. Clément Fages, "Courbet casse les codes des joailliers", *e-marketing.fr*, October 8, 2021.

opted for original distribution methods, with online sale and a responsible offering. It is a strategy that enabled it to grow from €400,000 to €2 million in sales in 2019. This figure was expected to double by 2021–2022.

After raising €8.5 million in funds in March 2020, which the Raise Ventures fund and Hylink, China's first independent digital communications agency contributed to, the brand, which is said to be owned by Chanel, is now turning its attention to Asia, and China in particular, with the launch of a localized site in summer 2021. Courbet also quickly became interested in the potential of blockchain for its business, creating and storing authenticity certificates in the blockchain, so as to quickly verify whether an item offered for sale is not stolen or counterfeit.

Another French DNVB is La Bouche Rouge, the first cosmetic project born from Station F in the LVMH lab and launched in 2017–2018 by Nicolas Gerlier, who designed the first plastic-free lipstick case and the first eco-responsible refill made in France. It is an innovative initiative, as the lipstick tube is refillable and customizable. From their smartphone, via the app or the website, the customer sends a photograph of any object or location, it could be a dress, shoes, purse, artwork or the sunset, and the brand reproduces the color. The customer receives the lipstick at home three days later, numbered and labeled with their name.

La Bouche Rouge is the first French eco-responsible make-up company offering formulas made with natural ingredients in plastic-free refillable and recyclable cases. The success of this project, which brings together luxury, eco-responsibility and fairness, which it also applies to foundations, facial care products and perfumes, has already made the big names in the luxury industry think twice, "*83% of the world's water is polluted by plastic. One billion tubes of lipstick are bought every year around the world and then thrown away"*, explains the founder, *"which is a real environmental catastrophe. But we are convinced that using design and creativity in our everyday objects can put an end to marine pollution[88]."* Five years after his debut, Nicolas Gerbier confirms with conviction, *"Luxury can be cool, sexy and sustainable,"* and continues, *"We have succeeded in our challenge – the brand is expanding internationally, with a humanitarian commitment. We initiated the "A Kiss for Life"project, supporting the NGO Eau Vive Internationale to provide clean drinking water to villages in Togo. Since the beginning of La Bouche Rouge, I told myself that if we managed to build even one well in Togo, we would at least have achieved something. And that all this would not have been in vain.[89]"*

Digital native luxury brands are targets for the big groups. Their experience in digital technology or their creativity in terms of products and services can be a strategic asset for other companies. And in return, their resources can accelerate the smaller companies' growth. But their autonomy is often a requirement for their creativity.

What future for DNVBs?

DNVBs, after the health crisis that saw them come to the forefront, intend to continue their development. Their DTC ("Direct to Consumer") model allows them to communicate with their customers without any intermediaries. Today, like any brand, they are faced with strong growth that they must manage. The challenges are to manage their production, to be present in the distribution channels and to enlarge their customer base.

88. Interview of Nicolas Gerbier by the authors.
89. Johanne Courbatère de Gaudric, "Nicolas Gerlier, le fondateur de la Bouche Rouge," *Les Echos*, February 26, 2021.

Will the aura and power of the big historic brands be enough to keep a distance between them? Some have been quick to understand and adopt the codes and winning business models of the DNVBs.

THE NEW ICONOCLASTIC BRANDS

Young generations are prime targets for digital natives, active, in a hurry, narcissistic, sometimes bling bling, but they are also ready to boycott a brand if it doesn't match their beliefs. The brands follow them closely, especially in the urban or streetwear inspired segment, imposing crazy prices on the market and even creating a second resale market, as Supreme did. Nicknamed the "Chanel of streetwear", Supreme has established itself thanks to an ultra-elite distribution mode, inspired by the luxury sector and its clientele is truly devoted to it. It is endorsed by many celebrities, from Rihanna to Justin Bieber, and rappers like Kanye West or Tyler, The Creator. Supreme produces several hundred different items each season and offers them for sale each week in very small quantities. As a result, it is now almost impossible to get its flagship item, a hoodie with its famous embroidered logo, unless you are the lucky winner of a prize draw organized by the brand. Disappointed customers have no choice but to pay more on the Internet for items resold by the first served in the stores. On average, the price is then doubled. Sometimes, some clothes are offered for sale at up to six times the price on online resale sites. A hoodie sold for €150 in store can easily be found for €600 on the Internet. This reached a climax with the auction of some Supreme items in 2018 by Artcurial, where designer hoodies sold for €1,200 and basketballs between €300 and €5,000!

Two other brands, which have well understood the importance of social networks, respond perfectly to the desires of the younger generation–Off-White, launched by Virgil Abloh, and Vetements, created by Demna Gvasalia. Both have their feet firmly in the luxury segment. The Vetements brand is certainly one of the most edgy brands around. Its creator, Demna Gvasalia, also named creative director of Balenciaga, has made redesign his favorite game and his credo. Provocative messages, delivery man jackets, skinhead jackets, mini dresses, tattooed models–it is a strategy that has paid off. In 2016, the Georgian designer even had the luxury of organizing a flash sale of "Official Fake" items in Seoul, with copies of his own models. It was a way to embrace the culture of counterfeiting and play with the codes of bad taste. Taking on the fake is also a way of taming this increasingly elusive border between vulgar and hype. In an interview with the *Guardian*[90], the creative brain of Vetements and Balenciaga explains how his creations reflect elements of everyday life, breaking with current or yesterday's fashion, *"I don't think elegance is relevant [...] Vetements is about the street and I don't think elegance is what people are aiming for."* He invites us to question the idyllic, elegant vision of Paris as the "capital of fashion" through his collections. But his transgressive creativity appeals in particular to millennials and generation Z, influenced by the pro and streetwear culture, buying in particular from Gucci and Supreme. In fact, luxury and fashion are becoming increasingly inseparable from popular culture. Austrian artist Sara Zaher cleverly mocks this obsession with big fashion brands by transforming famous logos on her Instagram account to show off controlled counterfeiting looks.

---

90. Demna Gvasaliain Jess Cartner-Morley,"'I don't think elegance is relevant': 'Vetements' Demna Gvasalia, the world's hottest designer," *The Guardian*, February 6, 2018.

Answers from heritage brands

Several answers have been provided by the so-called, "heritage" luxury brands.

"Focus on the essentials"

Gilles de LAROUZIÈRE, CEO, Maisons et domaine Henriot

What has the crisis taught us? That we need to focus on the essentials. Marketing chatter has been set aside. The question of the "target customer segment" has been removed. If we need to target someone, we already lose a little bit of truth.

Real authenticity is about telling the story of a family, the unique land that provides its fruits and the talent of those who transform these fruits. It is about describing the exceptional precision of expert hand movements repeated ad infinitum, the obsessive search for balance and distinction in blends, the confidence in the extreme attention paid to the smallest detail that each person puts into their work.

We don't target anyone. We simply offer what we are, our inspiration and our creations, our values of sincerity, generosity and distinction, which we strive to embody as perfectly as possible. We need to work in ever more depth and with more precision on all aspects of our business. From work in the vineyard to the presentation of our vintages, we must pay careful attention to each step of our work and always search for perfection.

Today's customers are looking for authenticity and deep roots. It isn't necessary make up a "story" to tell them. We just have to tell our story.

Gilles de Larouzière is Chairman and CEO of Maisons et domaines Henriot. He is also the Chairman of the Association des climats du vignoble de Bourgogne, a UNESCO World Heritage Site.

Transgressive creativity

Innovation and creativity have always been at the heart of luxury brand development. One example of risky boldness was a handbag unveiled by Balenciaga in 2017 that looks strangely like Ikea's blue shopping bag. It was a pastiche which quickly made a buzz. Even though the copy was almost identical, its price was very different; €1,695, instead of 80 cents for the original. It isn't an example that should necessarily to be followed. By imitating Balenciaga, brands risk confusing their customers and jeopardizing the authenticity and sincerity of their messages. Condescension and negative hype are never far away from this kind of creation.

Other companies have been more successful and brands like Fendi, Louis Vuitton or Gucci have been quick to react to these new transgressive directions. Louis Vuitton has collaborated with the streetwear phenomenon Supreme. Chanel features Cara Delevingne with a skateboard under her arm in a video for the launch of its new Gabrielle bag.

To promote its watch line, Gucci creates its own images or gifs on Instagram linked to humorous comments to create a funny and contagious association, which are then shared and liked, becoming viral on social networks. To carry out this campaign, Gucci has enlisted the help of world-renowned artists such as Amanda Charchian, Korean photographer Kim Tae Kyun (aka Less), Qatari duo Christto & Andrew and pioneering Instagrammers Lola Tash and Nicole Argiris of MyTherapistSays.

Brands are also rejuvenating their "institutional" images. Lily-Rose Depp (born in 1999), Willow Smith (born in 2000) or the actress Lily Taïeb (born in 2000) model for Chanel. Jaden Smith (born in 1998), Willow's brother, poses for Louis Vuitton.

All of these brands play on the doubling of famous personalities to seduce a younger clientele without scaring away the old one. The muses are specially chosen to play on this. And if, in the 1990s, brands didn't use their connections with rappers, they are now doing so, because generation Z seems attracted by the luxury often adored by its idols. Even the stage names of some rappers merge with brand names, as in the case of Gucci Mane.

As for rappers, they seem to be fascinated by luxury that they ostentatiously display. Jay-Z, one of the biggest fortunes in American rap, often name-drops brands in his songs: Mercedes-Benz, Lexus, Bentley, Porsche, Cristal Roederer, Gucci, Rolex are all widely quoted. Take his title *Young Forever: "Slamming Bentley doors, hoppin outta Porsches"* for example. A$AP Rocky is the face of Dior. Nekfeu from Nice was dressed by Louis Vuitton and Dolce & Gabbana for his last concert at Bercy. The song *Onizuka* by the group PNL was used at the opening of the Balmain men's fashion show in January 2018. Chanel even invited the duo to its Fashion Week show – an invitation that they declined.

The frenzy around luxury and the desire to belong to this new community has also struck the younger generations. Ten year olds are already very familiar with brands and want to own luxury items. Some even go as far as to claim to be part of the "rich kids" on social networks by posting fake photos. It is a fascination that is all the more paradoxical because young people from working class neighborhoods champion extravagant, ostentatious luxury, far from the life and style of their homes.

Luxury thus plays on trends and fashions; sometimes at the risk of getting lost. The future will tell us if brands like Balenciaga have played too much with fashion, ending up as just a fleeting fashion fad.

Luxury on demand

Hermès has long offered a service called "Le sur-mesure Hermès" to meet even the most unusual requests. Customer projects, large or small, ranging in size from hot-air balloons to key chains, are made according to requests, with the leather goods manufacturer placing all of its teams and services at the disposal of its most affluent customers and their specific desires. The brand makes their dreams come true while of course staying in keeping with the spirit and style of the house.

Its great rival, Louis Vuitton, also offers its customers a wide range of personalized services. The easiest way is to personalize creations by putting your initials or the symbol of your choice on the brand's mythical trunks. Special orders can be more grandiose. All sorts of objects can be created for clients: anything from a trunk with 36 drawers to hold a shirt and matching cufflinks in each drawer; to a celluloid duck-shaped suitcase to accompany a traveler around the world; a make-up kit and table for a Japanese kabuki actor; a red and white signature trunk with the Supreme logo and the traditional LV monogram, designed to hold a skateboard.

Car manufacturers are also increasingly offering customization to meet their customers' demands. Ferrari is becoming increasingly inventive. Not a single model leaves the Maranello factory without having been through the customization workshops. The Italian firm has even created several levels: Carrozzeria Scaglietti with original accessories, Tailor Made "for those customers who want to customise each element of their car for a perfect fit, creating an unmistakable, one-of-a-kind vehicle which reflects their personality and tastes", then One Off; unique models that the brand produces at a rate of one or two per year.

Luxury brands, whether heritage brands or new brands, are responding in many different ways, freeing themselves from their pasts to better live in the present and prepare for the future.

"Eco-responsible" brands

Launched in Shanghai in 1997 and inspired by the ancestral Chinese thought that values the harmony between man and nature, Icicle is based on the concept of ethical, eco-responsible and high-end fashion. In 2020, its turnover was €290 million, with 275 stores in 98 Chinese cities, a first store in Paris in 2019 and a second in 2021. *"Icicle is an eco-native fashion brand, and a forerunner in the field,"* says Isabelle Capron, International Vice President and Director General Paris at Icicle Shanghai Fashion Group. *"In almost 25 years the brand has cleared a path, explored and developed a value chain that allows us to source, create and produce clothes in the most natural way possible, without defacing or destroying the environment: natural materials undyed or with vegetable dyes, design that saves fabric, timeless style transcending the seasons, longevity and repair of clothes. Its vertically integrated model (three of its own manufacturing plants) allows for quality control and industrial-scale production, demonstrating a new model of "industriali-zable eco-fashion".* She concludes, *"Icicle seeks to inspire the fashion industry by showing a more virtuous path to profitable and responsible growth... The fashion industry, through its agility, can affect its own ecological and responsible transition. There are numerous levers: vegetable and natural replacement materials, recycling, upcycling, production on demand, etc.*[91]*"*

---

91. Camille Lingre, interview with Isabelle Capron, *The Good*, November 16, 2020.

VISION & PERSPECTIVE

"Luxury brands have even more of a duty to set an example than other brands"

Laure BROWNE-PONTHIEU, CEO, Veja

The notion of luxury is evolving according to the expectations and aspirations of the new generations. It is very often a reflection of the evolution of society, its desires, but also its concerns.

We seem to be moving from an individualized luxury of ostentation and glamor—something a little superfluous, status-oriented and inaccessible (this is a bit of a stereotypical definition though)—to a luxury that goes beyond the simple notion of sales to provide more enchantment, simplicity and commitment, something that focuses more on others.

Taking our time, taking care of ourselves and others, and silence, aren't these the greatest luxuries nowadays?

If luxury is about heritage and a symbol of quality passed down from generation to generation, if the new generations wish to consume better for themselves, but also for the world around us, then I am convinced that the luxury brands that will continue to develop are those that know how to move beyond their simple economic stakes to express their commitments through concrete actions with sincerity and humility.

The pandemic has only accelerated new expectations towards brands in general and even more so towards luxury brands.

For me, emerging or enduring luxury brands are those:

– who care about the world around us, the impact of their choices and actions on the environment, but also on society.

– who take action rather than make fine proclamations. Why not let the general public become your communications agency?

→

302

→

– who start by believing in their employees, convinced that economic performance is the result of the sum of the actions implemented by their teams.

– who are sincere, consistent and humble, and who don't hesitate to communicate about their strengths, but also about what they can improve.

I am convinced that luxury brands have a bright future ahead of them, but that they have a duty to set an example.

Laure Browne, CEO of Veja, has over 30 years of marketing and sales experience in large international groups and brands (Gilette, Microsoft, Bic, Yves Saint Laurent Beauté, Marionnaud, Nocibé, Numéricable-SFR, Auchan).

16

Numerous Growth Drivers

Challenges to be met

The luxury industry faces major challenges: the digitalization of its entire activity, social and environmental responsibility, and its presence in Asian markets. Despite the health crisis, these challenges remain and are becoming even more acute.

Do or die

The two types of responses by companies in the sector are hesitancy and proactiveness. "Product focused" companies are often cautious and put on a brave face in times of crisis. "Customer focused" companies are often more reactive. Some family-owned businesses that generate essential income for their shareholders are reluctant to take risks.

For independent brands, the temptation in times of crisis is to cut back and wait for normal conditions to return. Their conviction that product quality and their positioning will pay off can lead to immobility.

The Covid-19 health crisis was, however, extremely wide-reaching and long – an unparalleled event in the past century. It is taking longer than expected to end. Of course, production equipment wasn't destroyed. Various types of support schemes were put in place by governments for companies and employees. Household consumption didn't collapse. The recovery of the last few months gives us reason to believe things can only get better. In times of crisis, taking risks with new innovative products or services is a gamble. But it can generate a decisive lead over the competition.

Managing expenses to invest

The current challenges facing the luxury industry affect its survival and its place in the economy. Traditional markets are being disrupted and entire sectors of business will decline, if not disappear. During the pandemic, the fashion industry saw business collapse, leading to significant cost savings. The lockdowns and the closing of borders transformed the fashion shows and Fashion Weeks into virtual events. The pace of new collections has slowed down significantly. While investments in traditional media have been partly reduced, those in digital media have increased significantly. The costs of manufacturing materials are also the subject of increased attention with the challenges represented by the implementation of a circular economy, from the recovery of scraps and unsold goods to recycling, and the priority given to quality of design over that of materials.

Another area of cost reduction is the streamlining and reduction in the number of products, or even product lines. Ralph Lauren has sold off some of its sub-brands and closed its Club Monaco stores. Valentino, under the leadership of its new CEO, is refocusing its offering on luxury. Reduction in the number of brands is more difficult to decide on, because of considerable investments made to create them. While supply is being reduced, there is a new search for meaning. The health crisis triggered an earthquake in the fast fashion industry.

Seemingly well-established brands such as Fauchon or Lenôtre have closed stores that weren't profitable enough, poorly located or with outdated layouts. New formats have been developed: smaller stores for Fauchon or more and more pop-up stores, as they can better follow the different seasons. Some brand managers are questioning the possibility of closing their dedicated outlets and relying solely on distribution through multi-brand retailers and online. Click and collect was imposed on all types of businesses. The pooling of expenses may be necessary for the upstream part of the value chain and for technological investments.

Investment, the best "counter-attack"

The digitalization of the luxury industry is now a given. The priority for all luxury brands has been to radically increase their investment in technology, accelerate their digital transition and jump on the digital bandwagon by acquiring their own resources. The creativity of their products and services is as important as the omnipresent digital technology in their relationships with millennials and generation Z.

The sustainability of their activities and their work towards sustainable development are the second essential imperative of the luxury sector. On the strength of its exceptional profitability and the structural growth of its markets in Asia-Pacific and emerging countries, the sector must meet all of the challenges of sustainable development that it faces with unrivaled speed. The process is well underway among the large groups, although the pressure of financial markets, ever in search of increasing returns, is partly diverting them from the massive investments that would be necessary to move towards greater sustainability. The challenge between now and 2025 is to focus research and development on materials, manufacturing processes, packaging, transportation, distribution, recycling and upcycling. Combining all of these new solutions, luxury must become the standard-bearer for sustainable development in the entire economy.

The rise of globalized Asian brands

Chinese luxury groups make up almost 7% of the global market. This is far from being a minor feat, as this is already twice as much as all of the British groups and this share is destined to increase. Chinese groups are expanding their coverage of local markets with traditional jewelry, while implementing modern management methods inspired by international groups. The vast Chinese market gives them a colossal customer base. New brands with Western connotations are being acquired or created to protect the local market from foreign competitors, while laying the foundations for their export presence. Once the value of the domestic market has been increased and secured, with the possibility of cutting prices, westernized Chinese brands will have considerable firepower. This approach is perfectly in line with China's political orientations; namely to move its production upmarket, fight against inequalities and refocus on the domestic market.

Western assets and luxury goods skills are gradually migrating to China. Fosun International Group made a name for itself with its 2015 takeover of Club Méditerranée. Owner of Lanvin since 2018, Fosun Fashion Group adopted the name Lanvin Group in 2021. It also owns the Wolford brand of Austrian high-end lingerie, the Italian shoe manufacturer Sergio Rossi, St. John Knits, a women's clothing brand, Caruso, an Italian men's tailor, and Tom Tailor, a fashion brand for women, men and children[92]. The conglomerate, with an estimated €10 billion capitalization,

---

92. Bettina Bush Mignanego, "Zhao Yizheng, the luxury tycoon who set out to conquer the fashion world," *Luxury Tribune*, June 5, 2020.

has significant financial clout, with its €2 billion of annual net income. In the luxury sector, its two potential areas of development are the growth of Western brands revitalized by massive investments and the creation of local brands in the luxury or accessible luxury sectors.

The Chinese group Redstone, initially a distributor of French and Italian brands in China, is looking to expand, notably with the Italian brand Giada, which is based in Milan, "*In China we only want prestigious venues, and now in the USA we are planning to open in New York in 2021, then in London, Paris and then in Italy, Rome, Venice and Florence to bring Giada into the world,*" explained its founder, Zhao Yizheng, in an exclusive interview with *Luxury Tribune* in June 2020. He added, "*We are working on other joint ventures, not acquisitions: with another Italian haute couture brand, Curiel, we have already opened several stores in China; with Gabriele Colangelo we are developing a brand for younger women and three boutiques are being planned and expected to open this summer in China. We have projects afoot with Lanificio Colombo. We believe that in Italy there are many historic brands with a strong identity, and they should be promoted while maintaining their history. That is why we look for partnerships, not acquisitions.*"[93]

Mergers and acquisitions as accelerators

Shareholding stability, skills sharing, costs pooling and margin restoration ensure the durability of the major groups' brands. The amortization of infrastructure costs, product or geographic diversification and the increase in bargaining power justify mergers

---

93. Bettina Bush Mignanego, "Zhao Yizheng, the luxury tycoon who set out to conquer the fashion world," *Luxury Tribune*, June 5, 2020.

and acquisitions. For several years now, old luxury houses with solid reputations have been the object of acquisitions and resales, such as Balmain and Lanvin. Acquirers are trying to revitalize them with different levels of success, as the crisis has weakened independent companies and required even more resources for their development and success.

New European groups

Accessible luxury groups have been formed in recent years. SMCP (Sandro, Maje, Claudie Pierlot, de Fursac) is a well-known success story. Listed on the stock exchange, the group has been controlled by a majority Chinese shareholder since 2016. However, the health crisis hit it hard.

Mirabaud Asset Management recently invested in affordable luxury brands under the leadership of Renaud Dutreil. Its brands – Mauboussin, Korloff, Tara Jarmon, Vanessa Bruno, Carel, Clergerie and Ducasse – have strong potential to move upmarket. The group is banking on synergies between its brands, via common shareholding. The EPI group is another example of refocusing of family activities on the luxury sector. The group owns luxury brands such as J.M. Weston, Pinet for shoes and Bonpoint for high-end children's clothing. The group has also diversified into wine and champagne, with Château La Verrerie, the Piper-Heidsieck and Charles Heidsieck champagne brands and the Italian company Biondi-Santi.

Italian fashion houses could go down a similar route to challenge the big French groups. Renzo Rosso, founder of Diesel, has been commissioned by Confindustria Italy to convince independent Italian brands to engage in mutually beneficial cooperation. The costs of digitalization – though essential – might otherwise be out of their reach. Renzo Rosso has already begun this policy of regrouping. Giorgio Armani, long precious about his independence, can no longer resist the idea of a merger with another company (though it must be Italian and large). Remo Ruffini, the CEO of high-end down jacket manufacturer Moncler, is looking for new targets to form his own group after the €1.15 billion acquisition of its competitor Stone Island at the end of 2020. The Italian brands, often remaining in the same family for several generations, haven't weathered transmission to the next generations well as expected and are being sold off to the highest bidders.

New intercontinental groups

Icicle Shanghai Fashion Group, a Chinese house specializing in the "natural way", acquired the famous Parisian fashion house Carven in 2018. Cooperation between the two houses was given new impetus from 2021. The two companies merged into the new Iccf group – Icicle Carven China France. The distribution of roles is clear. Icicle's mission is to expand the group from China to international level. Its founding "Made in Earth" concept has close links with social and environmental ethics. Carven spearheads the group's penetration of Parisian fashion in China. Both brands will keep their own design office. They will share natural fiber supplies, production platforms and multicultural sales teams. Through this, each company will be strengthened.

The question of large enough critical size to enter the global market arises even for large groups. Hermès and the Agnelli family's Exor Group intend to accelerate their development in the Chinese market with Shang Xia, which they have been co-shareholders of since the end of 2020. This alliance will teach them how to work together. Exor's March 2021 takeover of 24% of Louboutin bodes well for its willingness to invest in the luxury sector. The deal valued the luxury shoe brand at $2.25 billion.

"Preserving creativity while focusing on core issues"
Alexis Mourot, CEO, Christian Louboutin

The health crisis has accelerated the fundamental trends that were already emerging, resulting in the strengthening of luxury groups and an increase in the market share of certain already well-established brands.

Concentration has accelerated but the arrival of new entrants such as Exor has been possible, offering interesting solutions such as governance and financial security for independent houses like Christian Louboutin, which wish to continue to be independent without being "integrated" into "fashion groups" or forced to follow predefined strategy models.

In general the luxury sector has weathered the crisis very well. On the one hand, there are many independent firms that, in my opinion, could be interested in such structures, and on the other hand, some very nice "family office" structures which could seek diversification into luxury goods. The objective is to enable companies to retain their creativity, while focusing on key issues such as digitalization, omnichannel and eco-responsibility.

In terms of markets and nationalities, we were talking a lot about Chinese clientele and their importance in the future of luxury goods, but the end of the crisis means that we can't forget the American clientele, who have shown us that we really need to factor them in. This is our primary market and we are seeing excellent performance in all of our distribution networks there.

Alexis Mourot is CEO of Christian Louboutin. After working in auditing at KPMG, he was responsible for financial management at Yves Saint Laurent and then Managing Director Europe for Marc Jacobs. He also oversaw a number of American subsidiaries of luxury brands before taking over the management of Louboutin and leading its diversification.

Complementing its industrial activity (FCA now Stellantis, CNH Industrial, Ferrari), the Italian company Exor is rapidly diversifying with Partner Re in insurance and *The Economist* in media, with the Juventus soccer club among its historical assets. John Elkann, president of the car manufacturer Stellantis and heir to the Agnelli industrial dynasty, is also interested in a partnership with the fashion designer Giorgio Armani. The businessman reportedly offered to acquire a minority stake in the Milanese fashion house. It was a proposal that was rejected in July 2021, according to several sources, but which clearly shows Exor's efforts to increase its exposure to the luxury market.

New technologies boosting European luxury

LVMH is using Google Cloud Platform to develop new artificial intelligence solutions based on cloud and machine learning. In a similar vein, Ferrari relies on Amazon Web Service for its cloud, machine learning and artificial intelligence needs[94]. If the protection of the national market and Chinese state capitalism have ensured the takeoff of BATX, Europe, has missed the large digital platform train – at least for the moment. But the next technological upheavals in digital technology could allow Europe to re-establish itself in global digital services similar to those of GAFAM.

94. *La Revue du Digital*, September 2021.

"Technology, the key to the future of luxury"

Chris BURCH, CEO, Burch Creative Capital

I believe the future of luxury is closely tied to many exciting innovations in technology. For example, cryptocurrencies and blockchain technology have taken the world by storm, with applications across many different industries. Within luxury, these new technologies can tie physical products to NFTs, with exclusive drops. There is a strong push towards owning unique, limited-edition products both on and offline, and this will become more prevalent in the luxury sector. Additionally, technology today has given way to greater personalization across products and experiences. Within fashion, travel, hospitality and more, luxury will be increasingly tailored towards each individual consumer – this is what the future of luxury means to me. As capital expands and new markets emerge, luxury will become more relevant across the globe.

Chris Burch is an entrepreneur and brand-builder who invests in the lifestyle and retail sectors and is the founder and CEO of Burch Creative Capital, which controls a portfolio of companies specializing in fashion and technology.

Artificial intelligence as a lever

Artificial intelligence (AI) is an obvious lever for the luxury sector. The digitalization of organizations is a source of data, both in production and marketing. In fact, "Big Data" is an increasingly important reality in large luxury groups. There are many opportunities for its use: beyond simple chatbots that provide information and advice to customers, AI offers a new powerful tool to enrich customer experience in a sector where this is crucial.

For luxury groups, the first area of progress is in customer knowledge; in terms of product choices, services, other consumption and lifestyles. Innovations can be tested with rapid feedback, enabling products and strategies to be refined. In this respect, e-commerce is an incomparable source of customer knowledge. *"According to Meta Group data, Facebook Shops and Instagram Shopping have a combined total of 1.2 million stores and more than 300 million visitors visit them each year worldwide. Significant volumes that reflect the new consumption trends on social networks."* reported JDN recently[95]. The sourcing of materials and semi-finished products can be compared between suppliers, taking into account their price, sustainability and inclusion in supply chains.

These production decision parameters are of course already taken into account by luxury group management. But artificial intelligence gives an unprecedented depth of analysis, depending naturally on the quality of the algorithms.

The luxury sector has the financial resources to invest in AI. As in the field of sustainable development, it is up to the sector to be the standard-bearer for irreproachable ethics in data collection and use. The European Union is leading the way with its GDPR (General Data Protection Regulation). Similarly, the Digital Services Act and the Digital Markets Act are moving towards tighter regulation of the European digital space. But, in the new fields of private metaverses and the "fullscale" metaverse, the luxury sector must play a steering role in protecting people, because of its role of pioneer in virtual reality.

---

95. Sarah N'tsia, "Social shopping: quel retour business pour les marques ?" *Journal du Net*, February 18, 2022

Luxury 4.0–towards mass customization?

Digital technology does not only have a monopoly on luxury products and services logistics, it also invades the heart of luxury–design. As technology develops, digital technology is moving step by step up the luxury product value chain and can profoundly change it. The first stage is product customization. According to Bain, 25–30% of consumers have a high interest in personalization[96]. KPMG's Consumer Barometer notes that nearly half of consumers want personalized products and are willing to pay a higher price for them. McKinsey points out that 51% of Chinese Generation Z consumers prefer brands that offer personalized products and 53% of them prefer on-demand services.[97] Nothing is easier than using 3D computer models to modify a product. One click is enough to change the color, add a pattern or even modify the object's shape. Guerlain offers several items that can be customized as desired. Kenzo or Baume offer the same service. There is already talk of "mass customization", a phenomenon that would be unthinkable without the digitalization of the entire supply chain and which opens up very broad prospects for luxury houses.

The next stage is the production of a personalized object using digital tools, especially with 3D printing. 3D printers use all kinds of materials that can be layered up–metals, plastics or organic fabrics. They are used by some jewelry brands, and are expected to spread to other sectors.

The Chinese company Chow Tai Fook Jewellery in Hong Kong is preparing stores where customers will be able to watch their jewelry being made by a human/machine duo, using the best 3D technology and the best artisans.

---

96. Yahong Zhang, *Haptic Media*, August 2020.
97. "McKinsey China Consumer Report," 2021.

316

The starting point of the value chain is the design. New technologies based on digital technology are increasingly numerous, such as new materials, connected products, laser cutting, no-sew clothing. They will give birth to entirely new products. Customers will be able to take advantage, but above all, it is the high-level artisans from the luxury houses who will be able to give free rein to their creativity.

The fight against counterfeiting using digital technology

Counterfeiting is the nagging disease of modern economies, especially in the luxury sector. After mass tourism, e-commerce has led to a surge in sales of copies of luxury goods of all kinds – clothing, leather goods, watches, jewelry, fine wines and spirits.

New responses are underway. The European "Digital Services Act" attempts to provide legal responses to the explosion in sales of counterfeit products on the Internet. New technologies, especially blockchain, are able to provide a definite answer, but at what financial and environmental cost?

Tens of billions of euros in lost revenue and image

Counterfeiting affects many types of products including pharmaceuticals, automobiles, cosmetics, perfumes and leather goods. Globally, the volume of imports of counterfeit or pirated products for the year 2016 was estimated at $509 billion, or 2.5% of world trade by the OECD and EUIPO. The share of counterfeit or pirated products has been growing rapidly since then and reached 3.3% of world trade in 2019[98]. In the same year,

---

98. "Trends in Trade in Counterfeit and Pirated Goods," OECD, EUIPO, 2019.

counterfeit goods imported into the European Union represented 6.8% of total imports, amounting to €121 billion[99] and the loss of 450,000 jobs.

The luxury sector is particularly affected by counterfeiting. The most counterfeited products are shoes (22% of total seizures), clothing (16%), leather goods (13%), watches (7%), perfumes and cosmetics (5%) and jewelry (2%)[100]. The loss of revenue in the European Union in 2019 is estimated at €28 billion for clothing, shoes and accessories and €7.1 billion for perfumes and cosmetics[101]. The annual impact on the French economy is estimated at €7 billion, with 40,000 jobs destroyed and €10 billion in tax losses for the country. In addition to economic losses, there is also the intangible damage done to luxury goods. As Jean Cassegrain, CEO of Longchamp, points out, *"the image damage is considerable, because our business is to create unique and original products. Counterfeiting trivializes our image"*[102]. Not to mention the often much poorer quality of the counterfeits compared to the originals. In France, 9% of consumers say they have been misled into buying counterfeit products[103].

E-commerce, the main counterfeiting channel

E-commerce is now a major channel for the distribution of counterfeit products, particularly for perfumes, cosmetics and sunglasses. 56% of seizures made by customs at the European

---

99. European Union Intellectual Property Office, June 2021.
100. 2016 Data. The other products in the ranking are electrical equipment (12%), medical equipment (5%), toys (3%) and pharmaceutical products (2%). Cigarettes are 12% of other industries.
101. *Journal du Luxe*, June 2019.
102. "Comment les groupes de luxe luttent contre la contrefaçon…et la détournent avec ironie," *Les Carnets du luxe*, February 20, 2018.
103. European Intellectual Property Office, June 2021.

Union's borders were sold through electronic transactions. 75% of these seizures come from China[104]. The other origins of the products are Hong Kong (5.7%), Turkey (5.6%) and Singapore (3.3%). It is particularly difficult to control, with global traffic in 2019 at 21.3 billion mostly small parcels. In 2020, French customs alone seized 5.64 million counterfeit items.

The Internet, source of illicit adverts

Illegal adverts encouraging the purchase of counterfeit products are rife on platforms and social networks, boasting of their quality and low prices. In the first ten months of 2021, 27 million illegal advertisements were removed from the Internet, websites and e-commerce platforms such as Alibaba and Wish, or from social networks[105]. Controlling counterfeit product advertisements is therefore essential. This is one of the purposes of the "Digital Services Act" (DSA) that the European Union adopted in 2022. This act aims to ensure that digital markets remain innovative and open to competition, while guaranteeing balanced and fair commercial relations. To this end, digital platforms will be responsible for the risks incurred by their users from the distribution of illegal, dangerous or counterfeit content and products, with fines of up to 6% of their turnover.

As requested by the Comité Colbert, the new regulation is not limited to platforms but also extends to social networks. While legal limits and enforcement are essential to reduce counterfeiting, technology will be the key to making major advances in the fight against counterfeiting.

---

104. In terms of value, seizures of products from China represent 68% of the total.
105. Unifab, stratégies, November 2021.

New blockchain and NFT technologies, a hope for the eradication of counterfeiting

Blockchain is a technology for encrypting the transmission and storage of information. A file using a blockchain is divided into sequences stored on multiple servers, located around the world and accessible using keys that are themselves tamper-proof. The breakdown of the data and their location is random. Only the creator of the file can access the data and reconstruct the base file.

A luxury product could be attached to an unfalsifiable identity card in the form of a NFT ("Non Fungible Token"), guaranteeing its origin and tracing its history, i.e. its possible changes of ownership or modifications by the brand itself. This digital authentication certificate would also allow the brand to keep a link with the customer or their successors. Blockchain technology is therefore attracting a great deal of interest from luxury companies. Blockchain is potentially even more useful for tracking the life of a product once it is on the market and for fighting counterfeiting. The objective would be to authenticate all production of a brand to allow consumers to identify fraudulent copies. The Arianee Project aims to build standards for the certification of valuable objects, offering digital guarantees of authenticity and security.

In the spring of 2021, LVMH, Prada Group and Cartier, in the name of better traceability of products sold, created a blockchain platform, Aura Blockchain Consortium. Its purpose is to allow customers to access the history of the product they purchase, by means of a digital certificate. And they are calling on all luxury brands to join them. *"By joining forces with other luxury brands on this project, we are leading the way on transparency and traceability. I hope other prestigious players will join our alliance,"* said Antonio Belloni, Chief Operating Officer of

LVMH, in a press release. LVMH, Hublot, Bulgari and Louis Vuitton are already active on the platform. Hublot, for example, has launched a digital warranty stored on the Aura infrastructure, allowing customers to verify the authenticity of their watches using a simple photo taken with a cell phone. This guarantee covers the materials used to build it, to trace it and follow it from the factory to the customer. This "Hublot e-warranty" will also serve as a vehicle for new services. Brands using Aura develop their own version according to their specific features and their customers' expectations. They also keep their data and adhere to the highest standards of customer privacy, with information stored on the blockchain in a way that cannot be altered, falsified or hacked. The contribution of blockchain to the fight against fraud is contingent on its refinement in different areas. For the moment its implementation consumes much too much electricity because of the huge number of the data exchanges between the servers and the volume needed for storage. The file access keys must be integrated securely and permanently into the products themselves. The procedures for updating information by authorized persons must be simple.

Considerable investments are required to implement blockchain on a large scale. But effective reduction in counterfeiting will ensure profitability.

NFTs, a global creative space

NFTs, stored in blockchain, are unforgeable computer files, representing a real or virtual object or product. The NFT market has gone through tremendous growth. According to data aggregator NonFungible.com and Atelier BNP Paribas, which published a study on non-fungible tokens in February 2021, the value of NFT transactions grew from $62 million in 2019 to more than

321

$250 million in 2020. In 2021, NFTs could be found in all areas, at all prices and for all audiences. Digital art was the pioneer in their use. Christie's auctions off original works, such as those by Mike Winkelmann, aka Beeple crap. The NBA markets still and animated cards of its most famous basketball players. In France, Sorare offers collectible soccer player cards, similar to the Panini stickers of the past, giving access to various benefits, including games[106]. In the luxury sector, the Karl Lagerfeld company sold 777 NFT figurines of its creator for €77 each.

New global media for artists

On Sotheby's marketplace, Sotheby's Metaverse, it is possible to acquire entirely digital artworks displayed in five spaces and offered for sale as NFTs without physical equivalents. Among the transactions made was an $11.8 million bid for a work by CryptoPunk.

Christie's presided over an auction of $69 million for a similar work. NFTs for works of art are obviously a new speculation area. But this technology is also a decisive contribution to the diffusion of artists' work. Digital technology has offered new techniques for digital design and production. With NFTs, the distribution of their works is no longer limited to galleries and exhibitions. On the contrary, works using NFT reach the whole world through the Internet and social networks, with an authenticity guarantee to boot.

The organization of NFT-certified auctions by Guerlain in November 2021 was a major step forward in linking art and luxury. The association of a major luxury brand with the art

---

106. Bérénice Marmonier, "La folie des NFT", *France Football*, n° 3910, September 11, 2021.

world is carried out with concrete, real benefits for the artists and not just an image boost for the brand.

NFTs, the virtual fashion motor

Thanks to NFTs, virtual fashion is booming with a young and trendy public. Gucci has launched an augmented reality sneaker series in the form of NFTs. It is an initiative that enables it to remain at the forefront of virtual reality trends. With these virtual shoes, Gucci is targeting Generation Z consumers who are tech-savvy and may not yet be able to purchase the brand's physical products. This digital sneaker, which costs €12.99 on the Gucci app, can thus reach a wider audience, unlike some exorbitantly priced NFTs.

Balmain has established a strong foothold in the virtual haute couture market. The fully digital Flame dress by its artistic direc-tor Olivier Rousteing is an animated NFT, covered in flames and swirling around the mannequin. This first NFT creation was submitted for auction in September 2021. Other creations were revealed in the Fall/Winter 2021–2022 collection.

Aelis, the fashion house created by Sofia Crociani, Karl Lagerfeld's collaborator for many years, has launched an NFT operation associated with its virtual fashion show presented at the Fall/Winter 2021–2022 haute couture week. The house is offering five unique NFTs for auction, *"Ownership of this dress will be divided into five NFTs that must be reunited to become the one, the only and the official owner of this extraordinary piece, much like a puzzle."*[107]

---

107. Frederic Bonelli, interview with Sofia Crociani, "Quand la Haute Couture rencontre les crypto-monnaies avec les NFT," on the *Forbes site*, July 13, 2021.

Dolce & Gabbana unveiled a nine-piece NFT collection – produced in collaboration with UNXD, a marketplace for digital luxury and culture – at its Alta Moda show in Venice in August 2021. Five of the items in the Collezione Genesi – two dresses, a men's suit and two crowns – are physical creations designed by Dolce & Gabbana which have digital versions. Four other items are virtual creations entirely made to measure.

Fine watchmaking, a natural territory for NFTs

Fine watchmaking is faced with several challenges which NFTs can provide solutions to. The high price of the most beautiful items means precautions need to be taken. Speculation on watches can be made on virtual watches as well as on real ones. Experts point out that there is little difference in enjoyment between locking up a physical watch in a bank vault and acquiring an NFT.[108]

Jacob & Co created the world's first luxury NFT watch in April 2021, in association with the NFT ArtGrails platform. This watch is inspired by the company's flagship product, the Epic SF24, which now sells for over $100,000. But although the starting price for the 24-hour auction was $1,000 on April 7, the highest bidder offered $100,000. Benjamin Arabov, CEO of Jacob & Co said in a press release, "*Jacob & Co is a pioneer in discovering this brand new arena for all high-end jewelry and watch brands. Our goal is to prove that there is a market for high end luxury digital assets and we want to be the first to break into this industry.*" Similarly, the digital twin of the Hublot watch "Bigger Bang All Black Tourbillon Chronograph" was sold in 2021 as an NFT.

---

108. *Journal de la Haute Horlogerie*, May 2021.

The era of digital and musical perfumes

The creative studio Look Labs has just created a perfume transformed into a non-fungible token on the Rarible platform of the Ethereum ecosystem. The NFT takes the form of a 3D video including the visual of the bottle and the infrared spectrum obtained by near infrared spectroscopy of the perfume.

Another step in the digitalization of fragrances is that of synesthesia. L'Oréal has created the soundtrack for its perfume Spice Bomb Infrared by Victor & Rolf in partnership with Ircam and its subsidiary IrcamAmplify. The objective is to evoke the deep fragrances of this perfume with sound waves online.

NFTs, the virtual world as an echo of the real world

NFTs of works of art or luxury products are a step towards digitalization. Their promoters predict a transformation of luxury items, whose digitalized versions could soon be more fashionable than the physical versions. NFTs don't just have limited use in real life. They can be displayed on a TV screen, as a decoration or as an electronic picture; NFT collections take up less space than a collection of objects in a closet or a trunk; dressing up your digital twin can be rewarding to parade in a video game played in a group over a pizza; reselling the NFT figurine of a footballer who became a star offers something that can be speculated on within anyone's reach. But, in reality, the real challenge for NFTs, virtual elements, just as for the metaverse, is the link between the physical world and the virtual world.

Brands will be able to associate their physical products with digital products, enabling their customers to dress their avatars at the same time. Laurent Boillot, president of Hennessy and future president of the Comité Colbert emphasizes this, "*In addition to Direct to Consumer transactions, we will have to add Direct to*

325

Avatar transactions into our strategies. It is essential to adapt and work with the different identities. There was only one consumer before. Tomorrow morning there will be two. " NFTs are also an opportunity to create unique and exclusive experiences for a brand's NFT owners. Finally, brands will be able to integrate NFTs into their sales space to allow more traditional customers to view the token and better understand the associated benefits.

The metaverse, a new luxury Eldorado?

Reserved for specialists until 2020, the term metaverse is now omnipresent in traditional and digital media. The pandemic and its lockdown periods brought digital technology to the forefront of the lives of individuals and businesses: telework, teleconferencing, video games, music and movie streaming. Parallel realities have been added to the physical world in everyday life. Resulting from the meeting of the prefix *meta* (with, after, beyond in Greek) with a declension of the Latin *vertere* (gathered, put together), the word "metaverse" describes a specialized virtual world, existing beyond the physical world, but closely united to it. A plethora of metaverses already exist on company servers or in the cloud, i.e. data fields in which all kinds of applications are deployed.

The metaverse can be another concept. Invented by the science fiction author Neal Stephenson in his novel *Snow Crash*[109], it refers to the parallel reality resulting from the stitching together of all the metaverse or virtual worlds created by the digital world. Because anyone can access it at any time and without difficulty, for its most enthusiastic promoters, the metaverse will be a complementary and alternative world to the real world. People will be able to choose to work, play, socialize, educate, shop or

---

109. Doug Stephens, *Business of Fashion*, June 7, 2021.

travel there. The user will have the choice to easily move from one to another without returning to the physical world.

Metaverse video games, architects and promoters

Video games are a powerful engine for the emergence of the metaverse. The sector, with its $175 billion in annual global revenue, is already bigger than the film or music industry. In France, it has reached €5.3 billion. Its growth, which was accelerated by the lockdowns and the health crisis, will continue thanks to new virtual socialization features.

The expansion of video games is seen in the development of major technological tools. Many of them can be transposed to other purposes: player interactivity with the platform and between themselves, the construction of elaborate sets, the possibility of creating games by the users themselves.

VISION & PERSPECTIVE

"Our lives and property will be gamified"

Stefano Rosso, founder and CEO of D-Cave, OTB Group Board Member

Looking at the recent events and the way the world has evolved and changed our lives after Covid, it is clear that the future of luxury will be more and more linked to the fusion of the physical and digital worlds.

Living through digital platforms and environments like the metaverse, adopting cryptocurrencies, and using NFTs is going to impact the way we consume forever. Everyone will have avatars that will use digital assets and will project the way we want people to see us in the different digital worlds.

There is a revolution happening. Our life and everything in it is being 'gamified'.

→

→

Luxury companies will face huge opportunities (or threats) if they are able to define their unique selling proposition and what they want to stand for in the virtual environment. Many will be highly successful and will leverage a new economy that could potentially outgrow their traditional business model. Others, not quick enough to change and adapt to this new way of living, will simply disappear.

Stefano Rosso is the co-founder and CEO of D-CAVE, a lifestyle brand destined to the gaming community. He held various positions at Diesel, from production to marketing, before joining OTB in 2011.

With its game *Fortnite*, which has 350 million users, Epic Games has continuously expanded the possibilities for its users. Players have avatars in the virtual and multiplayer worlds. In a major step towards networking separate metaverses, Microsoft, Nintendo and Sony have been convinced to allow their players to access *Fortnite*. Epic Games' dynamism has convinced tech investors and it succeeded in raising $1 billion in funds on April 2021[2], intended for the development of its metaverse projects.

The next step will be to set up social relationships between players, which are much more elaborate and peaceful than gun battles. We will then have partial metaverses; "*virtual reality universes where users have some form of representation of themselves and interact with other users and with a computer-generated environment[110]*".

---

110. Benoit Zante, "SXSW 2021: avec le métaverse, on ne sera plus 'sur' Facebook, mais 'dans' Facebook!," *INfluencia*, March 24, 2021.

Fortnite has built its own world where events like rapper Travis Scott's five concerts gathered 50 million gamers. The world premiere of the trailer for the film *Tenet* also took place there. Luo Tianyi, a digital avatar singer with 5 million followers, performs paid virtual concerts on Vocaloib (a text-to-speech software developed by Yamaha Corp), with tickets sold out in minutes. She can also sing duets with real opera singers, like Andrea Bocelli. Twitch, Amazon's streaming game platform, hosted the first presentation of the Burberry collection.

Video game platforms are also beginning to be channels for political communications. In June 2021, New York City mayor candidate Andrew Yang held a press conference using his avatar on the Zepeto platform, where 90% of users are from Generation Z. The goal was to draw their attention to his candidacy and convince them to vote for him.

Even more innovative, Roblox, a game platform, provides its users with creation tools. Millions of different games and experiences have been added to its initial offering. Upgrades of standard games are on sale as well as virtual products. New game creators can sell access rights, avatars and get paid in Robux.

The metaverse, a virtual copy of the real world

The administrative shutdown of economies due to the pandemic has had its consequences mitigated by the key role of digital technology in economies. Teleworking and meetings on Zoom or Teams became the norm in just a few weeks for white collar workers. "Remote" is now competing with "face-to-face". A few months of intensive use have convinced all stakeholders of the interest of keeping it going, at least partially. These technologies are extending to one day soon merge into a new expanded virtual world – the metaverse.

For example, the Ray-Ban glasses developed by EssilorLuxottica and Facebook can record 30-second videos that can be uploaded to the Facebook View application. The content, editable by the user, can be broadcast on Facebook, Instagram, WhatsApp, Messenger, Twitter, TikTok or Snapchat[111]. The 30-second limit will of course be quickly extended. Thus, users will be able to share their lives with their entire community. The metaverse will record as much of the real life of individuals as they want. The physical world will have its digital copy. The link between the physical and the virtual world is envisaged in two ways.

Facebook, one of the most active promoters of the metaverse (to the point of changing its name to Meta), is counting on its Oculus virtual reality headsets and its Horizon platform to create a virtual world that can bring its users together. They will have the opportunity to enrich this world with their own creations.

Other experts are in favor of an augmented reality metaverse, enriching our perception of the real world by mixing it with the virtual world. In the medium term, each individual will have a digital twin in the metaverse who can engage in multiple virtual activities.

The metaverse won't just a place for games and entertainment. It will make it possible for companies to address users directly, without going through platforms – therefore improving the relationship between brands and consumers. It is the meeting place between virtual worlds, social networks, e-commerce and decentralized services. The metaverse will therefore be a new sales and exchange space for brands. Digital twins will be able to try out and use both digital and non-digital products, which consumers will be able to acquire through decentralized financial

---

111. "Facebook et Rayban commercialisent leurs lunettes de captation vidéo", *La Revue du digital*, September 13, 2021.

services and digital currencies. It is also a new means of internal communication via services such as Zoom or Teams, which are destined to evolve and offer a more immersive experience that is closer to reality.

In the metaverse, companies will be able to have two dimensions – physical and virtual. Many companies are already designing their products with 3D models and simulations. The fields of industrial engineering, architecture, product lifecycle management, or bioassay, for example, will expand to simulate all business operations in order to prepare for decisions before they are made in the real world.[112] We can imagine that the company commercial relationships will be able to be had in the metaverse with their digital versions. In the event of further lockdowns, digital twins will allow for a continuation of activity to a much greater degree than that allowed by teleworking in the 2020–2021 crisis.

The complex conditions of its creation

The metaverse will not be an idyllic world, miraculously free of all the problems inherent of platforms and social networks. Users are increasingly opposed to the publication of their personal data. The lack of effective regulation of platforms such as Facebook or Twitter suggests that the metaverse could get out of hand in a much worse way, due to the generalized interconnection of virtual universes. Digital twins will be traceable and transparent to any hacker worth their salt.

Hijacking still or animated images of real people – deep fakes – already make it possible to make them say imaginary things (most often scandalous) with risks to brands or elections. This

---

112. B. Charlès, Chairman and CEO Dassault Systèmes, *BFMBusiness*, November 2021.

threat will have to be warded off in the metaverse with technical tools that have yet to be developed. The definition and application of ethical behavior will also be essential. The European Union is a leader in digital regulations. The RGPD (General Data Protection Regulation) and the Commission's digital package with the "Digital Services Act" and the "Digital Market Act" point the way towards regulations that will need to be made in other fields in the coming years.

Rules for the protection of digital twins will also have to be drawn up, computerized and rigorously applied. The viability of the metaverse depends on it. Thanks to SSI (Self Sovereign Identity), it is already possible to have a secure digital identity, distributed with verified information (name, first name, address, etc.). In fact, the metaverse can potentially put an end to the anonymity of the Internet, a place of inanity, verbal violence and a trigger for physical violence.

The development of the metaverse is dependent on advances in IT infrastructure. The cloud, which plays a key role in this, is currently benefiting from massive investments – $74.6 billion in 2021, increasing by 12.9% annually according to IDC[113]. This should continue and even increase. Cybersecurity is already a fundamental issue for societies and economies. It will then be of paramount importance if the virtual world is to last. A 3D browser and the widespread use of holograms will also condition the use of the metaverse.

The fight against climate change will finally require reducing the massive energy consumption of blockchains. This technology, still in its early stages of development, will have to evolve towards a distribution of information in different energy-saving clouds.

---

113. IDC, "IDC forecasts worldwide 'whole cloud' spending to reach $1.3 trillion by 2025," September 14, 2021.

New markets for luxury goods

The luxury sector is playing a pioneering role in the development of the metaverse. Its financial power allows it to be omnipresent. Its products can be offered at much lower costs than their physical counterparts, and its aesthetic codes can be promoted. The luxury sector is already bringing solutions to the fundamental question of the link between the physical world and its virtual copy.

"The metaverse: strategic for luxury"

Sandrine CRENER-RICARD, Program Director, Harvard Business School

New digital technologies are rapidly changing business, the economy and societies around the globe, and succeeding in this new world will require organizations to reinvent how they operate and compete in this fast-changing environment. Luxury brands are not immune to that change. New business opportunities in the metaverse will soon become critical to luxury brands' ability to remain relevant and drive growth. Simply creating digital products will not be sufficient; the new digital imperative demands a new level of strategic thinking, a new model of interacting with customers, a new mindset and creative approach.

While the reasons why people buy luxury may not change, opportunities in the metaverse will probably transform how people consume luxury, and therefore impact many aspects of luxury marketing strategies. In this context, it is important for luxury brands to learn and adapt quickly in spite of uncertainties.

Sandrine Crener is a Program Director at Harvard Business School and teaches luxury marketing at Harvard University (Cambridge,

→

→
Massachusetts). Previously, she worked at the Savannah College of Art and Design, the International University of Monaco and the World Bank.

The metaverse is expected to generate an additional $50 billion in revenue by 2030 for the industry, according to a Morgan Stanley communication published in November 2021. *"Revenue streams from digital mediums for luxury brands are negligible [...] We think this is about to change,"* say the bank's analysts. *"The Metaverse will likely take many years to develop; however, NFTs and social gaming (e.g. online games and concerts attended by people's avatars) present two nearer-term opportunities for luxury brands."* According to Morgan Stanley, non-fungible tokens and social gaming could increase the potential market for luxury groups by more than 10% within eight years and increase the industry's earnings before interest and tax by about 25%. *"We expect the whole sector to benefit from the advent of the Metaverse, but see the soft luxury brands (ready-to-wear, leather goods, shoes, etc.) as particularly well positioned as opposed to hard luxury (jewellery and watches),"* emphasizes the investment bank.

Something else striking at the end of 2021 was the price of NFT land that was skyrocketing in metaverses such as Decentraland or The Sand Box: about $106 million was invested on these platforms at the end of November 2021. These 3.0 investors have even designed virtual "malls" to house the major luxury brands, notes Stéphane Galienni, cofounder of Balistikart, who has conducted two studies on NFTs and the metaverse[114].

---

114. Isabelle Musnik, "NFT et métavers, des opportunités incontestables pour le luxe", *INfluencia*, interview with Stéphane Galienni, January 9, 2022.

The challenge for brands is to position themselves in this new space, to bring meaning to their arrival in the metaverse while maintaining their unique image. Selfridges attempted its first foray into the metaverse in January 2022 and is partnering with the Vasarely Foundation and Paco Rabanne to launch "Universe," a project that brings together fashion, art, retail, theater and NFTs under one roof. The London department store plans to simplify access for its customers, allowing them to buy NFTs with a regular bank card at the counter with no cryptocurrency needed.

When you consider that one in five Roblox players update their avatars daily, the growing importance of the metaverse is clear. By mid-2021, according to the Swiss Center for Luxury Research[115], 90% of Generation Z young people were gamers. By 2023, the number of video game players is expected to reach three billion. The application and social network Zepeto already allows the creation of virtual worlds, where the player can create avatars in Gucci colors. The luxury items can be worn by users' digital twins.

As the metaverse develops, the demand for luxury will inevitably grow in this parallel world. The need for affirmation, appearance, originality and exceptionalities will reign just as it does in the physical world.

The luxury industry already uses the metaverse to sell its products and services. Along with its Gucci Garden Experience on Roblox, the Italian brand offers virtual products for sale and sells a bag for $4,115 dollars—more expensive than in the real world![116] For Robert Triefus, Gucci's CMO, the Gucci Metaverse is not just a digital presence, but essentially a brand narrative. The objective is to lay the foundations of its future metacommerce,

---

115. *Luxury Tribune*, May 20, 2021.
116. Wunderman Thompson, "Into the Metaverse," study, September 10, 2021.

which the brand is convinced will grow, *"We know that people are willing to pay a lot of money for NFTs, digital collectibles and to have a second life in the Metaverse. The revenue potential is absolutely there,[117]"* he confirms.

Blockchain technologies will make a real demand for virtual items viable. The prices of virtual luxury items can then be established and take off. Digital art objects in NFT already show the possibility of price explosions due to speculation.

As of August 2021, Ralph Lauren announced a collaboration with Zepeto, titled Ralph Lauren x Zepeto. A digital fashion collection will be created as well as a virtual world, where it will be possible to create 3D avatars and use a networking application. Users will be able to purchase an array of apparel, including 50 unique designs, inspired by both Polo Ralph Lauren's vintage collections and the latest collections. Consumers will be able to test the creations on their digital twins, and change them for different environments and events.

It is crucial for brands to develop virtual products in the metaverse. It will allow customers to customize or even create their own items for their digital twin, acquire them in the virtual world and get their physical version through on-demand manufacturing. The metaverse will also revolutionize consumer information, selection and sales of physical products. With very deep virtual interactions, future customers will be able to meet all involved in the luxury industry, producers, sellers or influencers. They can make purchases in the metaverse or in the physical world.

---

117. Robert Williams, "Gucci's Robert Triefus on testing luxury's allure in the metaverse," *Business of Fashion*, December 7, 2021.

Conclusion

As we finish writing this second book on the luxury industry and its future, luxury has been confronted, as never before, with many challenges and opportunities under conditions of acceleration and instability rarely experienced until now. Previously marginal topics have become, if not the priority, highly important for many brands, such as sustainability, the circular economy, gaming and, more recently still, the metaverse and NFTs. They are probably future growth drivers and are today the main focus of attention.

There *is* a "new normal". It is today about how brands respond to new distribution and consumption modes for customers eager for novelty, in the real world as well as in the virtual world. These two will combine and respond to each other. The luxury industry is once again being a trailblazer, even if that means rushing.

More than in other sectors, luxury has been able to counterattack and react quickly, with creativity and agility. This period was conducive to introspection for brands because, beyond the crisis management of their operations, they were able to take the time to reflect on their reasons for existence and their positioning. The strongest companies are, of course, the best positioned to benefit, provided they have secured their bases. More than ever, it is crucial for them to develop ecosystems capable of withstanding the extreme volatility of the environment, supply, demand and increasingly fierce competition, also from markets like China or India. They need to have ecosystems that can also overcome the risks of economic crises caused by wars.

Russia's aggression of countries in Europe will certainly have new negative consequences on the world economy as well as on the luxury economy.

The wait-and-see attitude in a world that moves at the speed of digital technology is no longer possible. Many companies can no longer afford it. They will probably change hands or fall prey to investment funds, as shown by some recent equity investments. If they want to prepare for tomorrow, brands have no choice but to evolve, invest and meet the expectations of their customers, who expect them to behave irreproachably towards their employees and the planet.

In this new era of luxury, where brands are much more than what they sell, the future of the industry will continue to be driven by their heritage, creativity, innovation and ability to adapt and adopt trends while accelerating them. Their scope for action and expression has never been so wide and the trade-off between numerous opportunities will be decisive for their success and survival. In addition, the emergence of new brands driven by social networks and their influencers will continue, with global successes that have never been so fast, with new business models including the participation of celebrities in creation and distribution, acting both as ambassadors and investors.

Luxury is an empire on which the sun never sets.

Acknowledgements

We could not have written this book without the help of many major players in the worlds of fashion, luxury and hospitality.

We are particularly grateful to **Laurent Boillot**, CEO of Hennessy cognac, a prestigious LVMH group company, and president of the Comité Colbert, and **Cyril Chapuy**, President of L'Oréal Luxe, who both kindly wrote a foreword to shed light on the decisive role that luxury plays for France and on the new expectations of consumers.

Our warmest thanks go to the contributors who agreed to share with us, and therefore with our readers, their vision of luxury and its future, as well as their deep knowledge of the world in which they move. We endeavored to interview personalities from the key luxury sectors, from fashion to hotels, to tableware, leather goods and perfumery.

Numerous contributors from the biggest brands in the luxury goods industry gave us their precious help as well as their vision on the evolution of their own brands that they manage at the global level:

Nerio Alessandri, President of Technogym, **Max Aniort**, CEO and Co-founder of The Collectionist, **Javier Bach**, Chief Operating Officer of the Puig Group, **Andrea Baldo**, CEO of Ganni, **Chris Burch**, Founder and CEO of the Burch Creative Capital Group, **Gregory Carpenter**, Professor of Marketing at the Kellogg School of Management, **Jean Cassegrain**,

CEO of Longchamp, **Davina Cisier**, Director of Development for Accor's luxury and lifestyle hotels, **Sandrine Crener-Ricard**, Program Director at Harvard Business School, **Gilles De Larouzière**, CEO of Maison et Domaine Henriot, **Guillaume De Saint Lager**, Vice President of Orient Express-Accor, **Pauline Dollé Labbé**, Marketing Director of 24S, **Marc Durie**, President of J.M. Weston, **Alexandre Fauvet,** CEO of Fusalp, **Guillaume Houzé**, Director of Image and Communication and Executive Board member of Galeries Lafayette, **Jean-Claude Le Grand**, Chief Human Relations Officer at L'Oréal, **Sharon MacBeath**, Human Resources Director, Hermès Group, **Paul Michon**, Corporate Communications Director, Kering Group, **Alexis Mourot**, CEO of Christian Louboutin, **François-Henri Pinault**, CEO of the Kering Group, **Cédric Prouvé**, President of the Estée Lauder Group, **Alexandre Ricard**, Chairman and CEO of the Pernod-Ricard Group, **Stefano Rosso**, Co-Founder and CEO of D-CAVE, Board member OTB Group, **François Ruault**, Chief Sales and Marketing Officer of Devialet, **Elie Saab Jr**, CEO of Elie Saab, **Nicolas Santi-Weil**, CEO of AMI Paris, **Catherine Spindler**, Chief Brand Officer of Lacoste, **Éric Vallat**, CEO of Rémy Cointreau Group, **Angelic Vendette**, VP Marketing of Alo Yoga and **Shannon Washburn**, CEO of Shinola.

We are very grateful to all those who have given us their time in "real life", or during telephone conversations or on Zoom or Teams – because of Covid. Among these, we would like to thank in particular **Laure Brown Ponthieu**, CEO of Veja, **Isabelle Capron**, International Vice-President and General Manager Paris, Icicle Shanghai Fashion Group**, Bénédicte Epinay**, President and CEO of the Comité Colbert, **Laurent Grosgogeat**, Executive Vice President of Cerruti, **Marc Jacheet**, CEO of De Beers Brands, **Darshan Mehta**, CEO of Reliance Brands

Limited, **John Terlato**, Vice Chairman of the Terlato Wines International Group and **Henrik Wenders**, Senior Vice President of Audi.

Finally, we would like to thank Dunod, the publishing house that once again trusted us with the writing of this second book dedicated to luxury, and in particular Delphine Levêque and Laure Duclaud, the editors who accompanied us throughout this project and gave us so much advice.

édition pré-presse
livres numériques

44400 Rezé

84164 - (I) - ENSO 80° - KEP - MPN
Imprimerie CHIRAT - 42540 Saint-Just-la-Pendue
Dépôt légal : octobre 2022

Imprimé en France